DATE DUE		
AUG 0 1 2011		
AUG 2 3 2011		
FEB 2 5 2012		
MAR 2 8 2012		
MAY 2 9 2012		

COME TO THE EDGE

Come to the Edge

A Memoir

CHRISTINA HAAG

SPIEGEL & GRAU

NEW YORK

2011

Published in the United States by Spiegel & Grau,
an imprint of The Random House Publishing Group,
a division of Random House, Inc., New York.

SPIEGEL & GRAU and Design is a registered
trademark of Random House, Inc.

Grateful acknowledgment is made to the following for permission
to reprint previously published material:

ALFRED MUSIC PUBLISHING CO., INC.: Excerpt from "Love Is Here to Stay," music and
lyrics by George Gershwin and Ira Gershwin, copyright © 1938 (renewed) by
George Gershwin Music and Ira Gershwin Music. All rights administered by
WB Music Corp. All rights reserved. Reprinted by permission.
DGA LTD: "Come to the Edge" by Christopher Logue, copyright © 1996 by
Christopher Logue. Reprinted by permission of DGA, Ltd.
VINTAGE BOOKS, A DIVISION OF RANDOM HOUSE, INC.: Five-line poem from
*The Ink Dark Moon: Love Poems by Ono No Komachi and Izumi Shikibu, Women of
the Ancient Court of Japan* by Ono no Komachi and Izumi Shikibu, translated by
Jane Hirshfield and Mariko Aratani, translation copyright © 1990 by Jane Hirshfield.
Reprinted by permission of Vintage Books, a division of Random House, Inc.

All photographs courtesy of the family of Christina Haag, except page 84
(Robin Saex Garbose) and pages 158 and 234 (© L.J.W./Contact Press Images).

LIBRARY OF CONGRESS CATALOGING-IN-PUBLICATION DATA
Haag, Christina
Come to the edge: a memoir / Christina Haag.
p. cm.
ISBN 978-0-385-52317-2
eBook ISBN 978-0-679-60490-7
1. Haag, Christina 2. Television actors and actresses—United States—
Biography. 3. Motion picture actors and actresses—United States—Biography.
4. Kennedy, John F. (John Fitzgerald), 1960–1999. 5. Kennedy family. I. Title.
PN2287.H14A3 2011   792.02'8092—dc22   2010045787

Printed in the United States of America on acid-free paper

www.spiegelandgrau.com

2 4 6 8 9 7 5 3 1

FIRST EDITION

Book design by Dana Leigh Blanchette

For my mother

Come to the edge.
We might fall.
Come to the edge.
It's too high!
COME TO THE EDGE!
And they came,
and he pushed,
and they flew.

—CHRISTOPHER LOGUE

Amor vinciat

August 1985

Seeing a place for the first time at night gives it a kind of mystery that never leaves.

John's mother's house in rural New Jersey was on a private stretch of road between Peapack and Bernardsville in an area known as Pleasant Valley. Bernardsville, a charming town an hour west of New York City, claims Meryl Streep as its hometown girl, and buildings from the turn of the century have been converted into video stores and pizza parlors. Peapack is smaller, quieter, with an antiques store and two churches. Close by are Ravine Lake and the Essex Hunt. The Hunt was founded in 1870 in Montclair but soon relocated nearby, and Mrs. Onassis rode with them for years. And in the surrounding fields of Somerset County, John had gone on his first fox hunt.

On the left side of the road as you approached the house, there was a meadow and a ridge with a dark line of trees at the top. On the right—country estates, deeper woods, and a small river, a branch of the Raritan. The house was nestled on a hill. What I remember is the peace and comfort of being there. It was a place to rest and recharge. Mrs. Onassis had a great talent for making you feel welcome, for creating an atmosphere of elegance and ease in all of her homes, although each had its own special character.

The cottage in Virginia, which she used during foxhunting season, was simple, with pressed linen sheets that smelled like rain, a sloping roof, and a large sunlit bathroom with a sisal carpet and a comfortable chair to read in. When John and I lived in Washington during the summer of 1987—he was interning at the Justice Department, and I was performing at the Shakespeare Theatre—we spent weekends alone there. It was a particular pleasure to sink into that deep tub on an afternoon, the rain beating on the roof, and listen as he read to me from the chair, a book of poems or Joseph Campbell or whatever novel he was reading.

The house in New Jersey had five bedrooms and an airy living room with yellow walls and French doors that opened onto a pool and a stone patio. It wasn't grand or ostentatious; it was timeless and the colors subtle. You hadn't realized that you wanted to put your feet up, but there was a stool waiting. You hadn't realized that you wanted to read, but there was a light nearby and just the right book. Comfort and desire were anticipated, and you felt cared for.

But I didn't know any of this on that summer night in 1985—I'd never been to either home. Tonight would be the first time I would stay at the house on Pleasant Valley Road.

Rehearsals had ended earlier that evening at the Irish Arts Center, a small theater in Manhattan's West Fifties. It was a Thursday, and the play that John and I were in rehearsals for was opening that Sunday.

Winners is set on a hill, and our director, Robin Saex, had always talked about running our scenes outside. She had been toying with spots in Central Park and Riverside when John volunteered a slope near his mother's house in Peapack. It was steep, he told us—so steep we could roll down it! We would rehearse there on Friday, which would give the crew the entire day to finish the set and hang the lights in time for our first technical rehearsal on Friday night.

The three of us set off in his silver-gray Honda. When we arrived close to midnight, we found that supper had been laid out by the Portuguese couple who were caretakers of the house. They were asleep, but a very excited spaniel was there to greet us instead. Shannon was a pudgy black and white dog—a descendant of the original Shannon, a gift from President de Valera of Ireland to President Kennedy after his trip there in 1963. John scolded him affectionately for being fat and lazy and told him that the bloodlines had deteriorated, but the spaniel was thrilled by the attention.

On a quick spin through the house, he showed us his old room. It was a boy's room—red, white, and blue, with low ceilings, some toy soldiers still on the bureau, and in the bookshelf *Curious George* and *Where the Wild Things Are*. Robin dropped her bags near the bed, and we went downstairs and ate cold shepherd's pie and profiteroles, a meal I would come to know later as one of his favorites.

After supper, Robin yawned and said, "Guys, I'm turning in. We have a lot of work to do tomorrow." I was tired as well, but too excited to sleep, and when John asked if I wanted to go see the horses in the neighbors' barn, I said yes. He put some carrots and sugar cubes in his pocket, and we headed down the driveway and across the road to the McDonnells'.

Murray McDonnell and his wife, Peggy, were old friends of John's mother. She boarded her horses with them, and their children had grown up together. The McDonnells' hound, who spent most days visiting Shannon, began to follow us home, and Shannon, who never strayed far from his kitchen, trailed behind. John teased both dogs, saying they were gay lovers. He leaned over and shook a finger at Shannon, admonishing him again for being fat. "Don't be too sweet, Shanney, don't be too sweet. Or I will bite you. I'll bite you." Shannon thumped his stub of a tail and waddled back up the drive.

It was one A.M., and I was getting the moonlight tour. When I asked if we'd wake the McDonnells, John shrugged and told me not to worry. He showed me an old childhood clubhouse, and we ducked through the small wooden door. He showed me the roosters and the barn cats and the caged rabbits. And when an especially eager bunny nipped my fingers through the chicken wire, he said that Elise, his mother's housekeeper, ate them for treats. I whimpered—the desired response, I now think.

We moved into the cool of the barn and met Murray McDonnell's gelding and John's mother's mount, Toby. Like us, the horses could not sleep—or had been awakened by a whiff of carrot. I was not a horsewoman by any stretch of the imagination, but I'd ridden summers until I was fourteen, and I knew how to feed a horse. Still, it felt like the first time, and I let him show me. I had begun to value when he taught me things—his patience, the joy he took, how he never gave up.

"See, you keep your hand flat and your fingers back."

I stood close to him by the stall and he reached into his pocket.

"Let him take it, he won't bite. Like this . . ." Toby sniffed, lowered his velvet head, then looked up expecting more.

"You try." In the darkness, John had stepped behind me. "Go on, keep your fingers back."

"I'll just feed him a carrot." The carrot, for some reason, seemed safe.

"Here," he said, opening my hand and placing a sugar cube

there. "Don't be scared." And with the back of my hand resting in his palm, the horse kissed mine and the sugar was gone.

Our hands broke. But his touch stayed with me as we fed the horses the rest of our stash. It was with me when we left the barn and walked out into the ring. And when I climbed onto the split rail fence, John hopped up beside me.

The moon was full, and we were quiet, watching the sky.

"It's a blue moon tonight," I said. "I heard it on the radio."

"Oh yeah?" He crooned, "Without a dream in my heart, without a love of—"

"What *is* a blue moon?" I wondered aloud.

"It's when there are two full moons in one month. Not as rare as an eclipse, but definitely rare." Because of his time in Outward Bound and a NOLS stint in Kenya, along with his innate curiosity, he knew so much about the natural world that I didn't.

"So it's got *nothing* to do with being blue?"

He shook his head, smiling.

"But it seems special, like a stronger moon."

"Maybe it is," he said, looking into my eyes.

"Look." I pointed. "It *is* brighter. Everything is silver—the leaves, the barn, the stones, the horses, the road, everything." I shifted my weight on the fence. *Everything.*

Again we were quiet—the shyness that came from knowing each other well in one way, as we had for ten years, and then the knowledge deepening. We had been friends in high school, housemates in college, but now—walking home together these past few weeks, practicing the kiss in rehearsals, falling in love through the imaginary circumstances of the theater (a professional hazard for actors: *Is it real? Or is it the play?*)—attraction had become undeniable. We sat for a while under the stars and felt no need to speak. But then he did.

"Can I do this for real?"

He didn't wait for an answer; he leaned in. Only our lips touched. It was gentle, hands-free, exquisite. I opened my eyes for a second, not believing that what I'd dreamed of was happening, and saw, by the lines at his eyes, that he was smiling. I held on to the fence, woozy. A world had opened.

"I've been waiting to do that for a long time," he said, looking not at me, but at the sky. He was still smiling, and I remember thinking then that he looked proud. For the past week and a half, we had kissed in rehearsals, but in my mind, we were the characters, Mag and Joe, teenagers from Ireland about to be married because she was pregnant. At least I had tried to believe that. But this kiss was different. This kiss was ours.

"I guess that wasn't supposed to happen," he said finally, tucking one of his ankles behind the fence rail.

No. It's right. Again. Don't stop, I thought. Then my mind went to the actor I'd been with for almost three years, who was kind and good and could make me laugh, even in a rough patch, and to John's girlfriend from Brown, whom I liked and admired. Reality. People would be hurt. Or did he mean it wasn't supposed to happen because we were friends and should remain so? It occurred to me only later that he was testing the waters.

"Do you want to talk about it?" I asked.

He didn't answer. Instead, he took my hand and said he wanted to show me something. I followed him into the woods, twigs snapping under our feet. The sky had grown brighter, and light danced through the thicket of elms onto the rocks and the river. Sound rushed, loud and exhilarating. In my dreams, I'd promised myself one kiss—just one—and now I'd had that.

John stepped into the shallow river and sloshed around in his sneakers. I took off my sandals and jumped from rock to rock as he steadied me, and when I finally gave in and stepped down into the cold water alongside him, it woke me. I felt alive. I'd been quiet in the barn, but now I could not stop talking. Nerves, excitement, happiness—I'm not sure which was stronger. We talked about our childhoods. I told him how I hid in books, loved the ocean, didn't like sports but adored ballet. "You sound like my mother," he said, somewhat under his breath. "But I seem to recall a table or two you danced on in high school."

I told him stories about my younger brothers and about the nuns at Sacred Heart, where I had gone to grade school and where his sister had also gone. He remembered the building on Fifth Avenue, he said, and its covered driveway. He'd gone to St. David's, two blocks down, and in the afternoons had walked with his mother or his nanny to pick his sister up. He told me about playing in this river and making forts, about being bloodied in a fox hunt nearby—an initiation rite in which boys are dabbed with the blood of the kill—and about how, when he was a toddler and the first Shannon was a puppy, and a mess was made or sweets were taken from the table, his mother didn't know whether to scold him or the dog. He laughed when he told that story. But his mood darkened when he told of another Shannon, the one he loved best, the one who was irascible. He had been away for part of the summer, and on his return, he found that his mother had given the dog away. "I didn't even get to say goodbye," he said sadly.

It's strange how one kiss can make you remember what is long past but what has made you who you are.

Upstairs, before we went to bed, he shared his toothpaste with me. Looking at his face in the mirror beside mine, I wondered if he always brushed his teeth so long. He didn't seem the type. I knew I wasn't. I just didn't want the night to end.

"Good night," he said finally, grinning in the hallway between the bedrooms.

"Good night," I said, grinning back, but neither of us moved.

We kissed again. This time, he pulled me to him, and our bodies met like they'd always known each other. I'd never been kissed so slowly. He stroked my back and buried his face in my hair and kissed my neck. He was wearing a soft cotton shirt he had gotten in Kathmandu the year before. It was white, and on the back there was a large evil eye embroidered in turquoise and black. I felt the loose threads and his muscles beneath them. I felt his hand at the small of my back. Then I smelled something. Mint. In our passion, his toothbrush had become entangled in my hair. We looked at each other, realized, and began to laugh. I had toothpaste in my hair and I was happy. I was drunk with it. Then I pulled back.

"I hate to say good night—"

"Would you like to spend it with me?" he said softly.

Was this something he did easily? What would it mean? Would it be one night? And the play, would it change the play? Out of the corner of my eye, I saw a large and what looked to be quite opulent bed in the guest room, where his bags and the dutiful Shannon waited. At that moment, there was nothing I wanted more than to be with him. But other thoughts flashed through my mind, and I behaved not as I desired, not as I'd fantasized, but like the coy Catholic girl I was. The eroticism of waiting.

I stepped up on the landing that brought me closer to his height and whispered, "I would, but it's . . . complicated."

He smiled. "Well, if it ever gets uncomplicated . . ."

I was confused. "Isn't it for you?"

"Oh, I've had a lot of time to think." He dropped his head to one side, as if that way he could see me better. "I've walked you home so many times and trudged away alone."

What did he mean? Before I could speak, he brushed the hair from my face and pulled me close.

"But one more kiss."

This time it was harder to resist.

I stayed alone in Caroline's room that night—a girlhood room with twin beds in white eyelet, and trophies and colored ribbons from horse shows. The setting was virginal, but my thoughts were not. I stared at the ribbons late into the night, unable to sleep. It wasn't just the play opening, or the moonlight flooding through the window, or the smallness of the bed. It was the knowledge that our rooms adjoined through the hall door and he was sleeping so near. It was the knowledge that a kiss we had shared near a field by some horses might change my life forever.

Beginning

Within you, your years
are growing.

—PABLO NERUDA

In the cool of a June evening long ago, a man holds a child in his arms. Across the field, light is falling behind a bank of trees and resting on a water tower, a dome of red and white checks. She's in a cotton nightgown and her legs dangle. He is wearing tennis whites, but they're rumpled. They always are. No socks, his shirt untucked. Behind them, a shingled summerhouse rambles down to a dock and a muddy bay. Near the kitchen door, a painted trellis is heavy with the heads of pale roses bowing.

Every night they do this. He sings her made-up songs and tells her stories. Some are silly, and she laughs. *Daddy,* she says. Some are of women in long dresses. Some of a princess with her name and a knight who slays dragons. But on summer nights, as he does on this one, he points to the tower and tells her it is hers. Her very own. He tells her, and she believes him. His eyes, sharp like the blue of a bird's wing, gaze into hers. She lays her head against him, hair damp from the bath, and breathes the salty warmth of his skin. She wraps her legs at his waist and curls into him as the story ends and the light dies.

My parents were married under a pink and white tent on the East End of Long Island on a July night in 1959. The tent, sheer and billowing and filled with stephanotis and daylilies, was propped for the night on the grounds of a robber baron's estate in Quogue, New York, a resort community some eighty miles from Manhattan. The estate was not on the ocean; most of the grander homes there were set back across the canal from the spit of barrier beach that ran from the Moriches Inlet in the west to the Shinnecock Inlet in the east. There, on the eastern end—standing on the jetty past Ponquogue Bridge, looking at that wide, ancient bay and the cut where the Atlantic rushed in—you could see across to another sandy spit, and miles later, there was Southampton, where lavish shingled cottages were indeed built by the sea, on Gin Lane, on Meadow Lane, on Dune Road.

The rented house where they were married, with its diamond-mullioned windows and its graceful veranda, was close enough to the water so that when the wind changed—when dinner ended and the dancing began—the scent of the sea would have mixed with the music and laughter and the heady perfume of the sweet, high-hedged privet.

The bride's organdy gown was from Bergdorf Goodman, her portrait by Bachrach, and the engraved invitations by Cartier, and if you thumbed through the glossy black-and-white proofs of cake cutting and veil straightening, you might think children of privilege, society wedding. But you would be wrong. My parents' story was different.

They were both Catholic, both of German and Irish descent. They came from small towns in Pennsylvania and Nebraska. My father was the son of a railroad foreman, my mother the daughter of a rancher, farmer, wanderer, and occasional Prohibition bootlegger. They had come to New York to find their fortunes, and on a winter day, seventeen months before the wedding by the sea and twenty-six months before I was born, they found each other.

After graduating from St. Mary College in Xavier, Kansas, my mother took a monthlong TWA flight attendant's course. When asked to put in for their home base, she and her best friend swore they'd stick together. My mother wanted Kansas City, but her friend pushed for New York. "Aim for the top," she said. "You can always come back." They tossed a coin, and my mother lost.

By the time she met my father, she had been in the city for almost four years and was living in a one-bedroom apartment behind the Waldorf-Astoria with two roommates. No longer a stewardess, she was a Foster-Ferguson model with dreams of becoming an opera singer. She did commercial and editorial print, but not high fashion. She was the girl next door with the winning smile—Miss O'Neill Lyons Club, the Dial soap girl, and the second runner-up in the Miss New York Summer Festival of 1958. And in every snapshot from my childhood, no matter who was crying at the time, she looks perfect—her face catching the light, her ankle turned just so.

My father was thirteen years older. He'd been in New York longer and was in his element, as though he'd been born rushing somewhere in a single-breasted charcoal suit, a topcoat easy on his arm. He'd been a pilot during World War II and had flown a Martin B-26 Marauder over Utah Beach. In the winter of 1945, on R & R in Miami, he met a girl at the Delano Hotel and scrapped his plans to join the Flying Tigers and fly the Hump to China. He married her three months later—the daughter of a showgirl and a Chicago industrialist—and they settled in her city, where he went to Northwestern Law on the GI Bill. But the marriage was unhappy, and when I was ten and allowed to know such things, my aunt whispered that when it ended, my father was crushed. For him, New York was a fresh start. At thirty-one, he became publisher and president of *Everywoman's* magazine (later *Family Circle*), before moving on to run a thriving boutique advertising agency. He had no intention of remarrying. There hadn't been children with his first wife, and although he wanted them, he believed it wasn't possible.

My father ran with a fast crowd, mostly Madison Avenue types like himself, and twice a month they held "scrambles." To all appearances, these were martini Sunday brunches at someone's Midtown apartment. But the point was women, and the rule was that each bachelor had to bring three "recruits," preferably models and no repeats. My mother went with her friend Tex, and although she was impressed by my father's Tudor City aerie, she recognized the situation for what it was and left quickly. She also found him annoying. He didn't like *The Music Man,* and she did. He, however, was smitten. Richer men, kinder men pursued my mother then, but my father was fun, and after a date or two, she decided that was what she wanted.

On May 4, 1960, six days before Senator John Kennedy won the pivotal West Virginia primary, I was born, the child my father hadn't thought possible. He filled the room in the old wing of Lenox Hill Hospital with balloons and flowers, and smoked Partagas downstairs with his best friend, Lloyd. That summer, as they did for many summers to come, my parents rented an old farmhouse with nine bedrooms, a potbelly stove, two fireplaces, and a rickety old dock on Quantuck Bay, not far from the gabled house where they had married the year before.

When I was small, my mother read the story of Cinderella to me every night, at my insistence, and when she tried to skip a page out of boredom, I knew. I didn't want the Disney version, although we had that, too. It stayed on the shelf by my ballerina music box, and she would alternate between the Perrault and the Grimm—the one with the talking doves, the wishing tree, and the blood in the shoe. And when I could read, I devoured every color of Andrew Lang's Fairy Books.

I would ask my mother then to tell me the story of how my father had proposed. Her answer was always the same. *One day we just started talking about it. One day we just knew.* This horrified me. There was no kneeling, no meaningful locale, no diamond slipped into a champagne flute or buried in chocolate mousse. No glass slipper. I kept thinking she was hiding the truth from me and if I just bothered her enough, she'd tell. Despite my badgering, that never happened, and I vowed, as seven-year-olds do, that it would be different, far different, for me.

Still—in the wedding pictures that filled the cream and gold binder, separate from the albums of my brothers and me and our birthdays and our bikes, there was a small crown in her hair that held the short veil in place, and her impossibly small waist was made smaller still by the starched crinoline of the dress.

The dress stayed in a long, plaid cardboard box tied with twine on the top shelf of her closet at 142 East Seventy-first Street, the prewar building off Lexington Avenue that we moved to when I was three. It sat next to a portable green sewing machine and the hard case that held my father's letters home from the war. I'd look up at the box sometimes and wonder, even though I already knew that the puffed sleeves, sweetheart neck, and fluffy, girlish lines were not for me. I wanted satin—a dress that looked like the nightgown of a 1930s movie star—and an ivory mantilla that trailed the floor. During the Depression, my Nebraska grandmother had eloped a month shy of her seventeenth birthday in a red traveling suit with a cloche hat, and this fascinated me—along with the fact that she was one of the only divorced people I knew.

When she was twenty-nine, my grandfather took whatever he could sell and left her with two kids and 320 acres of family homestead on South Pasture Creek. It was 1943. The land was worthless from drought and crop failure, the farmhouse would burn the next year, and she was a woman alone. But she worked hard and saved her money, and eventually she had a dress shop in town and a slew of admirers: the auctioneer for the county, the town solicitor, and the one she loved—a married man who took her dancing when the big bands came to town.

She held on to the land until she died, and by the time my brothers and I visited in the summers, she lived in town, leasing it to ranchers and alfalfa farmers. We always drove out there in her gold Oldsmobile, and when we reached the cottonwoods by the creek, she'd direct one of us to run and take down the barbed wire gate, hold it open as the car passed through, and then hook it back on the fence post so the cattle didn't get out.

My grandmother walked with a pronounced limp, the result of a near-fatal car accident the year before I was born, but she'd point out the milkweed and the musk thistle or the face of a particularly forlorn calf she'd fallen for that spring. My grandfather had been dead for years, and she never mentioned him. My mother rarely did. Although a cousin might say something, it was always hush-hush, and no matter how much I prodded, she remained silent.

I became obsessed with old family pictures. Afternoon farm picnics, with straw boaters and white dresses, and slicked-haired men, stiff in their studio portraits with the hard paper frames. It was my mission; I didn't want the faces to be lost. I'd cart the photos to the kitchen table, and while my grandmother smoked her Pall Malls, I'd scribble dates and names, whatever she remembered, in pencil on the back.

I found one picture—small and insignificant, with white matte borders—of a man on a big paint horse with a lasso in one hand and a bottle in the other. Even though it was blurry, I could make out the jaunty grin. "Is this him? Is this him, Grandma?" I was like a miner hitting pay dirt. She stared at the image for a long time, and although it wasn't exactly a smile that crossed her face, it was enough. As I held my breath, she lowered her chin and made a small clicking sound at the side of her mouth, the way you do when you urge a horse to go faster. "Son of a bitch," she said softly before returning to her cigarette.

My mother's dress was brought down from the shelf three times—twice for cleaning and once, five years after my father died, when she moved out of the apartment that had been her home for thirty-five years and where she had raised us. The dress was the last thing packed. I stood on a piano stool and handed her the box. It was lighter than I remembered. She took it to the bed, careful of the broken edges, and when she opened it, she wept.

The Otto Kahn mansion stands at the corner of Ninety-first Street and Fifth Avenue, on the far reaches of Millionaires' Row on New York's Upper East Side. The five-story rusticated limestone façade is softened by simple pilasters and corniced windows, and an inner courtyard fills the many rooms with light, even on cloudy days. Inspired by the sixteenth-century Palazzo della Cancelleria in Rome, it was completed in 1918 as the primary dwelling of the Wall Street financier and arts patron. The mansion wasn't the only tony building on the block. The Burden and Hammond residences stood next door, and Andrew Carnegie's spacious Georgian-style home with brick-terraced gardens, now the Cooper-Hewitt museum, was across the street.

In 1934, shortly before Kahn's death, the building was sold to a French order of cloistered Catholic nuns and became the Convent of the Sacred Heart, the school I went to from kindergarten through eighth grade. In 1940, the convent acquired the Burden mansion, and the two buildings were joined by narrow passageways.

When we visited the school in the fall of 1964, there was no doubt in my mother's mind that I would go there. After the tour, I was sent off with a novice, a slim girl not yet in full habit, to play on the silver slide on the roof deck by the kindergarten rooms. My mother stayed behind with the small woman in the dark robes. When the inevitable question came—was there divorce in the family?—she didn't lie. She listened as the Reverend Mother explained what she already knew. In the eyes of the Church, marriage was indissoluble without an annulment. Sacraments could not be received. And although I was blameless—still, they could not in good conscience accept me for the next fall. My mother, however, remained determined. After all, that same year, Mrs. Kennedy, newly arrived in New York, had enrolled her daughter, Caroline, in second grade, and this had made an impression on all Upper East Side Catholic matrons. Having been educated by nuns herself, my mother knew exactly what to do. She crossed her ankles firmly under the chair, raised her head, and, without shame for what she was about to do, began to cry.

The school is still there, but the world I entered in 1965 when I passed through the heavy oak doors on Ninety-first Street no longer exists. Now there is a small plaque on the corner of the building that says LANDMARK STATUS. After years of scaffolding, the stone, once sepia with dirt, is bone white. Balustrades have been repaired, murals have been restored, and the threadbare velvet railing I once ached to touch has been replaced. The courtyard and coffered-ceilinged foyer by the chapel, the banquet hall, and the mirror-paneled ballroom where we danced barefoot in miniature Isadora Duncan garb can be rented for photo shoots, weddings, galas, and the occasional memorial service.

The nuns no longer teach. They are, in fact, gone. They no longer swish down the halls in long robes, no longer live in the fifth-floor wing that was forbidden to us and, because it was forbidden, fantasized over endlessly. By a blocked-off stairwell, two burly older girls once cornered me and my friend Diane. The larger one rapped on a hollow oak panel and convinced us that *this* was where the nuns hid the bodies and we'd better watch it.

Times were changing even then. The Second Vatican Council concluded at the end of 1965, and by 1967 there was an opening of cloistered life. In the years that followed, the Religious of the Sacred Heart heeded the call from Rome to adapt to the modern world. They began to venture outside the convent walls and were free to find vocations in areas other than teaching. But with renewal came an unraveling, and the eventual dwindling of their numbers.

Halfway through first grade, the order's habit was modified—the fluted bonnet became a veil—and those we knew as "Mother" were now to be called "Sister." Soon we saw their hairlines—a revelation. And by the time we entered middle school in 1970, most of them wore street clothes just like our lay teachers', only plainer, and formal traditions had given way to folk Masses and felt banners with cheery New Testament sayings.

I was never hit with a ruler, never taught the rosary or the difference between a venial and a mortal sin. When I was in second grade, an earnest nun with huge eyebrows taught us how to baptize. *Just in case.* One day, she said, we might find ourselves on a desert island with someone who wanted desperately to convert. She shut the classroom door, turned the brass knob until there was a click, and in hushed tones made us promise not to tell our parents. I did as she asked. I was quiet at dinner, but later solemnly baptized my dog Tango with bathwater so that we would be together forever in heaven.

The teaching methods began to change, too. We were still drilled on multiplication tables and French verbs; we still curtsied every morning and were silent on the stairs. But now there were journals for everything, and Arts Days and Medieval fairs; and if, instead of writing a paper, we wanted to paint a picture or put on a play or design a costume, we could. For Ancient History one year, we trooped to Central Park and scraped around in the dirt by Belvedere Pond pretending to be Sumerians. The sixties had seeped through the walls, and what we learned was love and not to hide our light under a bushel.

When I started at the school, more than thirty years had passed since Otto Kahn's death, but remnants of him were everywhere: a painted ceiling thick with leaves, a frieze of Greek muses, a grandfather clock like the one Drosselmeyer covers with his cape in *The Nutcracker*, and the shapes of waves on stone. Doors carved in lion faces, parquet floors perfect for dancing, and in the library, a flight of hidden steps up which Kahn, it was whispered, lured young actresses to the master bedroom (now a classroom) above. But at the top of the second-floor landing, between the library and the chapel, there was a painting of a young woman in a salmon-colored gown that reminded us of why we were here. It is a copy of a Renaissance-style fresco from the convent of the Trinità dei Monti in Rome.

Mater Admirabilis, Mother Most Admirable, she is called, and Our Lady of the Lily. The original, painted in 1844 by a young postulate of the order, was venerated and said to perform miracles, and in her small chapel above the Piazza di Spagna, words of thanks are carved in marble and etched in silver. Replicas of this Madonna can be found in Sacred Heart schools throughout the world. Ours was tall and had an arched frame. Set low to the ground, it rested on a platform of graduated steps so that even the smallest girl could approach. Unlit white tapers stood at either side, and on her feast day, the nuns placed flowers.

She's called Mater, but if you look closely, past the ease and self-possession, you can see that she's not yet sixteen. A girl. Through the columned arch behind her, dawn is breaking. She sits on a wooden chair, with a distaff on one side and a lily on the other. In her resting hand is a spindle, and at her feet, a book. Her dress is simple but ornamented. Beneath her is an elaborate floor of colored marble. She's the picture of contemplation, but she has not turned from the world; the hair that falls from her veil is curled, and behind her lips there is a secret. She wears a crown of stars, but it's before all that. Before she is Queen of Heaven, before the Annunciation and the Assumption, before the Magi and the star and the flight to Egypt. Before the wedding at Cana. And well before a body is handed down at the foot of the cross. Before grief.

I first saw her when I was four, and I liked her at once. She was pretty and she wore a pretty dress. But soon I knew her effect, the kind some have over small animals and storms. I felt watched over, loved without judgment or requirement. I felt allowed. It was to her I aspired, not the nuns or the priests or the images of suffering. I wanted to know her mystery only. In lower school, we passed her at least four times a day, shuttling from one stone staircase to another. I knew her then, knew her face, the way she appeared to blush in certain light and that her eyes were downcast but pleased. From the middle of a line of girls, I would always look back— craning my neck and dragging my feet—in case this was the day, the moment, she chose to reveal herself.

· · ·

I knew when I was young that I went to school in a castle, and I knew that this wasn't normal, but the small evidences of ruin—a chipped column, a faded tapestry—gave intimacy to the splendor, so it seemed it really was someone's house. The nuns would say God's house. And perhaps they were right. But from those years and from that place, I had the sense that brokenness meant approach and that beauty was something mixed of shadow and decay. That it was made, in part, from the pieces of the past and the things that are left behind.

I wonder if I was born nostalgic. It's possible it's in the blood, a predetermined trait like green eyes or flat feet. And it may well be that some ancestor on a sea crossing was filled with longing for what was gone—out of grief or pleasure, or simply to make the time pass on the ship.

I remember the first time I felt that kind of longing. I was standing in the hallway outside the first-grade classroom, eyes smarting and nose beginning to run. I'd been sent there by Sister Caroline for asking too many questions. *Too imaginative,* she'd written on my report card. *Disorganized.* Curiosity, it seemed—encouraged the year before by our kindergarten teacher, Miss Mellion, a smart Londoner who wore blue angora miniskirts and whose voice had a melody like one of Mary Poppins's chimney sweeps—was now punished.

Sister Caroline was stout, with a pinched, doughy face, and if you stood close enough to her, there was an odd, shuttered smell. She was a visiting nun from another order and wore a different habit—starched, short, and striped—not the flowing black robes of Mother Brown or Mother Ranney. She also lacked their kindness. Her sharp eyes were always darting, never seeming to rest or take you in. She was the only nun I ever truly hated, and I wasn't alone in this. What pleased her was order. What provoked her was expression. She was an expert in phonics, but her teaching was joyless, and her frequent reprimands, from which no one was immune, usually took the form of being banished to the stool in the Stupid Corner (while the rest of us had lessons) or coloring "baby papers"—simple outlines of flowers and puppies—with dirty crayons. Tougher girls, like Nancy or Christy, were able to laugh it off, but I wasn't. And after I refused to open my milk carton during milk break—because I could never finish it all and what about all those starving children in Ethiopia—her dislike of me became acute.

That day, the hand bell had been rung, all the doors were shut, and I was alone in the long white hall. This was one of the worst censures, second only to being sent to Reverend Mother's office, and it was the first time for me. I had no idea why I was there, and I wanted to hide. There was the cloakroom behind the elevator, the play deck on the roof above, or the dusty wings of the velvet-curtained stage in the assembly hall two floors down. Shame welled up in me, and I began to cry. I realized that the only way to get through the rest of the year with Sister Caroline was to dim myself, to silence whatever voice I had.

Blinded by tears, I turned down the hall. By the kindergarten rooms, thumbtacked neatly on bulletin boards, were rows of colored paper with cracked finger paint and names written in Miss Mellion's black felt pen. With all my heart, I wanted to push the classroom door open, grab one of the little-girl smocks that hung on hooks in the cubbies, and bury myself forever in Miss Mellion's soft, warm, British lap. And when I realized I couldn't, I began to sob harder.

Then something strange began to happen. I couldn't move, the floor seemed to swell beneath me, and a wave of everything I remembered from the year before came over me: Miss Mellion's throaty laugh, singing a song during show-and-tell, the rounded inkwells in our yellow wooden desks, the red rug where we lay at nap time, the delicate chiming of Miss Mellion's bracelets, the sun from the open window on Elizabeth's gold hair. I was frightened at first, but then I gave over to the barrage of color and sound.

When it was over, I was no longer crying. I had lost track of time, and that felt like relief. Although I sensed that six was a bit young for this style of reminiscing, I also discovered that memories of pleasure—of what I longed for and what no longer was—had calmed me. They were as real as the long hall I stood in or the Gospel words on the banner nearby or Sister Caroline's virulent disdain of me. I took the secret of that day, and later, on nights when I couldn't sleep, I would choose a memory. Lying on my back with my eyes shut to the dark, I'd pick one, imagining it was a selection on a jukebox. I would wait until, like a shiny 45, it dropped and slowly began to spin.

It might be that the desire to turn back is passed on. I believe that. But it could also be that this place so redolent of the past had claimed me, marked me, like the smudge of Lenten ashes burned from the blessed palms of the year before.

Famous people's children went to Sacred Heart, and in that way, it was like any private school in New York. The nuns were indifferent—they treated everyone the same—but names were whispered down, as in a game of telephone, during gym or in the lunch line. There was the daughter of Spike Jones, a big band leader of the forties and fifties (this impressed my father to no end; he had an eight-track tape of Glenn Miller, and he played it on all our car rides); the great-granddaughters of Stanford White; the nieces of William F. Buckley and Carroll O'Connor; and, for one infamous year at the height of Watergate, John and Martha Mitchell's shy, red-haired daughter, Marty. Caroline Kennedy and her cousins Sidney and Victoria were older than me. I saw them in the halls, during fire drills, or at congé, a surprise feast held twice a year, when we played hide-and-seek en masse and ate cake and tricolor ice cream in paper cups with lids that peeled off with a pop. But at that age, the world consisted of the thirty-two girls in my grade—and a few of the mean ones in the grade ahead.

On a spring day in 1969, when I was where I shouldn't have been, I saw her. No longer Mrs. Kennedy, she had married the previous October and was now Mrs. Onassis.

Arrivals and departures took place on Fifth Avenue through a small door that led to an industrial staircase. At the end of the day, the older girls headed off with colored passes for the downtown bus or the crosstown bus, but the lower school girls boarded private buses, double-parked and yellow, or were met by mothers and nannies gathered on the sidewalk for pickup.

The formal entrance was on Ninety-first Street through a recessed half-circular drive, once a carriageway, that led to two sets of dark double doors. The covered drive, where we sometimes lined up for fire drills and class pictures, was a well of coolness, a cavern of stone. At either end of the drive, flung wide in the day and locked by the nuns at night, were fifteen-foot arched dungeon doors. This was the grown-ups' entrance. We were allowed to use it only at special times, like First Communion and the Christmas concert, when the front lobby was home to a massive tree and a terrifying oversize crèche.

I don't remember whether, on that day, I went there because it was spring, or because it was off-limits, or because I simply wanted to stand by myself in the cool between the doors. Nor do I recall how, before that, I found myself, between lunch and gym, alone on the first-floor landing.

I stood on the landing (where I was allowed) looking at the lobby (where I was not), and instead of turning left up the steps by the courtyard, I lingered. Except for Miss Doran, the receptionist, the large hall was empty. No one on the heavy benches that looked like church pews. No one at the ancient creaky elevator with the brass grate (also off-limits). It was a window that wouldn't last.

My waist rooted to the handrail, I inched down a step. Miss Doran turned in my direction. She was chinless, and her head ended in a topknot. I watched as it bobbed. She was on the phone, a private call I could tell, and with her thumb, she kept tapping on the bridge of her cat-eye glasses. She saw me and she didn't. When she swiveled her chair away from me, I began to walk—the polished doors just feet away—not fast, not slow, but as though I belonged, as though I were an upper school girl instead of a lowly third grader.

I made it through the first set of doors into the tight alcove with the lantern above. My heart raced. Realizing that no one had followed me—no nun, no Miss Doran, no handyman—I pushed open the second set of doors. Triumphant, I stood alone on the top step, looking at the tight-budded trees on the street outside.

But there was someone there. A woman backlit by the sun had just stepped through the arch onto the cobblestone drive, her face obscured by shadow. Behind her, a photographer was taking pictures. He looked curious to me, like a monkey bending in all sorts of ways, but oh so careful not to drop his camera or cross the line that divided the sidewalk from school property. Even through the flashes, I recognized the long neck, the dark glasses, and her hair just like my mother's when she went to a fancy party. Tall, like an empress from a storybook, she glided toward me, without interest in the man who continued to take pictures of her back. Her face was calm, as if by paying no attention, she could will him from being.

When she was close, I saw her face, that her lips were curved. She took one step up, placed a gloved hand on the heavy doors, and was gone.

Years later, when we met, I remembered who it was she had reminded me of that day. It was the painting of the Lady with the Lily, with the same inscrutable smile.

The uniform we wore was nothing like the ones at the other girls' schools nearby. Not for us the blue pinstripe or the muted plaid. We wore a gray wool jumper, a boxy jacket to match, either a white shirt with a Peter Pan collar or a red turtleneck jersey, gray kneesocks with a flat braid up the side, and brown oxfords bought at Indian Walk the week before school started. The shoes were hateful—like the ones nurses wore, with pink lumps of rubber welling from the sides. The only consolation was that everyone had to wear them. My mother made me polish mine once a week with a Kiwi kit (also from Indian Walk), and as I sat on the white-tiled bathroom floor inevitably scuffed with brown, it seemed to me a supreme waste of time to shine something that was so ugly to begin with.

There were two things that made the uniform bearable. At the end of each year, Miss Mellion picked six girls to clean up the lower and middle school costume closet, a windowless box of a room in the Burden mansion. And each year, I was one of her chosen. A limited amount of folding took place. Mostly, it was an entire day without classes, spent thigh-deep in feathers, chiffon, dust, and torn velvet.

The other thing was the ribbons, wide, grosgrain sashes in pink and red that Reverend Mother would slip over your left shoulder and fasten with a pin at your waist. They were awarded sparingly for overall excellence. I got only two in nine years. But it didn't matter—they stood out in the sea of gray, a feast for the eye.

Every Monday morning in lower school, we had assembly, which the nuns called prîmes. We'd file down the stone steps from the fourth to the second floor, always by height, always silent, always to the left. We were girls in straight lines with wild hidden hearts—like Madeline. If the nun's back was turned, one of us would make a break for the stone banister which was perfect for sliding and swept into a curling flourish at the bottom.

The assembly hall had been Otto Kahn's music room, and there was a huge chandelier in the center and a shallow, curtained stage at the back. The teachers sat on upholstered chairs in front of the tall French windows overlooking the courtyard. They faced us and we faced each other. There were four rows of folding chairs on each side of the wide aisle, with the first grade in the front and the fourth grade at the back. Giggling and bored, we filed in and peeled off—half the class to one side of the aisle and half to the other. Reverend Mother came last. She was tiny, not even five feet, and we all stood when she entered the room.

As the teachers began to arrive, a shoe box was passed filled with balled pairs of white gloves, each with name tags sewn on by our mothers. Most of the gloves were thick brushed cotton, like mine, but some were trimmed with gold—a chain or a bow—and others were almost transparent, silky like a skating skirt or how it felt inside the top drawer of my mother's bureau. The gloves were always tight, as though the shoe box were magic and the stiff cotton shrank from week to week. Even when I used my teeth to nudge them up, they barely made it to my wrist.

At the end of assembly, we filed up two by two to be received by Reverend Mother. The procession was elaborate and choreographed, and the nuns rehearsed us endlessly—the spacing, when to turn, how deep to curtsy. Ball heel, ball heel. Like water ballet or a bride's walk. And when we finally got close enough, her eyes, magnified by the thick glasses she wore, were a filmy cornflower blue, and you could see the down on her cheek. She always smiled, but if she said something, you would answer, *Yes, Reverend Mother. Thank you, Reverend Mother.*

Prizes were given: medals, calligraphed cards, the pink and red sashes, and smaller ribbons in green and blue that we fixed to our jackets with tiny gold safety pins. I got ribbons for social studies, music, and drama, but what I wanted was the one for religion. For two months, I wanted it more than anything. I went to great lengths to furrow my brow in chapel and refrained from sliding down the banister, but the ribbon remained elusive. It always went to the same two girls—one with Coke-bottle glasses who told everyone she wanted to be a nun and the other who had the face of a Botticelli angel.

By the end of the year, I'd lost interest. I started reading books about Anne Boleyn, Sarah Bernhardt, and Lola Montez. I wanted to be an adventuress, an actress, or an archaeologist. But when *Masterpiece Theatre* began on PBS, I knew. I was transfixed by Dorothy Tutin in *The Six Wives of Henry VIII* and Glenda Jackson in *Elizabeth R*, and each morning during summer vacation, I would practice the two things that seemed essential to my future: how to raise one eyebrow and how to cry on cue.

There were games we played then. Hopscotch with colored chalk on the sidewalk and jacks on the slippery floor of my building's lobby. In second grade, there was *Dark Shadows* and *Lost in Space,* and we'd fight over who was Angelique and Mrs. Robinson. Elizabeth Cascella and I had queen costumes from FAO Schwarz. With the phonograph blaring, we would dance around the floral couches in her mother's living room and act out all of *The Sound of Music.* We adored Captain von Trapp—his profile and his uniform; we loved Liesl and her dress; but we wanted to be Maria in the opening credits, and we spun ourselves dizzy until the white ceiling of the room became an alpine sky.

And there were board games: Who Will I Be?, Trouble, and Mystery Date.

When I was ten, we had a new game, Paper Fortune. You rolled the dice, and that was your number. Then you made a list: five boys, five cars, five numbers, five cities, five resorts, five careers, and another five careers. On a piece of paper, you wrote each list on a separate line. Then, using your number, you began to count the words, crossing off the one you landed on. In the end, there was just one word in each row. You circled them with Magic Marker, and there it was: Your life. Who you married, what you drove, how many kids, where you lived, where you vacationed, what you did, and what he did.

The problem was boys. We didn't know any, or at least I didn't. For vacations, you could put down Monte Carlo or Colorado or the North Pole, places you'd never been. But the names of the boys had to be real, and though we didn't have to know them, they had to be our age, not Davy Jones or David Cassidy or any of the Beatles. Invariably, I'd put down Billy, who lived next door in the summer. (We'd kissed in the barn, and when we were little we'd played dress up at my house, until his mother called my mother and said that he couldn't.) A boy named Dwight I'd loved in nursery school. My friend Janie's cousins, who visited every summer from Lancaster, Pennsylvania, and taught me how to bunt in softball and cheat at cards. And someone's older brother. Sometimes, though, I'd put down the boy from the barbershop.

From the time I could walk until I was eight, I got my hair cut at Paul Molé, an old-fashioned barbershop on Seventy-fourth Street and Lexington. It's still there, on the second floor, but in a larger space a few doors down from the original. The photographs are still on the wall (some different from the ones I remember), and there's the same wooden Indian on the landing, and skinny black combs in blue water.

As I followed my mother's legs up the narrow wooden stairs, I would always stop by the pictures. They were black-framed and autographed, of newscasters and actors, and one down low of a boy my age with his hair cut long like my brothers'. Like every boy's in New York.

In the photograph, the boy is skinny, all energy. Something has his attention and he is caught mid-turn, eyes away from the camera, with somewhere to go. He may have just finished smiling or he is just about to. But there is something in him I recognize and I want to reach up and touch the picture.

He's the boy whose sister goes to my school, the boy whose mother is beautiful, and whose father was president before I can remember. But it's not that.

I stand and wait, wait for him to turn back. I wait—until my mother calls me. And each time we climb the steps, he's there.

Soon I'll forget about the game, forget about the folded paper and the Magic Markers. And the boy with the hair in his eyes whom one day I will find again. But years later, on a balmy night in Los Angeles in the late 1980s, when John and I are at a party in the Hollywood Hills, a girl I'd gone to Sacred Heart with walked in. We hadn't seen each other since we were fourteen. She was a model now, glamorous and high-strung, with an undiscovered David Duchovny like a jewel on her bare arm. He and John had been in the same class at Collegiate, and there, in a city so different from the one we'd grown up in, under a sky wider than the one we'd known, we caught up. When they leave to get the drinks, she takes my arm and pulls me close. Did I remember the nuns? she asks. How in first grade we pushed Sister Caroline down the staircase and in eighth grade we stole the wine from the sacristy? And what about the game? She leans in, her breath warm, and with something akin to shared triumph, whispers, "The game—you got what you wanted!"

I went to Sacred Heart for nine years. When I was old enough, I got a colored pass and took the city bus each day up Madison and down Fifth. It was a seed-kernel of a world, at once tight and about to burst. One of ritual and hegemony. We imagined ourselves different from one another, that each of our stories was special, but with rare exception, most of us lived in the small patch of privilege between East Sixty-fourth and Ninety-sixth streets. The West Side by Lincoln Center, where I had ballet class twice a week, was another country, and Downtown another planet.

It wasn't until I was fourteen and about to leave Sacred Heart that I fully questioned any of it. It was spring, close to our last day, and I was walking with the one Jewish girl in the school, who also happened to be in my class. Rachel was excused from chapel each

week, which made us all jealous, and her mother was glamorous—
a jazz pianist with a wicked sense of humor and a trust fund, who
let us play with her wigs, her muumuus, and her fake nails. Their
apartment was bigger than ours, and it was always dark. When I
slept over, I'd wait for the sound of Rachel's breathing in the next
bed. Then I'd sneak down the long corridor to find her mother in
the den. It would be dark save for the blue glow of the television
and the red tip of her cigarette. I'd curl up on the couch beside her,
and we'd watch *The Late Late Show* and I'd listen to her stories of
old boyfriends. If I was lucky, she'd pull out her Ouija board and
tell my future.

It came without warning on that spring day—a gauntlet. We
were close to Park Avenue, by the Brick Presbyterian Church,
when Rachel turned to me with what looked to be a smile and said,
"Do you *really* believe that Jesus Christ is the Son of God?"

My mouth fell open. I felt like I'd been slapped. I'd known her
for eight years, and she'd never said anything like that. We were
close to the corner, and I could hear the cabs whizzing by. It wasn't
just the theological issue—in fifth grade, we had studied Bud-
dhism, Confucianism, and Islam, and in seventh grade, for the
whole year, I had been obsessed with Chaim Potok—it was that
her words exploded the foundation of everything I knew: a world
solid and immutable, with all the rules in place. Whether I con-
formed or rebelled was another matter; it was there, safe, to push
against.

No one had ever asked me this question, and when she did,
doubt slipped easily beside me. In that instant, everything began to
fade: the mansion, the Arts Days, the felt banners, the Virgin with
her lily and her book, the quiet on the stairs and the darkened
stone, the shoe box full of gloves.

We stood at the light, awkward and silent. I believe she was happy, as if a war inside her had been won, but I was unmoored. I had no answer; I wouldn't for years. As we crossed the street, I wondered how long she had been waiting to say those words. What I didn't know then was how long I'd been waiting to hear them.

"Don't be afraid!" my father yells. He's waist-deep in water, far out on the second sandbar. I'm on the first—hands on my hips, foam at my ankles, and heels deep in wet sand. It's August. That's when they come, the sandbars and the jellyfish and the warm, shallow moats behind me near the shore. The waves are longer now, thicker—with storms roiling to the south. It's the best time to ride our navy canvas rafts, hurling and bouncing all the way, until we hit sand and fall off, scratched and breathless from the race. It's when we stand on our father's shoulders and dive off into the shimmering wall of waves. "Careful," he'll say when I scrabble up his back. "I'm not as young as I used to be."

My father is happiest in the ocean. It's something I have with him.

I can't see, but I know he's wearing the old suit, the blue-and-white-checked one. He has a new one with anchors he got for his birthday (same kind, different pattern), but he never wears it. Janie's father is younger. His suit has big Hawaiian flowers—pink and orange—and it hangs to his knees. He grew his hair long for the summer. But my father never changes. He'll wear the old suit until it fades to white or my mother throws it out, whichever comes first.

"*Come on!*" He's using his happy/angry voice, the one you pay attention to, the one that might hurt. So I dive in through the heavy surf, the water a cool, bright knife. "See," he says when I shoot up beside him like an otter. We're past the break and I stand on my toes. "Now how hard was that." It's not a question and he's laughing. He's always laughing then. It's the summer he turns fifty. He's happy with my mother. They have parties with wooden dance floors built just for one night, a bartender in each corner, and a band. He's still Fun Daddy and takes us for rides on his motorbike in the fields around our summerhouse.

My mother drives us to the station in the white wood-paneled Ford wagon. We wait for my father's train and place pennies on the tracks. My brother Bobby and I climb off the platform ledge. Below, it smells like oily gravel. We line our coins up carefully, dull copper against the silver rail. My mother gives us extra ones for Andrew. He's only three, too small to come with us, and he watches from above.

My father always takes the *Cannonball*. Before it stops, steam hissing like Hades underneath, I spot him between the cars, and when he sees me, he makes a Daddy face. That's another game we have. He jumps down—suit jacket still on (although it's hot), a briefcase in one hand and a newspaper in the other. After the whistle and the "All aboard Montauk," he helps us find the pennies in the tar, their faces ruined now and pink. On special days, we use nickels, but never quarters. Because that's illegal, he says. And we need to know the meaning of a dollar.

He tells us stories then. Depression stories, war stories, slipping-out-the-window-at-night-when-he-is-a-boy stories, sliding down the drainpipe to gamble with marbles in his Pennsylvania river town. Stories of when he is a pilot, a Democrat, a union organizer, a businessman, a rascal, a Romeo. The son of a railroad worker, who, by daring and chutzpah, made good and married a beauty. He tells us the stories, he says, to teach us about life.

My father is not a vain man. A handsome man, yes, with the profile of a young Brando. People stop him on the street, mistaking him for Ted Kennedy, to which my grandmother replies, "Much more handsome." He knows the effect, but he's interested in other things. And only more so as he gets older: the rumpled raincoat, the frayed cuff, and shoes worn and resoled when he can well afford new ones. "You'll understand when you have children," he grumbles.

It wasn't always so, a friend of my parents tells me later, when I am sixteen. I'm friends with her daughter, and we're sitting in their Beekman Place kitchen as her mother rhapsodizes. "Your father . . . Now, your father was a *catch*." I lean in and can smell the Scotch on her breath. Custom suits, white silk scarves, designer apartments, and parties. I've seen the pictures, and I remember the colored linen sport coats he used to wear. But it's as if she's talking about another person.

When I come home that night, he's up late working, a single light on in the apartment. He looks up over his reading glasses, asks how my night was, and then goes back to his papers. I stand there in the hallway watching him, trying to reconcile the whimsy of white silk with the man bent over yellow legal pads by a standing brass lamp.

"Put your fingers together. Keep your head down. And kick." We're bodysurfing, and his big thing is timing. I hold my hands as if I'm praying, but flat out, with thumbs crossed and elbows straight, and I hear him. "It's coming! Not this one!" We watch TV together late at night and guess the endings—that's another thing we have, we're both night owls. And now, in the water, we guess the waves.

There's a home movie: I am small, and he flings me in the surf by an arm and a leg. It appears almost painful, but each time I run back for more, my face shining. With Bobby, this doesn't work so well. He cries, imagining sharks. Aligned with my mother already, he sticks to the pool. "Respect its power," my father says. "Never turn your back." And I know, because he's told me, that when the big rollers come, I need to dive long and low so I don't get tangled in the break. If this happens, he says to hold my breath, make myself into a tight ball, and trust that the ocean will spit me back up. "It'll be over soon," he promises. "And I'll be there."

This is before a lot of things. Before he votes for Nixon, before the battles in high school, before he's angry most always, and before the stroke that years from now will leave him childlike, without interest in all that drove him.

It's when he takes me on night drives and tells me about love— the hometown girl; the wartime sweethearts in Paris, and the stockings and soap he gave them; the actresses and models at the Beverly Hills Hotel; the wild times on Fire Island. The ones who still, he knows, hold a torch for him. He keeps a shoe box, filled with snapshots of old flames, hidden in the attic. A secret I keep for him. One of the secrets I keep.

This is the summer I am eleven. I look up the sexy parts in Mary Renault books. I finish *In Cold Blood* when my parents aren't looking and hide my journal under the footed bathtub in the guest room. I wear a rope bracelet and cotton bikinis with ties on the sides. Before, I would wander the beach without my top and think nothing of it, but no longer. It's the summer I can still dive from my father's shoulders, the summer I still believe in his stories, the summer I am still his.

We've started diving now. He steadies me on his back with both hands and lowers down into the water. I'm taller than last year. It's tricky, but we get it. I wobble on the first dive, and he yells to keep my legs together. I swim back and we wait.

Remember this time. Soon it will start going fast. He says it like it's a bad thing. We're between waves now, and he won't look at me, his eyes as far away as Portugal. I scrunch my face and pray he's right. I want the days to rumble on, spin out, race ahead. I want to close my eyes and be there. It's all so endless: the summers, the school year in the city, the car rides, piano lessons, the nuns, the times tables, hot Sundays in church—endless, endless hours. I want to be twelve, to be sixteen. To kiss a boy, smoke a cigarette, have the curve when I lie on my side. I want to begin, to become who I will be.

But he tells me to remember, and I do. My arches curled on the slip of his shoulders, his back lowering like a whale, the clasp of our fingers wet and braided. The sun's in my eyes and there's a slight shift of knees before the wave comes and I go.

Waiting

The meeting of two personalities is like the
contact of two chemical substances: if there is
any reaction, both are transformed.

—CARL JUNG

In high school, we run in packs. It was no different in New York City in the mid-1970s at elite private schools such as Collegiate, Brearley, Dalton, Trinity, and Spence. We roamed the streets of Park and Fifth and ventured deep into the crevices of Central Park. We piled into Checker cabs, six or seven of us, or took the subway to Astor Place to wander the gridless Greenwich Village streets, untouched by designer outposts. SoHo was deserted; Little Italy was Italian; thrift shops were thrift, not "vintage." We passed the Bottom Line and Free Being Records on the way to Caffè Dante or Washington Square Park. The subway, green and tattooed with the tags of graffiti masters, rattled and rolled. We stood at the front of the first car, window down, the rush of speed on bright faces.

Stone chess tables at Carl Schurz Park, the Burger Joint on
Broadway, coffee shops near our schools, wisteria arbors behind
the Bandshell, Alice in Wonderland, the winged angel of Bethesda
Fountain, the boat pond, Belvedere Castle, and the long even steps
of the Metropolitan Museum of Art—these we made ours.

"Later at Alice."

"Catch you at the Met."

It was all about meeting. That's when the magic happened.

It's the weekend, and in that narrow Upper East Side hub, we're
looking for apartments devoid of parents. Some are done up like
Versailles, with gold accents, mirrored hallways, paintings glowing
under their very own lamps, and Nat Shermans, like pastel candies,
artfully fanned in small china cups. Others are more restrained—
pale sofas, family pictures framed in silver, and everywhere the
smell of soap. On the West Side, ornate gothic caverns rise, the
stone dark with soot. And the buildings have names: the Kenil-
worth, the Beresford, the El Dorado. The real estate boom of the
late eighties hasn't happened yet, and the West Side lacks the spit
and polish of the East Side. It's dirtier, more dangerous, exotic.
Often we head farther east or north, to smaller apartments without
doormen—or with doormen whose uniforms fit more loosely—
apartments of friends whose parents are not titans of industry or
scions of inherited wealth, but schoolteachers, designers, artists,
editors, or scientists.

We do our homework and we hang out. We smoke Marlboro
Lights and we smoke pot. We lie about where we are going. We
have crushes on boys we do not know but talk about incessantly.
We are juvenile and we are jaded. We are insecure and we are
worldly. With our friends as mirrors, we slip on identities like
wispy summer dresses and just as easily toss them aside. Like

teenagers everywhere, we are trying to find out who we are. Only we are doing it in a city that in 1975 has been almost felled by a fiscal crisis, where police and social services have been cut drastically, and homicide and muggings are rampant. Despite this, it is a city that knows itself to be the center of the world, the matrix where art and commerce thrive and power and excellence are de rigueur. This city. Ours. We can feel its promise; it's there beneath our feet. A shallow beat in dark asphalt.

In 1974, I left the Convent of the Sacred Heart and its gray wool uniforms for Brearley. Although Sacred Heart went through twelfth grade, I wanted a change. Many girls in my class left that year. Some ventured as far as Spence across the street or Nightingale-Bamford around the corner. Some left the city entirely for boarding school. But I wanted to stay in New York, and my heart was set on the girls' school in a ten-story building by the East River. One of the most competitive schools in the city, Brearley at that time resembled a prison and bristled with excitement. Caroline Kennedy had transferred there as well, but by the time I arrived, she had already left for boarding school. I didn't know it then, but my world was edging closer to John's.

"The Brearley," as it is known, may have lacked the poetry of the Otto Kahn mansion, but it had a major plus: no uniforms. The younger girls ran around in navy jumpers, with bloomers for gym, but there was no dress code in high school. The feel was more bluestocking than deb, and although there were pockets of Brooks Brothers and smatterings of Fiorucci and Cacharel, the standard fare was tattered jeans. It was something I looked forward to.

The summer before ninth grade, a letter in the school's signature shrunken envelope arrived. Inside, I was both welcomed to New Girl Orientation and asked to choose an elective. Music, dance, drama, and art were stacked one under the other. Next to each, a miniature red box. Mark one, the letter instructed. I was stunned. To my mind, they were inextricable from one another, part of one whole—what I loved best and far from optional. I stared at the word "elective" for a long time. Then I picked up my pencil and, with something akin to pain, checked drama.

Whereas Sacred Heart classmates were cruel behind your back, Brearley girls were more direct. They said what they meant. Opinion and curiosity thrived, and our class took it to the extreme. In an empty locker on the fifth floor, we kept a stash of racy books, calling it our pornographic library and even issuing library cards. Being Brearley, the smut was classic—along the lines of *Fanny Hill*, *The Story of O*, and Anaïs Nin's *A Spy in the House of Love*—and we devoured each behind folders during chorus, until a zealous math teacher ratted us out.

Drama was taught by Beryl Durham. Small, muscular, and Welsh, she had silver hair that ran the length of her back and a face in constant rapture. She told us tales of Julian Beck and the Living Theatre, and of her friends "Larry" Olivier and Vivien Leigh. When goaded, she divulged that sex was just like strawberry ice cream—an improvement, at least, over the Sacred Heart nurse's "like scratching an itch." We worked on Elmer Rice's *Street Scene* that year and a bad play by Giraudoux in which the tall girls played men and I was the heroine. For most, drama class was time to goof off, gossip, get Beryl to tell her stories and then make fun of her—anything but the embarrassing prospect of pretending to be someone else. But I was a fourteen-year-old who could not wait to lose herself in make-believe. In me, Beryl saw one of her own. Before classes ended for the term, she took me aside behind the heavy curtain in the auditorium. She was retiring at the end of the year. "You won't get what you need here," she said, her voice raspy and certain, her witch eyes wavering from blue to white. I nodded gravely, but before I turned to go, she pressed a small piece of paper into my hand. On it were the words *HB Studio* and an address on Bank Street.

My best friend in ninth grade was more experienced than I was. She took me under her wing, told me whose parents were famous and why, which girls were Legacy, and what the Social Register was. Most important, she made sure I never walked up Eighty-fourth Street to the two-block no-man's-land ruled by neighborhood toughs. Chapin and Brearley had addresses on East End Avenue's thin strip of privilege, but the half block west into old Yorkville was iffy. The toughs were just kids, really—kids who sat on stoops, who had knives, and whose favorite pastime was scaring nubile private school girls. "Why can't the police stop them?" I asked her. We were huddled at the corner of Eighty-fifth Street. I was blocking the wind that tore down East End from the river so that she could light her cigarette. She shrugged. "It's their turf. Besides, the fathers are all cops."

My friend went everywhere on her bike, dodging traffic in a faded jean jacket, her stick-straight pale hair flying behind. She lived in a town house off Madison Avenue, and her parents were divorced. We'd sit on her bed after school and talk about boys. I'd never been kissed, and she promised to tell me the secret of kissing, but only if I was her slave for the year. She knew John. He went to Collegiate, the boys' school across the park and brother school to ours. He'd been to a party at her house the year before and had left a black leather ski glove, which she kept hostage on her dresser. Part of learning the secret meant listening to her go on about how cute he was and how she would become Mrs. JFK Jr. Sometimes when she passed notes to me during Spanish class, she signed them that way as a joke.

At the end of ninth grade, the secret was revealed.

"Imitate what the boy does."

"That's it?" I said, my eyes widening.

"That's it," she said, tilting her chin and blowing a flawless smoke ring in my face.

By the next fall, I had been kissed, and that November one of the cool guys from Collegiate asked me out, although we never called it that. He and his friends were known as "the Boys" and they had nicknames that rang like handles: Sito, Wilstone, Johnson, Doc, Duke, Mayor, Hollywood, Clurm, Ace. He came with three of them to pick me up. All had long hair and puffy down jackets, and he whirled a red Frisbee upside down on his finger, mesmerizing my seven-year-old brother, who showed an excitement I tried to hide. "We're going to Kennedy's," the whirler told my parents. "His mother's home." I kissed my father and promised to be home by eleven. I had never been to Kennedy's before.

We walked up Park to 1040 Fifth Avenue, and when Lenox Hill dipped and flattened, they spread out—one across the street, another behind me, the one they called Sito short-stopping the divider—and they tossed the Frisbee across the wide avenue as we went. The boy I liked took my hand. It was cold that night, and soon the holiday trees would go up on the center islands that stretched north from the Pan Am Building all the way to Ninety-sixth Street. The sidewalk sparkled, the streetlamps catching bits of silver mica buried in the cement.

The elevator at 1040 opened onto a private foyer. There was

a huge gilt mirror and the smell of paperwhites. The front door was unlocked, the rooms dark, and Kennedy's mother wasn't home. I followed them to the dining room, where girls from other schools—Spence and Nightingale and one in baggy corduroy from Lenox—lounged by a table near an Oriental screen. Some smoked. The boys stayed close to the open window, stepping on the drapes and making noise, and we watched as they lobbed water balloons and paper towels stuffed with Noxzema fifteen stories down to splat on the sidewalk below. They howled when they nicked someone. "Score!" they'd shout.

One boy was especially keen. He darted back and forth, cracking himself up. Skinny, his hair in his face, he seemed younger than the rest. And he was *really* into throwing those Noxzema bombs. "Nice one, Kennedy!" they'd yell. And if he seemed younger, it was because his birthday was at the end of November and he was still fourteen. But I wasn't looking at him that night. I was watching the one I had come with. I had forgotten about the boy from the barbershop.

A group of us hung out that winter and spring. There were rumors that John liked a girl at Spence, but when he was with us, he was alone—a follower, under the tutelage of the older boys. We went to parties en masse, to sweet sixteens at Doubles, and to Trader Vic's on someone's father's charge. We tumbled out of the Plaza with gardenias from the Scorpion Bowls tucked in our hair and continued on to Malkan's, the East Side kiddie bar before Dorrian's caught on. We trolled Central Park at all hours, slipping through the Ramble, a wooded section where muggings and beatings were frequent. In 1978, the year we graduated, members of the 84th Street Gang also ventured there and, armed with baseball bats and a couch leg, savagely attacked six men they believed to be gay. This time their fathers could not protect them, and they were arrested and jailed.

We felt safe those nights in the park, the Secret Service trailing behind us at a respectable distance. John's mother insisted that they be invisible, and they almost were. But we always knew they were there. They had our backs. Or, rather, John's. And we'd wander off trails on moonless nights, clogs and sneakers stomping dead leaves, the glow of a joint drifting backward like a firefly in the darkness. Invincible, fifteen, and jazzed by the spark of danger.

Years later, after his plane went down, I thought of the sense of safety I'd always felt with him. Where had it come from? It was instinctual, I knew that. Like the clarity of faith the nuns possessed and tried to drum into me. Was it something in him, I wondered, his fearlessness rubbing off, the strength of his life force so strong that I believed nothing would happen to me if I was with him? Or was it the memory of those nights when we were young, sticks snapping underfoot, watching our breath go white, and knowing that unseen men with badges and guns kept us safe in the center of harm.

One night toward spring, John met us in the lobby at 1040, and we ambled down to the Met for Frisbee golf. The fountains were drained, and there was no one around, just the smooth stretch of cement lit by streetlamps. But that night, the 84th Street Gang had come west of their territory. They cornered us and we scattered. Some slipped across to the awning of the Stanhope. Others ran up the museum steps and hid in the alcoves behind the columns. I ducked behind the nearest car next to the handsome boy we called Doc. He was scared and kept smiling at me.

"Eighty-fourth Street," he mouthed, his eyes huge. "They *have* the Frisbee."

I peered around the bumper. Two of our own were there, demanding the Frisbee back. John was one of them.

"What are they doing, they're crazy," I hissed.

"It's not even their disc!" Doc agreed.

We heard voices rise, then—a flash of silver as the biggest one started forward and began to swing a large metal bar dressed in chains. Just as swiftly, from the other side of Fifth, two Secret Service men jumped from the shadows, flipped their badges, and the Frisbee was ours. As they trudged back to York Avenue, the 84th Street boys must have scratched their heads.

"Do you think they know?" I asked.

"Know what?" Doc said.

"That it was John. Do you think they're talking about it now? The night we were busted by the Secret Service for stealing John Kennedy's Frisbee. I mean, how often does *that* happen?"

Doc stood up by the car and dusted himself off. "Nah." He thought for a second and began to chuckle. "But I sure hope Mrs. O doesn't find out about this!"

I found the piece of paper Beryl Durham had given me in my ballerina music box under loose change and hair ties, and that spring I enrolled in Basic Technique for Acting at HB Studio. On Saturday mornings, I trekked to the Village, and as soon as I reached the top of the subway steps on West Twelfth Street, I took a deep breath. Unlike the tidy, canyoned avenues uptown, buildings here were low-slung, and I could see the sky. It felt like home.

I took a zigzag route west, past redbrick town houses, past Abingdon Square and the drug dealers who held court in the muddy playground to the south. Following the siren scent of the river, I turned right on Bank, and a few doors down from Greenwich Street, I came to a nondescript building where people clad in black were smoking in the outside stairwell.

Most actors in New York City find themselves at HB Studio at one point or another. It was founded by Viennese director Herbert Berghof and his wife, actress and master teacher Uta Hagen. Her book *Respect for Acting* would become my bible for the next five years. Annotated with exclamation points and underlined words, it went everywhere with me. *In the moment, objective, inner monologue.* I was learning a new language, and it was revelatory.

Edward Morehouse taught the teenage class, based on Uta's ten object exercises. A man of meager praise, he berated his students, often imitating them to make his point. He could be cruel, but he was always right, and I was hungry to learn. One Saturday after my third attempt at the fourth wall exercise, I waited at the front of the room for the usual onslaught of invectives. To my shock and that of the other students, there were none. As I walked back to my seat, his silence rang louder than any applause, and my face was hot with pride. I felt something stick that day, not just in my mind, but in my body. It was like a compass finding north for the first time; the needle would waver, but it knew where it was meant to land.

Soon he invited me to join his Adult Scene Study class. There, in a dark room off an airshaft, I found a world I loved as much as parties and prowling the streets with my friends. I may have had little in common with the others in the class—for one thing, I was much younger—but for the first time I found a kind of fraternity, the odd bond that exists among actors, those who are most themselves when they are someone else and most alive when they are telling stories in the words of others.

Perhaps it was the sober way Beryl Durham had said, "You won't get what you need here," but I knew not to speak of it at Brearley. I'd been in *Seventeen* magazine twice by that time—first in a two-page "makeover," where I had a crush on the photographer but was horrified by the amounts of pink lip gloss and purple eye shadow, and then modeling Victorian lingerie for an article titled "Becoming a Woman." This was a sort of infamy. Some girls smiled hard but behind the smile was, *Why her and not me?* An English teacher remarked with such sourness I thought it might cause permanent facial damage, "You might want to consider Professional Children's School." I kept it secret, along with the dance classes at Alvin Ailey and Luigi's and the agents who sent me out on auditions. *You won't get what you need here.*

The fall before he turned sixteen, John went to Phillips Andover, a newly coed boarding school in Massachusetts, and I saw less of him. When I did see him, it was with a mix of last year's troops and some of his new Andover friends. We'd meet up at 1040 and listen to *Exile on Main Street* in his bedroom before heading out for the night. Invariably, with his fist as a mike, John would do his Jagger imitation. No longer a follower, he was loud, confident, all over the place. But I began to notice that when he talked to me, he got quiet.

My friend Margot and I were walking down Lexington Avenue after school one day, the street thick with bus fumes and grade school boys juggling pizza slices and their book bags. Margot linked her arm in mine, and we steered our way through the sea of blue blazers. She was trying to hold back a secret. "I have good gossip," she finally confessed. "John's in love. It's serious." She had it from a friend who'd heard it from a friend who knew someone who lived on his hall at Andover.

We stopped for a moment, the boys jostling around us, and sighed. Not because we pined for him—we had boyfriends and were consumed by those dramas—but because we were like so many East Side private school girls: We felt protective. Despite the bravado, we knew his softness, and we didn't want anyone breaking his heart. He was one of ours.

Lucky girl, we said. *Very lucky.*

Mike Malkan's was on Seventy-ninth Street near Second Avenue, a long tunnel of a bar with red banquettes and a stellar jukebox—the old-fashioned kind, with the 45s that drop down and a selection that went on forever. You could put coins in as soon as you got there and leave without ever hearing your song, the lineup was that long. And there was no dance floor. Dancing was verboten. It was a place to go not so much for excitement or to drink, although they served at thirteen, but because you could always count on finding someone you knew there. And on the weekends the boarding schools let out, it was jammed.

On one of those nights, I slithered through the crowd to the back room. I was alone. The year before, I would never have thought of walking in without a friend in tow, both of us flipping our hair a block or two before so it was fluffy by the time we entered the bar, but by eleventh grade, I was more confident. I'd stopped wearing beige corduroys and clogs all the time and had on boots, a cut velvet skirt I'd found at a thrift shop near HB, and an old cashmere V-neck of my mother's that I pulled low. As if Donna Summer played continually in my head, I moved through the bar at half speed, swaying as I went. I imagined myself provocative.

The Collegiate boys had gathered around a table in a corner

booth by the divider, mai tais and rum and Cokes all around. I crushed in next to my boyfriend. "Hey, babe." His words made me feel grown-up. He kissed me and I melted. John and his friend Wilson sat across the table. They were down from Andover on a break. Both had gotten cuter since I'd last seen them. John was taller, not as gawky. He had turned sixteen.

Some song came on, and I had to dance. "Uncool," my boyfriend scolded. "Be cool. Chill" came the chorus from his friends. They never wanted to dance, not even when there was a dance floor, not even at parties where everyone else was dancing. They were more into getting stoned and watching *Saturday Night Live* and *The Twilight Zone*, and it had begun to bore me. John leapt up. "I'll dance with you," he said, grinning. He grabbed my hand, and together we cut a rug in the skinny aisle of the bar. We made it almost to the end of whatever Motown song it was before one of the waiters stopped us. "No dancin', guys. Mike says."

We slid back down to our drinks, laughing like bad children. "Hey." My boyfriend jabbed me underneath the table with his elbow. I took a beat, peered down my shoulder at him, and, summoning all my ESP/witch powers, transmitted, *Pay attention, babe.* With a whip of hair, I turned back to Wilson and John, whose heads were now bopping to the Stones. "Don't hang around 'cause two's a crowd!" they sang.

He's fun, I thought. *He doesn't need to be cool—he just is.* He had a way of looking up at you—his eyes barely out from under his bangs, his chin tucked in—and for a second I caught him watching. I didn't drink the White Russian in front of me; I picked up the sticky swizzle stick and twirled it over my lips. *And another thing,* I told myself as my boyfriend's arm staked itself around my neck, *he's a great dancer.*

· · ·

Mrs. Onassis had glittering Christmas parties then. They were always the first of the season—an easy mix of her friends and family, with Caroline's classmates from Harvard and John's from boarding school and the city. I delighted in seeing my cohorts on their best behavior, scrubbed and suited—the Boys especially. They were glamorous affairs, coats taken at the door and hors d'oeuvres passed, but without the pretension or stuffiness that accompanied many grown-up parties. Mrs. Onassis welcomed all of John's and Caroline's friends as if they were her own. While the adults tended to stay in the living room, with the sofas and the long terraced windows that looked out over the park, we stood crowded near the bar in the brightly lit gallery. Kennedy cousins and Caroline's smart friends milled about, and a buzz raced through the rooms.

Many years later, at one of these parties, I would sit in the corner of the living room with Mike Nichols sharing a plate of chocolate-covered strawberries. We had just been introduced by John's mother, but as the party swirled around us, he confessed that he had fallen madly in love, hadn't thought it possible, couldn't believe his luck. The light was dim, and I listened, transfixed by his giddy praise of an anonymous dulcinea. I was twenty-six, but he seemed years younger, a troubadour in thick glasses. And the next spring, he married Diane Sawyer.

These were happy parties and, as we grew older, markers of how we had changed.

In 1978, Mrs. Onassis threw a huge bash for John's and Caroline's eighteenth and twenty-first birthdays. I had graduated in the spring and was a freshman at Brown University. The party fell on the Sunday after Thanksgiving, just days after the fifteenth anniversary of President Kennedy's assassination. There were cock-tails at 1040, and after that 150 guests were invited to Le Club, a private discotheque half a block west of Sutton Place. Photographers and press were camped out in the cold on East Fifty-fifth Street. My mother had lent me her floor-length opera cape, and I felt very grand and grown-up. The black wool stiffened, a creature unto itself, and I ignored the chill that seeped through the arm slits and up the wide skirt to the flimsy silk dress I wore.

One of the reporters corralled me before I joined the bottle-neck at the door. He wore a cotton button-down under his tweed jacket, but he didn't look cold, and his thin hair was matted. He told me he was an old friend of Jackie's. There'd been an awful mistake, and his name wasn't on the guest list and would I please give her his card. He shuffled slightly as he took one out of a leather case and handed it to me.

"She'll sort it out—we go way back." Something caught his attention, and for a moment he looked past me. "Friend of Caroline or John?" he said, turning back. I noted the patrician drawl.

"John." He scribbled my name on a small flip-pad.

"What's it like inside? How many people?"

"I'm just on my way in," I said, edging back.

"You'll give her the card, then?" he shouted when I reached the door. "We're old friends!"

Past the velvet ropes, I was enveloped by a cocoon of colored light, thumping bass, and the crush of revelers. Unlike in the vast spaces of Xenon or Studio 54, with drag queens on roller skates and columns of strobe and neon lights, the ambience here was ex-clusive men's club. Tapestries were hung on dark-paneled walls with moose heads and baronial swords, and in the center there was a small dance floor.

I pushed through the crowd, looking for my friends. I was ecstatic to be home for Thanksgiving break in the city I loved. The Collegiate boys and the rest of the New York band I had wandered with for three years were there among the family members and celebrities to toast Caroline and John. Some I hadn't seen since graduation. It would be a warm reunion that night, and although we didn't know it then, a swan song of sorts. The party was one of the last times we would all be together. Interests and alliances ending, we had begun to scatter, settling in at universities across the country. Some friendships, by chance or effort, would remain; others would fall away. After the first weeks of college and the lonely freedom of being a blank slate, this night was an embrace. Later, on the dance floor, I looked around at the faces of my friends. A skein of shared history bound us, and we were there to celebrate John.

Before I could reach my friends, I found myself face-to-face with his mother. I'd never spoken to her alone before and was surprised that she was standing by herself. Out of nervousness or because I was faithful to a fault, I began to tell her about the man outside—after all, it was *possible* that he was her friend. She glanced at the card but didn't take it. Instead, her voice, suspended in a captivating intake of breath, finally landed with, "Oh . . . that's all right. Are you having fun?" Her kindness was such that she brushed aside my naïveté and the obvious fact that she had no idea who the man was, or if she did, his name wasn't on the list for a reason. Someone else would not have been as generous, and I was put at ease. She quizzed me about college—she wanted to know all about Brown. Did I think John would like it, she asked, her eyes wide. I knew he'd been held back at Andover—"postgraduate year" was the polite term. We talked about the party. "It's all going *so* well, don't you think?" She stood close to me and it felt like a confidence.

Together, we turned to watch John in the middle of the dance floor, a long white scarf flung about his neck. We agreed that he was having fun, and I saw her face light up. *Remember this,* I thought. *Remember this moment, that one day you might be forty-eight and filled, as she is, with this much joy and wonder.*

I had seen him earlier that fall at a party in Cambridge. What are you doing here? we both said, although I knew he was visiting his girlfriend, Jenny, at Harvard. Weeks later, he showed up at my dorm at Brown. "I'm here to see you," he said coyly. I looked at him for a second, then decided it was a tease. When I told him I already had plans that night, he admitted "Well . . . I'm here for my interview, too."

Jenny was with him at Le Club. Funny and smart, with a mane of blond hair and bedroom eyes, she sported an offhanded sexiness that anyone would have envied if she weren't so approachable. I liked her. *They look happy,* I thought wistfully. Things had ended that spring with the Frisbee whirler. He was miles away in Santa Cruz, and I knew I would never fall in love again. To make up for it, I danced all night.

Later, there was cake and sparklers, a speech by John's uncle and applause. By midnight, the older crowd began to clear out. We held on till four. The Boys, like lords of the manor, drank stingers out of goblets and smoked cigars with their legs propped up on the banquettes. Some of them even danced.

Outside, the street was deserted except for the press. They scrambled from their cars as soon as the doors to Le Club opened. I left with the first wave to find cabs. We crossed the street and began to walk to First Avenue. Then a shock of light and shouting. I turned back to see an older friend of John's I didn't know take a swing at a photographer. A fight broke out. John tried to stop it, to hold his friend back, but soon he had joined the scuffle and fell out of sight behind a car. *Where's John? Is he all right? Can you see him?*

Some of the Collegiate boys ran to get help. I hid behind a parked van. There was no rescue this time, no Secret Service to step from the shadows, his detail having ended two years before.

Then someone came bounding from the darkness with news. "Hey, it's all cool. John and Jenny caught a cab with Wilson on Second. They're on their way to 1040. Everyone's fine."

Like a movie, it ended as it should have—with a getaway and the enemy vanquished. There were high fives and smiles of relief as we said our goodbyes and split cabs north, west, and south.

The next day when I woke up, my father asked about the party. "Did you have fun? It's in all the papers." He smiled and tossed the *Daily News* in front of me. John in dark glasses. The silk scarf, the drunken buddy, the comely girlfriend.

I was confused. It appeared sordid in black and white. I had been standing across the street when the picture was taken. I had seen his arms outstretched, the light flashing off his aviators, but I didn't recognize this. I stared at the photograph for a moment, curious, before pushing the paper aside.

"That's not how it was," I told my father. "That's not everything."

That October there was a spike of heat in the Northeast, a brilliant backlash of summer. Providence, a city that would soon be bundled and galoshed—held captive by snow and rain for the next five months—was drinking in whatever warmth it could get. At Brown, on one of the highest of the seven hills that overlook the city, coats and sweaters were abandoned, classes were cut, and stereo speakers, perched high in open windows, blared the Allman Brothers and Grateful Dead, the drum solos drifting down through the air like a wild pagan call. Banners—sheets spray-painted NO NUKES/END APARTHEID NOW in black and red—were draped over dorm walls of brick and limestone.

On the Green, the patch of calm surrounded by the oldest buildings on campus, dogs chased after tennis balls and Frisbees or

lounged in the still-bright grass. On the Faunce House steps, theater majors bummed cigarettes, and aspiring novelists and semioti-
cians sparred over Derrida. Rich foreign students congregated in
the middle of the terrace: the men, with Lacostes tucked tight into
jeans and collars flipped high, the women, impossibly sleek, their
tousled heads thrown back in charmed laughter.

Brown, one of the nation's first nonsectarian universities, was
founded by Baptists in 1764. Its charter ensures religious diversity
and "full, free, absolute, and uninterrupted liberty of conscience."
This emphasis on intellectual freedom was shored up in 1969 by
student-led curriculum reforms. The New Curriculum, as it is still
called, did away with distribution requirements and rigid grading,
and encouraged choice and exploration. Education was placed
squarely in the hands of the undergraduate. You could major in
ethnomusicology or Egyptology, Portuguese or population studies, or take up gamelan or welding. And if the standard offerings
didn't suit you, you could design a course that did. It was also possible to get by with doing very little, but that was rare. Most students were busy, galvanized by opportunity and sparking off one
another's curiosity.

I was a junior in the fall of 1980. I had just gotten back from a
trip to Ireland, but for most of the summer I'd stayed in Providence to act in three plays. In New York, I'd done commercials,
but this was the first time in my life I'd cashed a paycheck for a
play. And Oscar Wilde, no less. I was incredibly proud.

Sophomore year, I'd moved out of the dorms to a rambling
house on Waterman Street, five blocks east of campus, one of three
student-run co-ops. There was a couch on the porch, a caricature
of Nixon in one of the windows, and a king-size water bed with a
sign-up sheet in the living room. My parents refused to set foot in-

side, proclaiming it "filthy," but I loved it. It had a measure of expressiveness and rebellion that I craved. In the basement, a mute computer science major slept, worked, and tended to large vats of sprouts, his sole source of nutrition. For the rest of us, jobs rotated and dinners were a festive event. That night, I was in charge of cooking a vegetarian casserole for twenty.

As I crossed the Green, a knapsack slung over one shoulder, my mind was racing. The coffee from the Blue Room hadn't helped. A paper due. Lines to learn. Cooking at the co-op that night. And the dark-haired French Canadian hockey player I'd met, who took art classes at RISD and spoke of training as if it were poetry. He slipped notes under my door that read like haiku. I, who had previously had zero interest in collegiate sports, now shivered in the stands of Meehan Auditorium and watched as he, outfitted like a gladiator, knocked equally well-padded men into the walls of the rink. Terrified and thrilled, I looked up at the bright banners and the fans cheering and the clean white ice below and thought, *this* is performance. On a cool night, when the embers were dying in his fireplace and there was no more wood to burn, he broke a table apart—wrenched the legs off, then the top, plank by plank—to please me, to keep the flames going. But the beginnings of love were distracting, and I kept forgetting things.

I couldn't find my bike for days, then realized I'd left it outside the Rock, the main library on campus. Hoping it would still be there, I walked quickly down the corridor between two of the buildings that bordered the Green. Light and noise began to fade. I kicked the heels of my new cowboy boots along the walkway, and the wine-colored gauze skirt I wore fluttered over the cement. When the path dipped down to the more shaded Quiet Green, I saw the Carrie Tower. Redbrick and granite, it reached high into the bright sky. I loved the tower, loved walking by it, and always went out of my way to do so. The four green-faced clocks on each of the sides were worn by weather. They no longer kept time, and the bell had been removed, but the tower had a story. At its chipped base, above an iron door, the words LOVE IS STRONG AS DEATH were carved into the stone, a memorial to a woman from her Italian husband after her untimely passing almost a century before. I stopped for a moment and looked up. I wanted to be loved like that.

When I passed through the main gates onto Prospect Street, I spotted my bike, an old Peugeot that took me everywhere. Relieved, I bent over the wheel and tugged at the lock. Then I heard my name. A voice I knew. I looked up, squinted.

"Hey, stranger." Someone wearing white was smiling at me.

I raised the back of my hand to shade my eyes. The sun glinted off a railing.

"I was wondering when I'd run into you," he said.

John was sitting on the bottom set of steps outside the Rockefeller Library talking with a large, preppy blond guy. "Catch you later," the blond guy said when he saw me, and took off in the direction of George Street.

I sat down on the step next to him, tucking the filmy skirt under my knees. I was happy to see him. He was now in his sophomore year, one behind me. He leaned in to hug me. His shoulders were broader. Around his neck, a shark's tooth on a string.

"It's been a while," I said, and we began to try and place when we'd last seen each other—a Little Feat concert where he'd teased me mercilessly about the Harvard guy I was with, a party in New York, his performance in *Volpone* the previous spring.

What had I done over the summer, he wanted to know. I didn't mention the French Canadian. I told him about Ireland, the double rainbow in Donegal, the pubs in Dublin, and a castle I stumbled upon near Galway Bay that turned out to have belonged to my clan hundreds of years back. Before that, six weeks of summer theater at Brown. His face lit up, and he wanted to know more. "That's cool. You seem into it," he said, adding that he wouldn't be doing any plays for a while. Something cryptic about needing to stay focused, as if the words of Shakespeare and Shaw were a sweet drug that he needed to pace himself around. He'd been in Ireland, too. Also Africa, and helping out on his uncle Teddy's presidential campaign. And Martha's Vineyard. "My mother's building a house there. You should come up sometime."

As we spoke, I searched his face. Something about him was different. In a summer, he had changed. Taller, more handsome; I couldn't put a finger on it. Maybe he was in love. Maybe it was the white garb. But he seemed at ease with himself in a way he hadn't before.

"I can't bear to be inside on a day like this." He exhaled deeply and cocked his head to the library, a rectangle of cement and glass whose revolving doors whirred behind us. He leaned back, propping his elbows against a step, and stretched his legs. His linen pants were rumpled. I saw that he was wearing sandals, the woven kind, and that his feet were still brown.

"Where are you living?" I asked.

"Phi Psi. I pledged."

"Oh." I tried not to wrinkle my nose.

"And you?"

"Waterman Co-op."

"Huh. Tofu."

The first bell rang, and I moved toward my bike. The lock came off easily.

"I'll walk you," he said, following. "I've got time."

I crouched down and slipped the U-shaped metal bar neatly in its holder on the bottom bar of the bike. His feet. *I've never seen them before*, I thought, and threw my knapsack in the front basket. They were elegant, and that surprised me.

I steadied the bike, and we began to walk up the uneven street, past the Van Wickle Gates, past the Carrie Tower, to the rise at the top of Prospect and Waterman.

The second bell rang, and people began darting around us.

"Well, stranger, this is where I get off. Thanks for the chivalry."

"My pleasure," he said, and with that, he slid his foot between mine, tapping lightly against the inside edge of my boot. "Nice."

As I ran up the steps of the Am Civ building late for class, I felt a lightness and a bitter/sad tug deep in my chest. I may have chalked it up to the splendor of the day. If I'd been wiser, I would have guessed that I was a little in love with him even then. But I was twenty, and whatever I knew on that autumn-summer day was a secret to myself. And when a friend who had also known him in high school and noticed his metamorphosis from cute to Adonis later whispered, "God, he's gorgeous," I agreed. "Yes," I said, "but I wouldn't want to be his girlfriend." I had seen the way some women looked at him, sharp sideways glances my way simply because he was talking to me. I'd heard about the campus groupies. Besides, I was with the French Canadian, and I thought it would be forever.

We didn't see each other much that fall. By winter, I'd moved out of the co-op. I'd outgrown its dusty charms. A space had opened up in a five-bedroom house on Benefit Street, where Poe and Love-craft had lived. I moved into a cream-colored row house with maroon trim, molded bay windows, and a stone sundial in the backyard.

A few months after I began living there, a tall curly-haired fellow named Chris Oberbeck appeared at the front door one morning. I'd met him at hockey games through my boyfriend, and he'd been to a party at the house the night before. Impressed, he'd come to inquire about it. He was looking for a place to live for senior year, with John, who was his fraternity brother, and Christiane Amanpour, a friend of theirs who was studying journalism and politics at the University of Rhode Island. Was the house available? As it turned out, my roommates were all graduating in the spring, and Lynne Weinstein, a classmate whom I'd known from New York, would be moving in. We joined forces and the next fall John, Lynne, Chris, and Christiane moved into the house as well.

Benefit Street, with its gas lamps and cobblestones, runs north–south partway up College Hill on Providence's East Side. It's a full mile of Federal and Victorian houses, some with plain faces open to the street and wooden fans etched above doorways, others turreted and overdone, with porticoes and pilasters. As you drive down the street, there are flashes of colored clapboard and street names like Power, Planet, Benevolent, and Angell.

By the mid-twentieth century, after major industry had left Rhode Island, the area fell into disrepair and was slated for the wrecking ball. Funds were raised, and preservation efforts began in earnest in the seventies. In 1981, Benefit Street was not quite the swank address it is today, but it was well on its way. Tenements and boarded-up buildings remained, standing shoulder-to-shoulder with grand homes. To me, a college student, that only added to the allure.

Our house had a maple tree out front. It was on a corner lot, built into a steep side of the Hill, and afternoons there were drenched in light. At the entrance was a lantern and tall, brass-knockered doors in glossy black. On the first floor, there was a separate apartment and an alcove. From there, the staircase spiraled up to where we lived. There was a tiny kitchen in the back that had recently been renovated and smelled of pine; a dining room, with a bust of a naked woman on the fireplace mantel, an enormous table, and our bikes resting along the walls; the landing where the phone was; and the main room, with its high parlor-floor ceilings and double bay windows. From there, you could see past the alleys and the streets to downtown—the art deco skyscraper everyone called the Superman Building, the marble dome of the State House, and just over the rooftops, parts of the red wire letters of the Biltmore sign. Upstairs, there were two large bedrooms and a bathroom. The top floor had low ceilings, a storage closet, and three smaller bedrooms.

Before we left for the summer, we chose our rooms, and because I'd lived there before, I was given first dibs. I picked a room in the back of the house, the second-largest one with a view of the garden. It had a curved wall that was stenciled at the top and a marble fireplace that didn't work. Kissy, as Christiane was called, got the master bedroom with the huge walk-in closet. John ended up in the smallest room, which had just enough space for a desk and a bed, with the proviso that he and Kissy would switch the next year after the rest of us had graduated.

It was an interesting mix. Chris, a staunch Republican, was clearly headed for the financial sector, but he had a rich baritone

and took voice lessons. Christiane, a few years older, was passionate and informed. Raised in Tehran and London, she and her family had experienced the Iranian Revolution firsthand, and she was
more worldly-wise than the rest of us. She also dressed with great
style. No slave to fashion, she knew what suited her and stuck with
it. Lynne was the calming element in the house. A photographer
and a dancer, she knew best how to arrange the couches in the living room, and of all of us, she was the most accomplished cook.

We each brought something to the house. Chris had a talent for
smoothing things over with Mrs. Mulligan, the hawkeyed mother
of our absentee landlord. Kissy made sure the chores were done. I
arrived with a box of glasses and a set of turquoise dishes that my
mother didn't want anymore. Lynne contributed pans and skillets,
and John's African textiles and posters brightened the living room.
His stereo was in there, too, along with all our records jumbled together in big white bins.

Early on, a friend had dubbed the house "Can of Worms," pre-
dicting disaster because of the egos involved. But he was wrong.
Except for some overheated political arguments and the occasions
when John and Chris went food shopping and came home with
hamburger meat and nothing else, all ran smoothly.

Since Lynne and I had both lived in the Brown co-ops, we suggested a similar but more simplified routine. Two people would
shop once a week from a list we all contributed to, and everyone
would pick a night to cook. Food tastes ran from vegetarian to total
carnivore, with Chris and me on either ends of the spectrum and
everyone else falling somewhere in between. Kissy's specialty was
crispy Persian rice with dill and yogurt. I took my cues from the
Moosewood Cookbook. Chris liked burgers but tried his hand at
pasta. Lynne's boyfriend, Billy Straus, who ate most nights with

us, excelled at all manner of trout. And Lynne taught John how to prepare tofu and even to like it. John showed the most improvement. He branched out, experimenting with a tattered copy of *Cooking with Annemarie* (Annemarie Huste had been his family's chef when he was seven), but everything he made had some variation of what he called "sauwse"—a mixture of tamari and whatever else the spirit moved him to throw in. Pretty much everyone in the house had a significant other, and we usually had a full table for dinner.

One Saturday, the phone rang early. I was half asleep when I answered, but was soon made alert. The man on the other end said he knew where I lived. He said he hated the Kennedys and he threatened to kill John. Before the man hung up, Lynne's boyfriend, Billy, picked up the extension upstairs to make a call, and afterward, he met me on the landing. I cried as I told him what the man had said. Should we tell John? We didn't want to upset him. We climbed the stairs to his room, but he had spent the night elsewhere.

Throughout the day, each of the roommates was let in on what had happened, until finally we stood huddled in the living room, trying to decide what to do. Go directly to the campus police? The Providence police? Wait until we could speak to John? Call Senator Kennedy's office, someone suggested. We were all worried and we argued. Then I heard the back door slam, and John bounded in, dropping his bags by the chair on the landing. He caught sight of our faces. "What's up?" he said. No one spoke, but when Chris finally did, John said not to worry. He brushed it off so easily, that, for a moment, I felt foolish for being alarmed in the first place, for not intuiting, as he had, the difference between a prank and a real threat. It was only a moment, though, and after that day, I felt more protective of him than I ever had, and, in a strange way, more in awe of his fearlessness.

That year I went to see him in plays, and he came to see me. One exception was an arty production of *The Maids*, in which I was briefly, but starkly, nude. *In character*, I said. I was applying to graduate acting programs that winter and had just finished a summer intensive at ACT, the American Conservatory Theater, in San Francisco. There was mild campus shock over my display of skin, but John seemed truly scandalized and refused to see the play.

He was awkward in the princely parts but shone in the grittier role of Big Al in David Rabe's *In the Boom Boom Room*. I remember watching him in the dark of the small black box theater. With a buzz cut and lumbering gait, he was transformed, channeling passion and anger into a riveting performance. It was the side I'd seen in high school that faced down gangs and took on the paparazzi.

Theater had become a kind of bond between us. James O. Barnhill, now theater professor emeritus, was my acting teacher and my friend—a southern gentleman who spoke in koans. He knew I was friends with John, and in the winter of John's freshman year, he asked me to invite him to join us for lunch at the Faculty Club. As he did with all those who were under his wing, Jim often took me out for meals (usually at Thayer Street's International House of Pancakes), and when we sat down, he would wave his hand with a sudden dramatic twist and announce, "Order anything you like! Anything at all." The real nourishment of these meetings was not the waffles, but the tales of his life and his interest in mine. He often spoke of India, where he had traveled extensively and had many friends. Once, he pulled out a Vedic astrology chart, yellowed and creased, to show me what had come to pass. He prodded me to nurture more than just my mind. And the Faculty Club was reserved for occasions when he had something significant to discuss.

In the paneled dining room bright with white linen, Jim spoke to us about the theater. In his roundabout way, he tried to encourage John. When lunch was over, John took off on his bike, and I stood with Jim on the corner of Benevolent. He asked that I encourage John as well and he said that whatever he did with his life, theater would strengthen his leadership skills and give him confidence. "He's our prince, you know," he said, with a weary smile and the signature flip of his wrist. He seemed to be aware that John would not become an actor, that despite his talent, it was not something he could choose.

I didn't argue with my mentor, but I was sure of something else. From where I sat, I believed my friend was free to choose whatever he set his heart on.

Spring fever is a real thing. At the end of the fall term, when one is equally sleep deprived and exam addled, passions are quelled by the shorter days and, perhaps, the genetic knowledge that it will only get worse and it's best just to burrow in. But in spring, with its rampant downpours and mud and bouts of warm air, anticipation is everywhere. It sparks and snaps off the pavement when you least expect it.

On a day when the forsythia raged and daffodils cluttered the spaces between stones and the white slats of fences, I had my first fight with John and it was about food. I was graduating in less than a month, and like everyone else in the class of 1982, I was in a state of acute scramble before commencement. There were exams, papers due, parties I didn't want to miss, goodbyes that had to be said and said well. My mind was in a quandary over whether to go to ACT or Juilliard the next year. I had gotten into both, and the deadline loomed. I was also in rehearsals for *Twelfth Night* as Viola, a role I adored: besotted, cross-dressing, and protective of her brave and tender heart.

My friend Tom, Feste to my Viola, was coming for dinner that night. I was making ratatouille and cheese calzones, and he was going to be my chopper. We had an enjoyment of each other that shadowed the roles we played. We walked through the backyard, running lines, and dropped our bags in the dining room. Chris and John had done the shopping earlier, but no one was home yet. Tom settled himself on the windowsill and opened his script. As I took out the cutting boards and knives, he began to quiz me on the ring speech. "'For such as we are made of, such we be,'" I said, opening the refrigerator. No eggplant. No tomatoes. No zucchini. No mozzarella. Only a case of beer, a drab head of lettuce, and steaks, bloody on a white plate.

I began to pace, and Tom watched as I fumed. The unfairness of it all. The countless times they'd done this. In an instant, I'd come undone because of a bare cupboard.

"I'm so mad I could break something."

"Do it." Tom's eyes twinkled.

"No!"

"Why not? Break a plate. Throw it against the wall. Who cares?" He spoke like a Zen master.

From the corner of my eye, I saw turquoise plates glaring from the drying rack. I picked one up; it quivered in my hand. Then I closed my eyes and let it drop. The look on my face sent Tom into peals of laughter.

"Oh my God, that was so much fun," I said. And because it was, I broke another. There is a reason why people break plates, I told Tom. Whether it was the sound of shattering, or the pleasure of doing something completely out of character, or the fact that the plates were just plain ugly, breaking them had made me feel better. My anger was gone, and my sense of freedom went further. I'd been bold enough to break things, and now I didn't want to cook either. I hadn't eaten red meat since I was fifteen, and I'd be damned if I was going to sizzle it in a pan for someone else! Tom proposed that the two of us go have a nice meal and a bottle of wine at the French restaurant on Hope Street. Why not, I said, as I scribbled a haughty note. Let them fend for themselves. I was becoming a whole new person, and I felt high with it.

Before we left, I reached for the broom, but thought better of it. As I stepped over the pile of shards, Tom held the screen door open, and we let it slam behind us.

When I returned, the house was dark and the broken plates were gone. So was my euphoria. I snuck into the dining room. A five-foot ebony mask of John's stared at me from a corner. Empty pizza boxes were scattered about, and I could hear my roommates upstairs talking, the sound muffled through closed doors. John's bike was gone, but by the phone he'd left a two-page letter filled with exclamation points. The next morning, I apologized to everyone, and after a few days things around the house got back to normal.

But John wasn't having any of it. He spent most nights at his girlfriend Sally's. When he was home, he refused to speak to me and left the room when I entered. As one week rolled into the next, nothing changed.

It was late and I was in bed. I loved reading in that room on Benefit Street—soft gray walls, tall windows over the garden, and furniture I'd inherited from my friend Nancy, who had moved to Berkeley the year before: an art deco armoire and, covered in clothes, a small veneered desk I never used. The shades on the windows were rolled as high as they could go, their silk tassels dangling. I could see a few lights on in the houses up Court Street. I lay under the comforter, curled into my book.

There was fumbling at the back door. A pack thrown down. Then, *"Shit."* The back buzzer had never been fixed, and John's entrance through my window had been a common occurrence throughout the year. But that night he continued up the fire escape to the floor above. As he passed, he made sure not to look in my room. He rapped on Chris's window, called his name, rapped again. I heard him jiggle the lock, then stop. There was a long silence before he lowered himself back down the metal rungs to the landing outside my window. It was cold that night, and he was wearing a wool cap pulled low over his forehead and a black sweater with leather patches. His face was close against the glass, and his breath made widening circles with its heat.

I got out of bed, slid a cardigan over my nightgown, and walked barefoot to the window. I unlatched the lock and held the bottom sash up as he stepped through. The cold air rushed in and we stood there eyeing each other like animals.

Then I began to laugh, so hard it hurt. I knew I was making things worse, but I couldn't stop. John frowned—he didn't take to being laughed at.

"You look like . . . a burglar," I said when I could get the words out, then kept on laughing.

"That's not very nice, you know."

"A nineteenth-century burglar. A Dickensian one."

He gave me a withering look. "That's a very silly thing to say."

"Look." I pointed to his reflection in the window. "Look!"

He turned, and when he saw himself in all his woolen ruffian glory, he pulled the cap off and ran his fingers several times through his hair. With his eyes fixed on the floorboards, he shook his head. He was trying valiantly to keep the corners of his mouth down, but soon he was laughing, too.

"Shh . . . they're all asleep."

"Okay," he whispered. "I don't want to be mad. I don't want us to be mad. But you *were* a jerk!"

"It's true, I was," I said, smiling.

"You were totally wrong!"

"I know. Shh."

"And childish."

"Can we be done?"

He said nothing.

"Can you just . . . please . . . forgive me?"

He nodded, his face suddenly tender, and reached out to hug me. I stood on my toes. His arms were around me, his face in the crook of my neck, buried. The smell of wool and rain.

We stepped apart.

"Okay?"

"Okay then."

At the door, he stopped and looked back. I was sitting on the bed, cross-legged, covers around my waist. "You were *still* a jerk," he said after a moment, but this time there was a trace of a smile at his lips. I let him have the last word—he liked that—and he closed the door quietly.

After he was gone, I tried to read but couldn't. I put the book down and shut off the light. Outside, rain had begun. Seven years I'd known him, and I felt closer to him that night than I ever had.

There was a kind of intimacy in our silly fight. And risk. He cared enough to show me how he really felt, how I'd disappointed him, how he wanted me to be better than I was. In the dark, I smiled to myself. I'd never imagined that anyone could out-sulk me, but he had. He had won.

I decided on Juilliard not with a coin toss, but with a shuffle of colored cards. My friend had a Rider-Waite tarot deck she kept wrapped in a silk scarf in the bottom drawer of her bureau. On one of those harried nights before graduation, when I was careening between ACT in San Francisco and Juilliard in New York, she made us tea and told me to keep a question in mind as I held the cards. I thought of Juilliard, the tomblike building where I'd gone to ballet school, and of the old Russian dancers who'd flicked our shins into alignment with their long tapered sticks. Then I imagined ACT and the sunlit classrooms where I'd been so happy the summer before. The cards told a different story. Those for ACT were ominous: the Tower, the Devil, crossed Swords. For Juilliard: Pentacles, the Magus, and a Wheel of Fortune well-placed.

Only the last one, the Two of Cups reversed, was inauspicious. *Lovers will part.*

A year later, after I had finished my first year at Juilliard and was living in New York, the cards proved true and my relationship with the French Canadian ended.

The Juilliard School, a conservatory for the performing arts, lies on the northern end of the sixteen-acre tract of concert halls, fountains, and stages that Lincoln Center comprises. Unlike a university, the school's Dance, Music, and Drama Divisions are separate. Musicians take up most of the building, but in the early eighties, the third floor was the province of the actors on one end, the modern dancers in the middle, and, in its own enclave far to the front, the School of American Ballet, training ground for New York City Ballet. Late afternoons, small girls with book bags in hand and pink tights under street clothes filed by just as I had done years before, their hair already twisted and pinned in place and a dream in their eyes of someday becoming a sylph or a swan or, the real prize, Clara in *The Nutcracker*. One night in their young lives, they had sat transfixed in the darkness and watched as the velvet curtain opened on a world of inarguable beauty, and in that instant, they were smitten. Undone. It was a look I knew.

The Drama Division, inaugurated in 1968, was the newest addition to the school. Conceived by John Houseman and Michel Saint-Denis, the training had a European bent, with an emphasis on classical plays, the idea being that if you could tackle the Greeks and Shakespeare, you could do anything. The walls outside the drama theater attested to this. They were lined with photographs of alumni—Kevin Kline, Patti LuPone, Val Kilmer—in Restoration garb and long flowing robes.

When I arrived in the fall of 1982, Juilliard was still the tomb-like building I remembered. With massive columns and stark stone steps, it was an airless place, lacking whimsy or adornment. None of the windows opened. Even the floor-length wool rehearsal skirts issued the first day with name tags sewn tight at the waist were of a dour, lifeless shade. MS. HAAG, mine said, and we were referred to with the same formality on the rehearsal call sheets posted on the main bulletin board.

The severe design was meant to impress, not inspire, and as excited as I was to begin, I also wondered whether I would survive. In the first days, members of the class ahead whispered what I'd already guessed—that acceptance to the school was no assurance that you remained. Our class, Group XV, began with twenty-six members but would dwindle to half that by the time we graduated. In the second year, there were warnings and cuts, and at any time the possibility of not being "asked back." Even the first play we did, referred to officially by the faculty as the discovery play, was secretly known as the test. The first two years focused on training, and the last two were geared toward performance. I already had an agent, and my covert plan was to stay two years and leave.

As imposing as it all was, there were pockets of warmth. Beyond the double glass doors and down a wide corridor was Nora, an ancient Irish sweetheart who manned the desk and always saved you a smile and a piece of fruit or candy. At the Greek coffee shop across Broadway, now a Barnes & Noble, Chris wrapped up a bagel in tinfoil and ladled out thick navy bean soup, and if his boss wasn't looking, he'd push your money back and wave you out. And the teachers—Michael Kahn, Eve Shapiro, Liz Smith, Marian Seldes, and Tim Monich among them—were not overly interested in your opinions or ideas. What they were passionate about was passing on what they knew. They insisted on your attention, and proposed to give you the means and the freedom to rise up to the words and the story. This alchemy would occur, they promised, through repetition and discipline. Like the violinists and pianists we rubbed shoulders with in the elevators—those who numbed their instruments with endless scales and drills—so we began to play our bodies and push our voices.

I wasn't sure on most days whether I was exhilarated, exhausted, or infuriated, whether I was prisoner, combatant, or acolyte, but one thing was certain: I was being changed. And it was happening from the inside out. *Submit,* the walls seemed to say, *submit and be changed. Lengthening and widening,* the Alexander teacher hummed, her weightless hands guiding stubborn bodies into ease. *Down to go up,* we were persuaded in movement class. *Find neutral,* a voice teacher demanded, her meaning a mystery. Once a week in Room 304, we met with John Stix for sense memory, an exercise codified by Lee Strasberg to elicit emotional responses. With eyes closed, we slouched in metal folding chairs and conjured to life cups of coffee, lost objects, past hurts, childhood joys. *Concentration and relaxation,* Stix intoned, as he navigated the room.

Some days, I chose a bath—heat rising up, steam grazing my lips. Other days, the coffee. But most of the time, I picked the necklace I'd lost near water long ago. The braided chain was from a watch my father's father had received for fifty years of service on the Pennsylvania Railroad. The religious medallion had come from county Cork, worn around my great-great-grandmother's neck on a sailing ship as she crossed the Atlantic. "Tell no one," my grandmother had murmured, snapping the clasp around my seven-year-old neck. "You're my favorite grandchild." Careful not to wear it around my cousins, I loved the heavy feel. The metal was soft, and there were marks on the saint's halo made by a baby's teeth as her mother held her.

I can still see it. Bright gold in blue water.

Classes began at nine in the morning, and rehearsals were usually from six to ten at night, but one particular autumn evening, I was free. John was meeting me at an Italian restaurant on Amsterdam Avenue—a crowded place I knew, with a narrow aisle and tables pushed close, each done up in a shiny checkered cloth. It was cheap with great lighting: an actor's hangout, where ten bucks got you a salad, the house red, and a huge plate of pasta. Candles in Chianti bottles covered with layers of red and green wax lit the room.

John had graduated from Brown in the spring. He'd spent the summer diving in the waters off Cape Cod in search of a pirate ship that had wrecked on the shoals near Wellfleet. He would soon head off to India to study at the University of Delhi and travel the country on a research stint in rural development. It was an invaluable opportunity, he said, to have distance from home, friends, family, and country, and he was excited to live in a place where everything from government to food to sex was considered in a completely different manner. At his going-away bash the week before, while we were dancing, he'd stowed the long strand of diamond-cut garnets my mother had given me in his pocket so it wouldn't break, and I'd left without it. We had arranged to meet so that he could give it back, but also to say goodbye.

I spotted him from the street. He was sitting at one of the tables near the window, lost in thought, and when I walked in, he stood up and gave me a bear hug. The scent of his jacket was familiar and exotic.

"Lest we forget," he said as we opened our menus. He dug deep, fished out the garnet necklace, and deposited it in my hand.

The stones flashed in the light, a curl of blood red, and I looped the strand twice around my neck. I was no longer a vegetarian, and when I ordered the Bolognese, he raised an eyebrow and muttered something under his breath about a woman's prerogative.

"What's up with that?" he said.

"What do you mean?"

"Uh . . . meat. Last I recall, you—"

"Oh, that. I've changed," I said lightly. "I'm allowed."

"So, no broken crockery?" he teased.

"Not tonight—if you're lucky."

"Touché, Miss Haag. Touché."

We drank wine and laughed and spoke of his plans and mine. He fiddled with the candle, chipping at the wax until it fell in red flakes on the map-of-Italy place mat. He wanted to go to Sri Lanka and Nepal. And he planned to meet up with Professor Barnhill, who was on a sabbatical year in India. His mother might visit, he said, and Sally would come for part of the trip. Along with his studies, he'd climb mountains, hit the beaches, and go to theater festivals.

"What about the temples? Will you see the temples?"

His eyes narrowed, as if to say, It's *India*—there are temples everywhere.

I began to describe the erotic carvings at Konark and Khajuraho I'd seen in books. I was fascinated that sexuality could be emblazoned on a place of worship. I thought of those stone women, robust and fecund. They were nothing like the slender, salmon-robed Madonna of my childhood who stood watch outside the Sacred Heart chapel. Her motto was patience, not pleasure, and the stars above her head were a coat of arms.

"Yeah, I'm sure I'll go there." He'd moved up the candle, his thumb pressing the soft part near the flame. He began to talk of tiger parks—he wanted to see the tigers. From his pocket, he pulled out two white pills and downed them with wine. "With these babies, I'll be able to drink well water!" He handed me one. Acidophilus, he said. When taken in advance, they would forestall any intestinal misery.

He was intrigued by Juilliard. "What do you *do* there all day?" He'd pulled his chair closer, his knees knocking mine under the table. He was especially curious about acting class. "How is it different from Brown?" he asked. I told him about finding neutral and metal chairs and sense memory.

"Let me get this straight—a roomful of people and everyone's moaning?"

"Well, not everyone." I tugged at the garnets around my throat and knotted them through my fingers. "Some are crying. Some are laughing. Some are just sitting there and nothing's going on."

"Hmm, emperor's new clothes. And you, Christina, what do you think about?"

"I can't tell you that."

"Come on."

"It wouldn't be a secret then, would it?"

"So?"

"It only works when it's a secret."

He started to speak, then thought better of it.

"What?"

"I don't know. You just seem . . . happy."

"I *am* happy. Tonight, I'm out of my cloister."

"You're hardly a nun." He frowned slightly and leaned back on the heels of the chair. "Maybe a devadasi."

He had seen *Lovesick* recently, with Elizabeth McGovern and Dudley Moore, and said I would have been better in the part. He appeared to have given it a great deal of thought, taking it as a personal affront that my agents hadn't gotten me a meeting with the director. "It's just timing," he said. "For you, it's a matter of being in the right place at the right time." I believed that, too, and we lifted our glasses and toasted each other with the cheap red wine.

Like the prince and the pauper, we might have switched clothes then and there. A part of him could have pushed the glass doors open each morning, dashing past Nora. She'd call him darlin' and toss him an orange as he raced to the elevators and the third floor, late for speech with Tim or fight class with BH. A part of me was dying to take off, pack on my back and feet dusty with the world, seeing all that he would see. But we were half-grown then, and it was time to choose what defined us. It was enough that night to trade tales, and as we spoke, it occurred to me that I had never sat alone with him in candlelight before.

Outside, a warm wind chased my skirt back, then flung it forward. I wasn't wearing stockings, and it felt almost balmy.

"Can I give you a lift?"

I was surprised he had his Honda and said so. For a New Yorker, getting around the city by car was uncommon; we had subways and cabs for that. Cars were for tourists and for leaving town on the weekends.

"Yup, my steed's parked around the corner. I had some repairs done at a garage on West End." (Years later, he would confess to the lie, saying that he'd brought the car just so he could drive me home, so he could woo me.)

We were both going to the East Side, to the streets we'd roamed as kids, he to his mother's at 1040, and I to the high-rise on Third Avenue where I lived for two years in the spare room of my father's office. I'd leave it each morning as though I didn't exist—corners tucked, surfaces wiped, and any trace of me jammed into a tiny closet with a rickety accordion door.

We went south on Columbus. He didn't take the transverse at Sixty-fifth Street, the straight but potholed cut through Central Park; he took the long way. There was some plan to ride the lights up Madison, but at Fifty-ninth Street, when we saw that the blue barricades that so often blocked the lower entrance to the park were open, he asked, "Shall we take the Drive?" It was a question to which there was only one answer. The Drive is six miles of meandering road that runs the length of the park, and ever since I was a child, I've loved going through at night. The pavement seems smoother, the darkness darker, and there is rarely any traffic in this cool scented heart of the city.

I smiled at him, perhaps because it was all so unexpected, and when the light changed, we pulled in front of a horse carriage and followed a yellow cab onto the curving road. It was October but warm, and we rolled all the windows down and turned the radio up. My legs were bare, too close to his hand on the stick shift. He drove fast, and I leaned back in the seat, letting my fingers trail the air outside. It would rain later; you could feel it. We took the loop around the park three times that night—up to 110th Street and back down near the Plaza where we'd started—before he turned east on Seventy-second Street to take me home. Each time he asked, "Once more?" Each time I said, "Yes, again." The wine had worn off, but the air and speed were intoxicants, and I was drunk somehow.

He'd be gone for seven months, and it would be longer than that before I saw him again. There were postcards—one of a masked Nepalese demon, all skulls and silk; the other of temples he remembered I longed to see. And, before he left for Bangkok, a letter describing Everest Base Camp and a dream in which I'd appeared. "Now what does this mean?" he offered in orange marker on tattered blue aerogram paper. It was a letter I looked at sometimes, smiling at the rangy script and trying to decipher a section at the bottom obscured by a mysterious bronze stain. *Now what does this mean?*

While he was in India, my relationship with an actor in the class ahead of me got serious. Bradley Whitford was from Wisconsin and he was irresistible. He would later go on to fame as Josh Lyman in *The West Wing*. We'd meet between classes on the Juilliard roof, and at night he would ferry me on the handlebars of his bike to his apartment twenty blocks north. Lanky, sweet, and original, he was blessed with a rapier wit, but more lethal to me were his gifts as an actor. I had never gone out with an actor before, and our fights were frequent and passionate, ignited by a shift in mood or a slight. They were also over quickly. After one stormy argument in Sheep's Meadow, he carved our names in a park bench near Tavern on the Green; and when he played Astrov, or as Orlando, gushed, "But heavenly Rosalind!" I hoped he was thinking of me.

I pushed the drive around the park out of my head. Like the weather that night, it was defined by exception. I decided I had made it up—not the smooth road or the candlelight or the warm night air—those I knew had happened—but the sense that it was something more.

He hadn't kissed me that night, and I hadn't asked him upstairs, although we had lingered awkwardly when I got out of his car. We hadn't crossed the line, but it was there, unspoken. Like the scent of warm rain on pavement.

Falling

They talked some and perhaps dreamed some,
because they were young and
the day was beautiful.

—BRIAN FRIEL

I had known him almost ten years by a June day in 1985. It was a warm Saturday—the kind of day New Yorkers live for. The sky was clear; there was a slight breeze and no trace of the humidity we knew would come. On days like those, you dream, and your step is light on the pavement.

After rehearsal at Robin Saex's apartment on Christopher Street, John got his bike and walked me, as he usually did, the couple of blocks to the subway at Sheridan Square. Passing the bustle of gay bars and leather shops, we stood for a moment under the hand-painted sign outside McNulty's as the heady smells of hazelnut and bergamot wafted onto the street. Robin, our director and friend from college, drank the strong vanilla tea they sold there, and now, after four and a half months of sporadic gatherings at her apartment, both John and I were hooked. When rehearsals ended, we'd sometimes stop in the store with the low tin ceilings and the burlap bags of coffee and glass canisters of tea from all over the world.

Since the end of January, we had begun to read through the play every few weeks. Everyone was busy and we met when we could. Because there was no production in the works, it was an open-ended venture—more like playing around, something we did for fun. Robin was directing her own projects, in addition to assisting prominent directors at Circle Rep and the Manhattan Theatre Club. I had finished my third year at Juilliard and was juggling auditions with a pastiche of jobs—paralegal work, catering, and coat checking—to pay the bills. John was busy, too. He was working for the City of New York in the Office of Economic Development. He was also weighing whether or not to apply to law school that fall.

For me, these meetings were a relief from the rigidity of Juilliard. Legend has it that Robin Williams, an alumnus, called it boot camp, and on many days that's what it felt like. For John, they were a way to hold on to his love of the theater. Robin Saex knew that he missed acting. Although he had majored in history at Brown, he'd appeared in plays there with authors as varied as Shakespeare, Pinero, Rabe, and O'Casey. She sensed that we would work well together and often spoke of finding the right vehicle. The play she found was *Winners*. It was a perfect fit.

Brian Friel is one of Ireland's most prominent playwrights. He was born in Omagh, county Tyrone, in 1929 but grew up in Derry. His more notable plays include *Philadelphia, Here I Come!; Translations;* and *Dancing at Lughnasa,* which would receive the Tony for Best Play in 1992. In 1980, along with actor Stephen Rea, he had co-founded Field Day, a theater company and literary movement that sought to redefine Irish cultural identity. He also happened to be one of my favorite playwrights. At twenty, while traveling through Dublin, I had attended the opening night of *Faith Healer* at the Abbey Theatre, and when, by chance, I was introduced to him, without thinking I bowed slightly. It was as if I'd met a rock star.

Winners had premiered at the Gate Theatre in Dublin in 1967 before coming to Broadway. It's really one part of a two-part play, *Lovers: Winners and Losers. Losers* is about a middle-aged couple married for many years, but *Winners* is about young love. It's often performed on its own, as we did in our production.

Maggie Enright and Joseph Brennan are seventeen and seventeen and a half, respectively, and Catholic. It's a warm day in June, a Saturday, and they are studying for final exams on Ardnageeha, the hill above their town. Mag is "intelligent but scattered" and Joe dreams of becoming a math teacher. They're to be married in three weeks because Mag is pregnant. As they look out over Ballymore, they fight, they sleep, they laugh, and they tease; they profess their love and talk about the future.

When we reached the subway stop at Sheridan Square, John suggested that we enjoy the day. He would walk me to Fourteenth Street, and I could get the subway there. Usually we parted here. He'd get on his bike, and I would head to Brooklyn, where I'd moved the month before, or to my boyfriend's on the Upper West Side. But today we got ice cream. He ordered a pistachio double scoop, and I got coffee swirl. As the woman at the register handed him his change, she seemed suddenly flummoxed.

"What's your name?" she said.

"John."

"John what?"

"Haag. John Haag."

"Spell it," she insisted, her eyes narrowing.

"H-a-a-g."

"You positive? You related to the General?"

He told her he was a Democrat, and we made for the door.

"Wait!" she cried out, trying to enlist me. "Do you know who he looks like? I mean, who does he look like if you didn't know him?"

"Richard Gere," I deadpanned. "Definitely Richard Gere."

"Oh no, he looks like John-John!"

Outside in the sun, we laughed. "You need a persona," I said, as he moved to unlock the heavy chains that bound his bike to a nearby street sign. He handed me his cone and nodded. When he turned his back I thought, *He has to do this all the time.* I must have known it in the years before, but the worlds of high school and college had been cocoons of a sort and it was only there, by the newsstand at Sheridan Square, that I grasped that life, in the smallest of ways, even getting ice cream, was very different for him.

"You may be right about that," he said, taking his cone back, the bike balanced with one hand. "But Richard Gere . . . I'm way better-looking." He winked, then bit into his pistachio.

"How's yours?" he asked as we walked.

"Yum," I said. "Perfection."

"Mine tastes a little funny. Smell it."

We stopped, and he held out his cone. As I leaned in, he took the chance to dab my nose with green. "Hey!" I said, looking up. He was thrilled that I had fallen for his trick, one that had been played on him by countless cousins when he was young. I brushed the ice cream from my nose, and we continued up Seventh Avenue, passing cafés and secondhand shops and looking in windows. We talked about our grandfathers. He told me that Joe Kennedy had prized mystery in a woman, and I smiled, imagining myself a siren. I told him that my Irish grandfather had been a rancher who had moonlighted as a Prohibition bootlegger and kept stills in Nebraska, Wyoming, and South Dakota. He liked that. "We have something in common," he said. "Word is mine was, too." Larger territory, I suggested slyly.

My grandmother had died that May near the Nebraska homestead where my mother had been born. I'd gone back for the funeral. I told him about the land that seemed to stretch forever, land that was as wide and as rolling as the sea. I described the shock of its beauty—how you knew it in the roller-coaster dips of the dirt country roads and the burnt-yellow fields broken only by barbed wire, cattle, and a windmill here and there; by the massive snowdrifts in winter; and, in spring, by the lilac shelterbelts, some twelve feet high, planted during the Dust Bowl to keep the soil down. He stopped for a moment and with surprising urgency said, "You know the heartland. You don't understand how lucky you are."

I remember being struck by the phrase, its quaintness, and realizing that I didn't know him as well as I had thought. I was sure I saw something in his eyes then, a yearning for a kind of life he had missed, for spaciousness. But when I look back now, I think of the black-and-white photographs of his father and his uncle Bobby, shirtsleeves rolled up, receiving hands reaching to them from the crowds, the faces weeping, smiling, believing. I think of the weight of those images and imagine that the call of service might have been there for him—was always there for him—even as he walked the city on a warm spring day with a girl he had known for years.

By Fourteenth Street, we had finished our ice cream. He asked if I wanted to keep going, and for no reason, we cut over to Sixth

Avenue. The incidental music to our production was all early
Beatles—*Rubber Soul* and *Help!*—and as we walked, we sang,
mangling lyrics to "I'm Looking Through You" and "Ticket to
Ride." We left the Village, with its kaleidoscope of lanes and avenues, and the buildings grew higher and the streets quieter. In
1985, that span of blocks had not yet been gentrified. Bed Bath &
Beyond, Filene's, Burlington Coat Factory, and the crowds they
engendered were a thing of the future. On that day in June, the
streets were ours, and the city looked new. At the Twenty-third
Street stop, he didn't leap on his bike and I didn't say goodbye. We
didn't even think about it.

Earlier, during rehearsal, Robin had informed us that she'd
found the right venue for the play. We'd be performing it in early
August in a seventy-five-seat black box theater at the Irish Arts
Center, a nonprofit cultural institution in Hell's Kitchen. There
would be six performances for an invitation-only audience. John
didn't want any publicity and Robin had ended an association with
another theater when an item was leaked to Page Six. We were
both excited about the news and discussed it as we walked north. It
meant that in July, we would begin rehearsing five nights a week.

We passed through Herald Square—lines converging and the
noise and color of traffic—and kept on going, through the Gar-
ment District and past the Broadway theaters. Finally, we found
ourselves at Columbus Circle, flushed and fifty blocks from where
we'd started. The sun was going down behind the Coliseum. I
looked up past the monument of the famed explorer that stands in
the center of the circle and took in the fact that we had not stopped
talking for the entire walk. Now, at Merchants' Gate, the southwestern entrance to Central Park, we were quiet.

It had gotten cooler, and I braced my arms around my waist
while we waited for the uptown bus. "That was fun," I heard him

say, but his voice was somber. We looked away from each other
and into the roundabout of cabs.

"Yes, that was fun," I said. I was not the kind of girl who found
tramping fifty blocks—or anything even remotely athletic—fun,
but it had been.

He turned back to me. "Well . . . see you next week," he said,
brushing his lips against my cheek, and before I could climb the
steps of the bus that had come too soon, he had gotten on his bike
and was gone.

From the window, I watched as he weaved through the traffic.
With my forehead to the glass, I followed the swerves and the zig-
zags until I lost sight of him.

*Why is my heart beating so fast? Why am I so happy? And why, in
God's name, did I walk so far? Well, maybe I do have a little crush on
him, but I can handle it, I can enjoy it. It's just a feeling, that's all.
Nothing has to happen. Nothing will happen. He's my friend, and
we've known each other so long. If anything were going to happen, it
would have happened already. And anyway, he couldn't possibly feel
the same way about me.*

Thoughts rushed in—fear and pleasure at once. I talked them
down as I rode north on Central Park West to my boyfriend's
apartment, a ground-floor studio with bars on the windows and
light from an airshaft. I thought I was safe.

No matter how many times you fall in love, it always comes at
you sideways. It always catches you by surprise.

After more than twenty years, it's strange to read my script of
Winners. With the highlighted chunks and dog-eared pages and
penciled-in stage directions, it could have been any script from that
time in my life. But this one I saved. This one made it through the
years and the many apartments and the shuffling back and forth be-

tween Los Angeles and New York and all the places in between, the constant shifting that makes up the vagabond life of an actor. For a time, I kept it with other scripts, old photographs, opening-night cards, cast lists, and telegrams in a wooden chest that had belonged to my great-great-grandmother on my father's side.

Ann Dargan had come from county Cork during the great famine, a spinster alone on a sailing ship with all her belongings in the humble chest. On the ship, she met a man from the north with two small girls and a wife. The wife died of fever, as many did on those voyages, and before they reached the Port of New York, Ann married this stranger called McIntosh. They moved to the hills of western Pennsylvania—green hills that looked much like the ones they'd left. They farmed the land that was pocked with stones and raised the girls and had five more children of their own, one of them my great-grandmother. I liked the story, and I kept the chest.

The papers were in no particular order, and I found the script buried at the bottom under an old tax return. The binding had split, and the last quarter of the play was missing. But I knew how it ended.

Winners is a play about first love, and although we were young when we performed it, this wasn't the first time for either of us. I had just turned twenty-five; John was months shy of it. But we weren't that much older than Friel's characters, and like them, we'd grown up together. We also shared their traits. I could be studious and overly serious, like Joe. I sulked when I was hurt, like Mag, and talked a blue streak when nervous. John had Mag's impulsiveness and love of a colorful tale. And he smoked the odd cigarette now and then. Like Joe, he could tease and joke himself out of any fight. He would explode in anger and strong words, but soon it would be over and forgotten for him, and he'd be baffled if you didn't feel that way, too. And much like Joe, he had a vulnerability, which was at times difficult for him to express—a kind of loneliness and a sense of being separate no matter who else was around. Because he loved people and had a wealth of friends, this wasn't always apparent, but I suspect that anyone who knew him well saw it, and loved him for it.

One of my favorite parts of the play is when Joe tells Mag how he feels about her. Throughout the morning, he has teased, scolded, and ignored her, but when he is certain she's asleep, he leans over and gently brushes the hair from her face. Then, covering her with his jacket, he reveals his heart. He tells her he's crazy for her and vows to be true. I remember that summer lying on the fake grass of the small raked stage for his three-page monologue, the stage lights hot on my face. As I feigned sleep and his words washed over me, there was delight in the secret knowledge, the tender mix where make-believe and reality—lives onstage and off—had begun to meet.

When I reread the play many years later, other things came back: how he stressed a particular word, how he sang a song about kisses, how effortless he was. And that I laughed. Laughter onstage is often harder to come up with than tears, especially when you've heard the joke a thousand times in rehearsals. No matter how gifted the teller is, spontaneity fades, and it can sound forced. But with John it was easy. I needed only to listen.

What makes this a powerful play—and what I've left out until now—is the knowledge almost from the beginning that in a few hours, Mag and Joe will drown in the shallow waters of Lough Gorm, a lake east of their town. Friel uses two narrators, a man and a woman, who function like a Greek chorus. In our production, they sat on stools at either end of the stage with bound scripts in their hands. Although the deaths are never solved, the narrators interrupt the dialogue with facts—about weather, topography, and sociological, medical, and family histories. They describe, in excruciating detail, the lack of wind, low water levels, an abandoned boat, search parties, sightings in Liverpool and Waterford, airport and border closings, search parties called off, and bundles of clothing washed ashore. Then the bodies found facedown in twenty-seven inches of water, the inquest, the coroner's reports, the requiem Mass, and the large turnout.

The final image of the play is of Mag and Joe laughing, hands joined, running down the hill at Ardnageeha on a June day to begin their lives together.

At twenty-five, I found the irony poignant, romantic, even affirming. *Carpe diem; life is fleeting*, it said to me. But fourteen years later, when I heard the words on the news—search party, clothing found, autopsy (along with the endless facts about water depths, haze, and flight plans) they were familiar to me. Words that the heart does not understand, words you keep reading in hopes that they will help you to fathom what you cannot.

During the summer of 1999, the country was gripped by a massive heat wave. The East Coast was the hardest hit—blackouts in New York City, roads buckling in New Jersey and Pennsylvania, and in Rhode Island, a spate of temperatures not seen since 1895. In western Massachusetts, it was cooler, but only by degrees. Drought had singed the once verdant lawns that July, and a dull persistent haze blanketed everything.

It had been years since I'd seen him—not from ill will, but our lives had gone in different directions. Still, when I learned he had gotten married, I was devastated. It was early on a Sunday morning almost three years before, and I was wandering through Penn Station waiting to board a train when I saw the headline. We had broken up at the end of 1990, but for a year or so after that, we would meet and there was the sense of possibility in the air. By the time I stood at the kiosk at Penn Station, I no longer felt this. Yet he remained in my heart, and seeing the photograph was like a small death, a vivid punctuation of an end that had already taken place.

For the last two years, I'd been living and working in Los Angeles. I'd also fallen in love with someone, an actor, and was visiting him that July at a theater in Stockbridge, Massachusetts. I hadn't thought about John in a long time, but two days before his death, I did. The actor's family would be arriving the next day, and I would meet them for the first time. But in a sunlit aisle in a supermarket in Lee, I stopped the cart, looked up, and for a moment almost violent in its clarity, it was as though he were with me.

On Saturday, July 17, a friend called early and woke me. She'd heard about the missing plane on the radio, and didn't want me to find out that way. As she reported what she knew, I crumpled to the kitchen floor, my back pressed on cabinet knobs. I held the phone against my chest, and when I stopped crying, she spoke. "But it *is* John. He's come out of things like this before."

I remember little of that day, only the heat. The actor's family shielded me from news reports, steered me from televisions, and tried to keep me busy, their helplessness etched on their kind, embarrassed faces.

I keep searching for a word I once knew, or perhaps imagined. It's to hold two opposing beliefs at once, fully and without judgment; to know that both are true. Like *ambivalence,* but without its reticence. That day, when I received my friend's call, I knew in my heart that he was gone. There would be no rescue. And I also knew that this was not possible. In my mind, I kept seeing the purple shadows of the small, uninhabited islands off Martha's Vineyard, ones I had been to with him years before. Surely, they would be found there. Surely, they would be rescued. And like everyone else, I waited.

The next morning when the light was still gray, I got up and drove for hours alone on the back roads of Otis, New Marlborough, and Tyringham. I drove fast, careless with myself. As in a dream, lush white fog covered the hills and wrapped itself around the young birch trees. I blinked to see the road. Things forgotten, tucked away and put to bed, tumbled by across the glass as if they were present. A glance, a touch. The way he said my name and woke me in the morning. Spaghetti he made with soy sauce and butter. Leaping on the benches outside the Museum of Natural History. Candles flickering at the Vietnam Veterans Memorial, which he insisted I see for the first time at night, his hand guiding mine over names of cold stone. Another night—skating over black ice. My back against his chest, his arms holding me up; cold on our faces and the sound of the blades. Black trees, black below, black sky. The brush of blue satin against his tuxedoed leg. And the adventures—dangers that fate had tipped in our favor. Once safe, they became the stories we told. But now, pulled over by the side of a country road, I remembered the terror I had felt.

By eight thirty, the heat was full on, and I stopped at a coffee shop in Lenox. *Coffee,* I thought. *The paper. Do things that are normal.*

Outside by the steps, the sun glinted off the newspaper stand. And I saw, on the front page of every national and local paper, the headline, the wedding photograph. I stood for a long time, never making it past the steps. In the thickness of shock, I tried to puzzle out why this was in bold print, why this was news, why this was public. I hadn't understood until then that it was real. And that he would be mourned deeply by people who had never met him but whose lives he had touched all the same.

Plane debris had begun to wash ashore on Philbin Beach near Gay Head by Saturday afternoon. On Tuesday, at a depth of 116 feet, the fuselage was spotted several miles northwest of Nomans Land, the island you could see from his mother's beach. News broadcasts began to play the biographical montages mixed with grainy long-lens footage of the house in Hyannis Port, the wide green lawn, and the white tent for the family wedding that had now been canceled. On Wednesday, after the bodies were found, I took the train to New York to attend a memorial service that Friday—not the one filled with dignitaries and family members, with a reception in the Sacred Heart ballroom, but one arranged by his friends Jeff Gradinger and Pat Manocchia and held at La Palestra, an upscale gym he frequented near Café des Artistes.

When I walked in, I felt welcomed, even though I hadn't seen many of the people in years. Some of his cousins, including Timmy Shriver and Anthony Radziwill, had come directly from the earlier service. I embraced Anthony. He was weeks from the end of his fight with cancer. I hadn't seen him since his wedding in 1994, when he had spun his bride around the dance floor and everyone had applauded. Now he was fragile, his weight resting on a cane. "I'm all cried out," he said quietly when we spoke of the events of the past week. "There's nothing left."

When I looked across the crowded room, I saw disparate groups—lawyers, bankers, journalists, musicians, artists; friends from grade school, law school, boarding school, and Brown—the many tribes that John had knit together. There was anger, grief, and disbelief in that room, but also a celebration of the friend we'd lost.

People stood up to speak. Some attempted humor. Others told of exploits, athletics, bravery. I read a poem he'd once read to me, one his mother loved. But it was Christiane, our Benefit Street roommate, whose words comforted the most. They still do. "He was an ordinary boy in extraordinary circumstances," she said, her voice unwavering. "And he lived his life with grace."

After it was over, I went back to my apartment in the West Village, and for the first time in days, I wept. Then I went to the old chest. In it, I found a slim volume of Gray's *Elegy.* I brushed the dust from the sepia cover. My grandmother had given it to me when I was eleven, but I'd never read it. When I was young, I had no interest in graveyards or dead youths, "to Fortune and to Fame unknown." On the first page, in her careful schoolteacher's hand, she'd inscribed it FOR TINA WHO LIKES POETRY. I turned one of the thread-bound pages, and a newspaper clipping, one she must have tucked there long ago, fluttered to the floor. Now yellowed, as fragile as a bee's wing, it was an artist's rendering of a commemorative stamp from the mid-1960s, a drawing of a three-year-old boy saluting a casket.

Deeper in the trunk, I found my copy of *Winners,* and I opened it.

At the end of July, a week and a half before the play opened, John bought a red motorcycle. Bullet red with clean lines. There had been no hint of it in the weeks since rehearsals had relocated to the Irish Arts Center, so when he rode up that evening, it was a surprise. "At least it's not a Corvette," he quipped. We teased him, but really everyone was thrilled. It was a welcome distraction from the nerves before opening, and after rehearsal we stood on the sidewalk and he took turns giving us rides.

Robin got on first. She was tiny and settled in tight. Then Denise, the stage manager. She didn't want to, but John coaxed her. After that, Santina, the lighting designer, who'd also gone to Brown. They were good friends, and she'd directed him in two of his best performances there, *Short Eyes* and *In the Boom Boom Room*. Next, Phelim, a lanky, red-haired boy with cowboy legs as long as the bike. He grinned when he got on board, and when they came trundling down the block, he pitched his legs out to the side and we all laughed.

I hung back, talking to Toni, the assistant stage manager. We stood by a chain-link fence that bordered the abandoned lot near the theater, a three-story converted carriage house on the north side of Fifty-first Street. It was late, but I could feel the afternoon's swelter on the bottoms of my sandals. I could smell the river a block and a half away.

I'd changed out of my rehearsal clothes—a short blue skirt and a red cardigan. It was 1985, the Madonna/*Like a Virgin* era. I eschewed the leggings, the bleached hair, and the ubiquitous skinny rubber bracelets, but sported a slinky black dress I'd gotten cheap at a street fair, a wide leather belt low on my hips, and a bronze-colored cuff on my arm. The cuff was a remnant of a costume from some Shakespeare play I'd been in, and I'd taken it as a totem. My hair was loose and long and out of the clip that turned me into seventeen-year-old Mag Enright.

The play had been going well since rehearsals had moved from Robin's apartment. John sometimes complained about the stepped-up hours (he insisted on having weekends off and won), but he always showed up after work ready to go. We'd had one squabble. It was over the word *God*, a matter of where the pitch lay in the mouth and if and how the lips were rounded. It was slight, but I corrected him and we argued. For days, neither of us would back down. I knew I was right. After all, the year before, while John had been exploring India and Thailand, I had been learning all manner of dialects—from Afrikaans to Cockney to Czech—and could transpose them into IPA, the International Phonetic Alphabet. I'd also spent hours studying a tape labeled "Donegal native speakers," compiled and given to me by Tim Monich, the speech teacher at Juilliard. Finally, Nye Heron, the artistic director of the Irish Arts Center and a native Dubliner, was brought in to settle the matter. He would set John straight. But as it turned out, I was wrong. My version, Nye said, was correct—for a county or two over. But John had it down to the township. Humbled, I took pains from then on to say it exactly as he did, and I was grateful when he didn't gloat. His ear, the gift of any actor, was superb, and at least in the matter of *God*, it had trumped mine.

In rehearsal clothes, we tumbled and wrestled on the small stage. There was ease, banter, and trust, and he'd lean against me when Robin gave notes. But over the past week, once we were alone and in street clothes, something was different between us. There was a seriousness, a glance too long, and, for me, the aware-ness always of where he was in the room. I couldn't stop thinking about him, and I fought it.

"Hey," he called out from the bike. "I'll give you a ride home."

That night home was Brooklyn, the walk-up I shared with an-other actress on the outskirts of Park Slope. Not over-the-bridge Brooklyn, but eight miles as the crow flies and forty minutes on the D train—if it was running express. And that summer, it never was.

A trek to one of the outer boroughs didn't concern him. He flicked his wrist and the engine growled. "Hop on," he said. I pressed my sandal onto the rubber-wrapped metal foot peg and slid on the back of the bike, pulling at the slithery fabric of my dress. "Hang tight," he said as he revved the engine once more.

My hands—where to put them. Certain they'd give me away, I tried the silver hitch behind me on the saddle. No good; I'd fall. As they fluttered forward, I thought, *He will know if I hold him. He will know by my touch.* It was as though I had no memory of the hour before. Earlier, in the theater, we'd begun to rehearse the kiss at the end of the play, the one we'd always marked or skipped over, a long kiss during the narrator's speech about death and drowning. Robin wanted it passionate, extending well beyond what the script called for, and as we knelt on the itchy stage grass facing each other, she told him to grab me and he did.

On the bike, I touched his back lightly, then placed my hands at the sides of his torso. We waved goodbye to Robin and Santina and the crew, and took off down Eleventh Avenue, past the warehouses and tire shops.

A few blocks later, he turned right toward the river. At the stoplight, his legs dropped, decisive, to either side of the bike. He reached back, grabbed my arms, and placed them firmly around his chest, pressing twice so they'd stay put. And then, as quick as air, we swerved into the fast lane of the West Side Highway. If we hadn't—if the light had been a little longer or he'd hesitated, taking time perhaps to adjust the mirror or run his fingers through his hair—he would have heard a sharp intake of breath before I gave over and let myself sink into his back. Before I surrendered. Then I knew. It wasn't my hands that were telltale; it was my heart, pounding against the thin white cotton shirt he wore that night. I tried to slow it down, to slow my breath. *He'll know, he'll know how you feel.* It didn't occur to me that he already did.

I knew that if we spoke of it, everything would change. It was like a dream. And you know that if you tumble forward into it, there will be no way back.

It was late, but the traffic was heavy. He dodged the taxis and potholes, and I held on, my knees wedged against his. Near the FDR Drive, he took the long, lean ramp up to the Brooklyn Bridge. The railings and cables were lit for the night. The sky was velvet. No stars. And the city moon, days from being full for the second time that month, scattered itself over the oily current of the East River like a soothsayer bestowing gifts. The wind flapped his shirt back, the cotton silk on my skin. I closed my eyes. And somewhere on the bridge, I rested my head against him and listened to the hum of the night.

When we hit the Brooklyn side, I directed him from Adams to Flatbush. We passed Borough Hall and Junior's Deli (still open, bustling and bright), the shuttered storefronts, and the Beaux Arts façade of the Academy of Music. And when I saw the domed clock tower where Atlantic meets Flatbush, I knew it was almost over. I wanted to keep going, to take him farther into Brooklyn, all the way to Brighton and the sea.

"Here," I said at Fourth Avenue. "Turn."

Union Street was wide and empty, and I pointed to a brownstone identical to many on the block. He parked the bike, and I slid off, dizzy from the speed, my eyes dry, my hair tangled. We stood close but apart, under the glow of a streetlamp, and he began to rock the toe of his sneaker against the curb.

"This is where you live."

"It is. I feel like I have sea legs." My face was warm, and I realized that if I said anything else, it wouldn't make sense.

But he nodded; it had been a long ride. Then I saw him look up to the door of the brownstone.

"I had a thought," he said. "What if we leave for Peapack on Thursday night after rehearsal instead of Friday morning. You know . . . spend the night, have the whole day?"

On Friday, the crew would be in the theater, and we were going to New Jersey to rehearse on the hill near his mother's house.

"I thought I'd check with you before floating it by Robin," he continued. "Whatever you think . . ."

I fiddled with the bronze cuff, twisting it on my wrist. He watched.

"I think it's a great idea," I said slowly. "Are there horses there?"

"Yeah . . . there're horses." He looked at me as if he was trying to recall something. He'd stopped fooling with his sneaker and we were still.

"So how do you feel?" I asked. "About the play?" Although it wouldn't be reviewed and the setting was humble, it was a big deal. His New York debut and mine, and though we didn't know it, his swan song.

Although he'd mentioned that many of his cousins would be at the opening, as well as his mother's friend Mr. Tempelsman, and this made him happy, I knew his mother wouldn't be there, and neither would his sister. "They're on the Vineyard." I was quiet when he told me. Were the rumors true? Did his mother disapprove? But he quickly brushed it off. It was better this way, he said. If they came, it would only cause a fuss.

"How do you feel?" I asked again.

I imagined him not as he was, standing before me by a skinny tree on Union Street, but in his costume: the wool cap and leather satchel, and the striped schoolboy tie askew on the collar of his wrinkled button-down. It was hard to make John look nerdy, but onstage, in our play, he did. He'd perfected the hangdog look, and in a blue blazer sizes too small, he stooped.

He was looking up at the tree, his lips pursed. "I feel good. I feel okay. I mean, I'm nervous—with you I'm fine." He nodded, as if trying to convince himself. "But that speech I have about Kerrigan shooting the cows, sometimes I blank. Even though I say the words, I'm out of the scene."

I smiled. He was wonderful in the role. "Listen," I said. "I'm going to tell you something an acting teacher once told me. If you're in trouble—don't just keep going. Stop, take a breath, and look into my eyes. It will ground you. It may feel like it's forever, but it's not, it's just a moment. And you'll remember. I promise. You'll know where you are."

"Okay," he said, nodding again. "I'll try. But same for you. Deal?"

"Deal."

I reached out my hand and he took it. Our eyes locked. I wanted to hold him, to be back on the bike, but when my hand slipped down again, we were no longer smiling and he spoke so low I could barely hear him.

"It's heady stuff. Very intense being with you like this each night." It was an offering, a way into new territory, and when I stayed quiet, sure and unsure of his meaning, deciding whether to dodge, play dumb, or lunge headlong, he kept on. "I don't mean in a bad way. I just—"

"Oh, yes," I began, astonished by my duplicity. "Friel is amazing!" And I continued to rattle on breathlessly about the magnificence of playwrights and the transcendence of the theater, before I turned to climb the steps of the brownstone, leaving him to his journey alone across the bridge to Manhattan.

A week after the play closed, the motorbike was stolen, and in September the police found it abandoned in a field somewhere on Staten Island. I mourned the idea of the shiny new machine, but John seemed indifferent. He decided not to claim it. "Anyhow, they're dangerous," he said. "A good thing it's out of my hands." And the following spring, when we were together and I no longer retreated up brownstone steps away from him, the motorcycle, whether it was red like I remember or not, became part of the story we told each other. "I didn't care that it was stolen," he would announce. "I bought it to woo you, and it was worth every penny." He said this, whether it was true or not, always adding, "I can't believe I took you all the way to Brooklyn, and you didn't even invite me up for a glass of water!"

"What's your favorite New York memory?" he asked. We'd met at noon on the steps of his old school under the guise that I would help him find a present for his sister. And now, hours later, we had walked in circles all over the Upper West Side. It was four days before Christmas, and the city was crammed with tourists and shoppers. The tree sellers were out in full force, drinking steamy coffee at their makeshift stands, and the sky was clear, although the news called for snow.

It had been more than four months since the play had closed, since he'd kissed me by the McDonnells' horse barn, and we'd seen each other only a handful of times.

We searched that afternoon in small artisan shops I knew on Amsterdam Avenue. In one, with room for only a handful of patrons, dull light flooded the floor-to-ceiling windows, and every crevice was packed with pillows and textiles, mohair coats, sheep-skin jackets, and imported leather bags. "Gold or silver?" he said, studying a tray of earrings in one of the cases. Before I could an-swer, he held one to my cheek—a small silver hand with a coral bead. He kept it there, cold teasing my skin, and leaned back to as-sess it. "I say silver. Like the moon." He bought a different pair for his sister and, months later, would give me the wrapped box with the silver hands.

When we stopped for lunch, he told me he was applying to law school, something that his family had encouraged and he had waf-fled about over the summer. Now, though not exactly thrilled or even certain of his future as a lawyer, he had decided. After hot chocolate, he asked about the play I was doing at Juilliard—one that was closing that night—how my love life was, if there were still problems, if I was happy. It was territory we had covered be-fore.

On an August night during the run of the play, we'd gone to Cen-tral Park. To talk, we'd said. It was a perfect night. The punishing humidity of July was gone, and there were stars in the city sky. He carried a paper sack with a couple of beers he'd bought at a corner store on Columbus, and as he walked, they chimed against each other. By the Ramble, he took my hand, and we walked off the path toward the lake. There was a large outcropping there, and we climbed it. I wore wedged espadrilles, and so I wouldn't fall, he led me over the pocked ridges to the farthest spot.

We sat for hours by the water on the big rock near the Ramble. Our own world, he said. And under a moon no longer blue—as it had been the week before by the horse barn in New Jersey—but quartered, words we had long held tumbled out. How he felt, how I did. Our lips bruised from kissing, we promised we would be together, but not, I told him, before we ended the relationships we were in. When we left the park with the night half over, clouds had begun to blanket the sky and everything seemed simple.

The play closed two days later. Photographers loitered outside, we got congratulatory telegrams from Friel's agents at ICM, and there was heated talk of moving the production to a bigger house for a commercial run. "I'll be guided by you," he told me privately as we weighed the decision. Before the performance on closing night, we stood for the last time in our costumes in an empty room on the third floor. He gave me a first edition of Synge's *Riders to the Sea,* and I gave him Edna O'Brien's *A Fanatic Heart.* Books are not always a customary closing gift, but we had both brought them.

At the closing-night party at Fanelli's on Prince Street, he kissed my shoulders when no one was looking. "Don't make me wait too long," he whispered. "Sort things out, but come back to me." I was leaving for Maine the next day, to a friend's house on Vinalhaven—a self-imposed exile, without phone or electricity, that I presumed would bring me the resolve to break with the man I'd been with for almost three years and whom I still loved.

It was weeks before I saw John again. I was in rehearsal for a PBS broadcast celebrating Juilliard's eightieth birthday, and we agreed to meet afterward by the Dante statue near Lincoln Center. When we got off the phone, he ran to an open window, his roommate later told me, and yelled to anyone within earshot, "Christina's free . . . the girl I'm going to marry is free!" But I wasn't; he had kept the vow, and I hadn't.

All through dinner at the Ginger Man, I waited for the perfect moment to tell him. I watched his face in the candlelight, felt his pleasure at seeing me, laughed at his exploits since I'd seen him—

tales of Hyannis and the Vineyard. I'd missed the happiness of being with him—the newness, the edge of ease and tension between us—and I knew that once I told him, that would all change. Greedy, I wanted more of the night. As in a spell self-cast, for hours I made myself forget what I had come to say.

We made our way to the park again, this time far from any path, to the darkened south end. He laid his jacket on the ground and waited for me to sit first. It was just after Labor Day—still green, still warm, with a few precocious leaves skittering about. "It never feels like this," he said as he held me, his face open. "I should tell you," I finally began, and wound my way awkwardly through the words I'd rehearsed hours earlier. Something about owing it to the relationship. I left out the part where, a week before, when I'd gotten back from Maine, Brad had fought for me, and that his apartment—an actor's usual disarray of laundry, scripts, and dust—had sparkled. The worn yellow floor had shone, and he had bought flowers. I left out the part where he'd said, "He'll leave you. One day he'll leave you." And that somewhere deep inside, I was afraid this was true.

I believed I was doing the right thing, but as I spoke, my voice suddenly sounded hollow. What I really wanted, although I didn't know it, was for John to make me see how wrong I was. To grab me as he had in the play and tell me he couldn't live without me. Instead, he listened. He was quiet for a while, then gracious. "I'm glad it got this far—at least I got you to the park again." His face, shadowed by trees, was a cipher, and when I reached for him, he pulled back, leaped up, and ran out of the park. I called out, sure he was just over the hill, but there was no one. Frightened, I grabbed his jacket and found my way through a maze of bushes to the walkway by the drive. At Sixth Avenue, I caught up with him—his arm outstretched for a cab. He looked angry. "There's nothing more to say," he said, cutting me off and jumping into the cab I thought he'd hailed for me.

It was well after one a.m., and I was alone on Central Park South, save for a couple of fancy working girls who slouched across the street and traded cigarettes. It had happened so quickly, and there was so much I hadn't said, but I watched the taillights travel up to Columbus Circle and disappear north onto Broadway.

A few weeks later, I heard that he'd gotten back with his girlfriend. In October, we met with Robin at the P & G bar on Amsterdam to look at pictures from the play. She gave us each an orange plastic flip-book of three-by-fives, and we went over the contact sheet with a magnifying glass, circling the others we liked in red pencil. When she left to use the pay phone, I asked him how he was. It was good things had worked out as they had, he answered coolly, fixing his eyes on the ceiling, the bar, the door—anything but my face— until Robin returned.

I buried myself in work: a leading role at school that fall and the PBS *Live from Lincoln Center* broadcast, in which, somewhat prematurely, I was cast as Blanche DuBois seducing the paperboy. Slipping into someone else's skin had always been a saving grace for me, and it was then. Some days I succeeded in not thinking about him at all.

One day, I got a note from the head of the Drama Division asking to see me in his office. A summons, though not uncommon, was cause for trepidation. Michael Langham was an exacting director and a brilliant mind. During World War II, as a lieutenant with the Gordon Highlanders, he'd been captured near the Maginot Line and had spent five years in POW camps. There with the approval of the German guards (and fellow prisoners as actors) he had begun to direct plays. For many years, he'd served as the artistic director at the Stratford Festival in Canada, and later at the Guthrie Theater in Minneapolis, and his innovative productions of Shakespeare were renowned. Now in his mid-sixties, with a shock of silver hair, he was still dashing and often wore pink cashmere, as he did on that day.

His door was open. I knocked anyway.

"Come in." I heard the clipped, familiar voice from inside. "Close the door behind you."

I sat across from him in the low-ceilinged room, its walls lined with framed costume sketches and the wide desk between us. His eyes, sharp with thought, were a deep, changeable blue.

"So, what's wrong with you, my dear?" he began, dispensing with small talk.

I'd lost weight in the past month, and I mentioned the cold I couldn't shake.

"That's not what I meant." He was impatient. His eyes hadn't left me, and he flexed his fingers under his chin. "You're distracted. I saw your last performance. You had glow but not enough glitter." As he spoke, I let my eyes wander up the curved cable pattern on the arm of his sweater. "I've spoken with your teachers. It's apparent on the stage."

I closed my eyes, mortified. *Not just Michael—the whole faculty.* I saw them seated around a long, oval table discussing my personal life. The year before, I'd been let in on a secret. Two students in the class ahead had broken into the office one night and read the files, recounting that the notes on each of us included not just missed classes and lazy consonants but who was with whom and in what extracurriculars they indulged.

"Do you drink?"

I shook my head.

"Do you do drugs?"

"Well, I—"

"Are you addicted?"

"No," I said quickly. Michael had been sober for years, but there were rumors of his indiscretions. One in particular, with a red-haired actress in Minneapolis, that had almost ended his marriage.

"Still, it's something." He got up and moved around the desk, his hands clasped tight behind his back, his head proceeding slightly in front of his body. "I believe it's love," he concluded with some distaste, as if I were an awkward bit of staging to be solved. "You're addicted. I believe you're in love with love!"

I burst into tears and began to apologize.

Michael handed me a handkerchief from his pocket. He didn't require details, and for that I was grateful. It was about the work. He patted me lightly on the back and told me to take care of things. "We have great hopes for you," he said before I reached the door. I turned and saw that his face had softened. There was a rim of red wetness around his jeweled eyes, a sort of kindness.

At the end of November, I got an invitation to John's annual birthday bash, this time at a club in Midtown. It was a curt, breezy note, something about losing my address. You can, of course, bring a date, he wrote. I went alone, and when I saw him through the crowd, laughing easily, surrounded by friends, I knew he had moved on. And I was sure of something else—I had made a huge mistake that night in the park. It had taken me that long to know. As I left the party, there were flurries in the night air, but they melted before they hit the pavement. I wondered if everything that had happened that summer had meant nothing, if it had just been a mirage of the play, a trick of the theater.

A smaller voice said, *Wait.*

Then in December, I ran into him at a Christmas party in the East Twenties. He'd come with his girlfriend, and I was meeting Brad later, but at some point, we found ourselves in a corner of the kitchen, and the steely awkwardness that had been there all fall had vanished. We flirted. The light in the room was bright and we weren't alone, but it felt as if we were. And before I left, he asked if I would meet him the next day. He needed help picking out a gift for his sister.

"Favorite memory?" I repeated the question.

After lunch, we wandered all afternoon near the planetarium, past the stores on Columbus and then down to Lincoln Center. Now we were on Broadway again—walking each other back and forth between Seventy-ninth Street, where my bike was locked, and Eighty-sixth, where his apartment was. It was after four and we kept putting off saying goodbye. As we walked, our breath came out in short white puffs.

My hands were cold; I'd forgotten gloves and he offered his. Stitched brown leather and fuzzy on the inside.

"Favorite now . . . or of all time?" I put the gloves on. Even with space at the fingers, they were warm. I kept one for myself and handed him back the other.

"Childhood. The best one."

I closed my eyes, and I was there. Running up the steps in a cherry velvet dress during intermission at *The Nutcracker* to touch the beaded metal curtain that hung by the tall windows across from the bar. I'd turned my back and pretend to look out on the giant courtyard. Careful at first, I'd make the beads sway—the weight on my fingers a pleasure—but when I saw, balconies below, that the curtain rippled into a full-on spin, I'd get bolder, my touch now a jangle, until a guard or my mother would stop me. It was as much a part of the tradition as the Sugar Plum Fairy or the Christmas tree that grew.

Sunday dinners with my kindergarten best friend at a Chinese restaurant on Third Avenue. Wide round tables at half-moon booths, a fountain of magic rainbow-colored water at the entrance, and uniformed waiters who'd load up our Shirley Temples with maraschinos. We'd gnaw the stems and line them at our plates like twigs. Halfway through dinner and bored of our parents, we'd slide off the shiny vinyl banquettes to whisper secrets under the table. The starched tablecloth—a cave entrance—and our mothers' legs poised, even in the darkness.

And skating at Rockefeller Center—always cold, always shadowy—but the music and hot chocolate were better than at Wollman Rink. Plus they had rental skates that didn't make your ankles buckle.

"Well, Madam?" he persisted. Under our boots as we walked, the crunch of salt and ice.

"The World's Fair," I answered. "I'm almost five, and my mother's in a beige suit and heels, very pregnant. I remember going with my father up to the highest deck of the observation tower—the one that's still there and looks like a spaceship. We went in one of the small exposed elevators that rode up an outside track, but my mother stayed below. I held my father's hand, and the whole time I could see her, but she got smaller and smaller. And when we reached the top, I could see the tip of the city over the trees, and my father leaned down and said he was proud of me. Then we went on It's a Small World After All, and I got to sit between them in those little boats."

"It's a Small World . . . I remember that!" To prove it, he

hummed a bar. "We went with my cousins Anthony and Tina. Maybe we were there at the same time."

"May*be* . . ."

"Remember the goats?"

"Oh my God, I do!"

"I liked those goats," he said, as if he still missed them. He began to shake his head softly, a smile beginning on his lips.

"I was wrong about you. I was sure you'd say Serendipity." He was referring to the fancy ice-cream parlor near Bloomingdale's, with the faux Tiffany lamps and the spiral staircase, where Upper East Siders had birthdays in grade school. "Girls always like Serendipity. I thought that would be your favorite."

I smiled. I liked it fine, I told him, but there were other things I liked better.

His face had gotten wistful in the sudden dimming light. After a moment, he turned to me. "I have to tell you . . . I didn't think you were going to show today."

His eyes caught mine. I'd thought the same thing about him.

"But I'm glad you did. I've missed this."

Those were the words I needed, the ones I'd waited to hear; and we walked faster, whether from cold or happiness, I did not know.

West by the river, there was a last gasp of sunset. We'd arrived at the corner of Eighty-sixth and Broadway for the third time, and the streetlights came on. When he turned, like an admission, to walk me back once more, we laughed.

"What about you—what's your favorite?" I asked.

"Beatles. Shea Stadium." For him, there was no pause.

"You were *there*?" I gasped. "How old were you?"

"Five," he said, satisfied. "And hansom cabs." Except, he told me, every time there was a major change in his life—a new school, his mother marrying Onassis—she'd take him for a carriage ride around the park to break it to him.

"Ah, you couldn't escape."

"Too true," he chuckled. "Too true, I couldn't."

We stopped in front of a dress shop that had always been there. In the window, there were sale signs written out in Magic Marker and old-fashioned mannequins covered in polyester jersey.

"I remember this place, it was here in high school," I said.

"Wanna know something?" He leaned in, and where my scarf had loosened, I felt his breath. "I bought my mother a dress here once. A present in fifth or sixth grade. Two dresses, actually. For $19.99."

I was charmed and asked the obvious. Did she wear them?

"That night she did." He closed his eyes, remembering. "But only in the house. She was very convincing. She said she loved them. She said they had style."

We'd reached Seventy-ninth Street for the last time, and there, on a crowded corner at twilight, between a Baptist church decked in Christmas wreaths and a news kiosk, he kissed me. Before we parted, I handed him back the glove, and he took both my hands in his and pressed them to his lips. And the snow that had been promising all afternoon to fall had finally and quietly begun.

I left for Mexico the next day, a family vacation, but stayed on an extra week to travel on my own. I slept in a hammock in Yelapa, downed shots of tequila before parasailing, and spent New Year's Eve on a cliff top with strangers toasting the sky. I thought the time away would make me sure of what I already knew. When I returned two weeks later, there was a letter waiting. It was short and to the point. As he filled out his law school applications, he couldn't stop thinking of me. "I'm imagining you all alone in the hot Mexican sun," he wrote. Unlike the missives from India two years before, with their crossed-out words and serpentine scrawl, he had printed each letter squarely, perfectly, without confusion.

"PS," he added at the bottom. "I want to see Your Tan."

I waited a few days, then called him, and this time I didn't look back.

We stood on the pavement between Eighth and Ninth avenues waiting for cabs, a huddle of friends from college. We'd been dancing that night at a new Cajun restaurant, once an old post office annex. John had a new job at the 42nd Street Development Corporation. The office was next door in the McGraw-Hill Building, and the restaurant was his find. He would rent it out, or his friends would, for birthday parties, celebrations, and, as people we knew began to get married, the odd bachelor party. With the tables pushed back, it made for a great dance floor, and at night, with Talking Heads or Funkadelic blaring, the large picture windows that faced the vacant lot and the welfare hotel across the street made it a snow globe of light on what, in the mid-1980s, was a desolate stretch west of the Port Authority. When I arrived alone, the party was in full swing.

I had been in a play that night. Each spring at Juilliard, the members of the graduating class perform for two weeks in repertory, a nod to the European roots of the training. It was thrilling to shift gears and worlds like that; it was why I wanted to be an actor. The slate that spring was a Jacobean tragedy, O'Casey, Ibsen, and Sam Shepard. Tonight—the tragedy. I was Annabella, murdered for her incestuous love of her brother Giovanni. Believing their passion is pure, they forgo morality and society's judgment, and when they cross the line to carnal pleasure, it seals their fate. *Romeo and Juliet* with a twist.

When I came offstage, I removed the heavy makeup and the wig of human hair the color of mine but longer, thicker. I let the brocade gown drop to the floor and stand by itself in a poof. I untied the hoop skirt and unlaced the stays of the boned corset. I pulled off the wig cap and the bobby pins that held the pin curls to my head and made the wig lie flat. I shook out my hair, lined my eyes with black pencil, and slowly inched fishnets up my legs. A tear; I pulled higher. Then I put on the new dress I'd bought at a thrift shop behind the planetarium days before. I slipped the black sheath of silk crêpe over my head—slim straps on the shoulders and a bias-cut; it fell to mid-calf and flared slightly there.

With six dollars and a token or two in my pocket, I headed to Columbus Circle to catch the A train. I slung my Danish schoolbag across my back; it was purple and stuffed with dance shoes, leotards, scripts, scarves, the *Post*, a red paperback of Yeats's poems, and my journal. When I reached the subway steps, I changed my mind and hailed a cab. The bag was heavy, and I was eager to get to the party. Anxious, too. Chris Oberbeck, our roommate from Benefit Street, was getting married to his college sweetheart, and this shindig was in their honor. Although John and I had been seeing each other for almost three months, this was the first time we would be together as a couple with people we'd known for years.

Our courtship since mid-January had been hidden, sporadic, and intense. Separating from the long relationships we'd been in—John's for five years and mine for three—had proved more difficult and painful than we had imagined. And there was the fact that we'd known each other for so long. I was afraid that if I took the leap, I might lose my friend. What was undefined held safety.

One February night, as I was walking to meet him, the wind bit the backs of my knees and my mind raced. *This can't work . . . How can he . . . What should I . . .* But when I saw him at the street corner waiting, his chin tucked, his head dipped to one side, I only knew I was where I should be and this was right. There was nothing else.

Still, it was stop-and-start.

In late January, he's going to a conference in Pennsylvania, and he asks me to meet him there afterward. "To take a weekend together," he says. It's not a concept I understand. I have boyfriends, and we just do things. But for some reason, I find the phrase so sexy. He describes the hotel where we'll stay, a place he's never been. "There's a heart-shaped Jacuzzi in the room," he says, reading the brochure. On January 28, the day the *Challenger* crashes, he leaves a short message on my answering service saying the trip is off. I don't understand at first—it's a tragedy, surely, but not one that affects him directly. When we speak, he explains. His presence is required at the memorial service at the Johnson Space Center in Houston with President Reagan and other dignitaries. It's either him or Caroline, and his ticket is up, Jacuzzi or no.

. . .

We meet for lunch at Café Madeleine on West Forty-third Street, and he whispers, "I miss your ears. I miss your hair, your freckles, your laugh."

I leave school one day, and tied to my bike I find red roses and a postcard of a French courtesan. On the back, unsigned: YOU RULE MY WORLD.

We're at the Palladium. As we dance, he moves to shield me from a photographer I haven't noticed. Unlike mine, his eyes are peeled for that sort of thing. In the picture, I am laughing. I think it's a game. The caption reads, "Mystery Woman."

Headed to Martha's Vineyard in a small plane, we hit a winter storm. Buffeted by high winds, we're rerouted to Hyannis. With no place to stay, we arrive unexpectedly at his grandmother Rose's fourteen-room house. It's late. On our way up the dark staircase, we run into his aunt Pat in a Lanz nightgown. She's in her cups. Then his uncle appears. Neither knew the other was there. Upstairs, we find a bedroom that's used only in summer. We push the twin beds together and lie under the thin coverlet, as the wind rages. In the morning, before we leave for the Vineyard, we walk on the breakwater as far as we can go. The waves slap the sides and he steadies me on the wet rocks.

On a warm day, he bikes from Manhattan to Park Slope with tiramisu from his favorite restaurant, Ecco, melting in his backpack. We eat it on my brownstone roof, homing pigeons cooing nearby, and watch the light fall over the faraway city.

. . .

A morning: He kisses my forehead and tells me to sleep in, tucking me into his king-size water bed. When I wake up, he's gone.

After seeing Ronee Blakley at the Lone Star, he gives me the first of many driving lessons. In this, he is both brave and patient. I'm a born New Yorker, and driving is not in my skill set. With the Scotch from last call warm in our throats and Al Green in the tape deck, I sit on his lap, and we drive his Honda in circles around the Battery Park lot for what seems like hours. The stars are white and cold, and we laugh as he explains over and over how the engine works, what it does. And I learn somehow. I learn well.

But there are weeks I don't see him. Things are not resolved with his girlfriend, and they're not for me either. After one stretch in March when we haven't spoken, John appears at a performance of *Buried Child*. I am Shelly and spend much of my time onstage in a patchwork bunny jacket peeling carrots. A friend who is there that night tells me that John wandered the halls alone at intermission humming to himself.

Afterward, we meet and cross Broadway to McGlades, a bar where the Juilliard actors and dancers congregate. It's awkward at first, until after a beer or two, he suddenly reaches across the table. Half out of his seat, he takes my head in his hands and pulls me closer, the table wedged between us.

"I was going to leave right after the play. I keep trying to forget you, but I can't. I can't let go." His words come so quickly. He looks worried.

"What?" I say.

"I'm obsessed with you. I can't stop thinking about you."

"What?"

"I'm obsessed. You make me an emotional person, and I'm not."

"No, John . . ." I laugh, taking his hands from my ears. "I can't hear you." I hold them between mine over the table, and we smile knowing something has been laid bare.

"You're funny," I say.

"Why?"

"You're a funny boy. You can only say that covering my ears." He sighs, but he doesn't look away. "I'm scared."

"I'm scared, too," I say, but we're both smiling.

As if to assuage me, he kisses each knuckle, then turns my palm over.

"I can't stop looking at your hands. There's a poem . . . have you seen *Hannah and Her Sisters?*"

Yes, I tell him.

"When I saw it, I kept thinking of you. You look like the actress. Your hair. When Michael Caine's in the bookstore and he gives her the book—"

"I remember. 'Nobody, not even the rain—' "

" '—has such small hands.' "

He leans back and his eyes close. I touch his cheek. "What are you thinking?" I ask, but he shakes his head.

"What is it?" I make him look at me.

"On the street—I keep thinking I see you. You make me emotional, and I'm not like that. I want to say your name all the time."

The cab stopped on Forty-second Street, and I walked across to the restaurant. Through the glass, I could see faces I knew. Happy. Young. Some from high school, most from college. John's roommate, Rob Littell, with his shirt askew, was sliding across the floor doing his ski move. Art majors boogied in groups, punctuating with jumps and hoots. Classicists shimmied solo. Girls who grew up in Manhattan took up space, looping around the sides of the room and executing serpentine finger drills worthy of Indonesian temple goddesses. Frat boys got down with Iranian beauties, making up with enthusiasm what they lacked in finesse. I dropped my bag by a pile of jackets near the door and found my friends, the roommates from Benefit Street. Chris was talking to Kissy, and Lynne stood close to her boyfriend, Billy.

"He's here somewhere," I heard Lynne say over the din. "He was just asking about you."

Then he appeared, smiling so big, and anything I feared was gone. With one hand, he led me into the center of the dance floor. And when the fast song got slow, when the Stones bled into Joan Armatrading, I leaned into him. If there were people talking about us, about me, if there were eyes of judgment or of envy, I shut them out. Like Annabella, the character I had left on the stage that night, I looked into the eyes of my Giovanni and thought of the love that overcomes everything.

When the party was over, we drifted outside. The April air was balmy but still cool enough for a coat. There were no cabs in sight. John stepped off the curb to scout, and I turned to say my goodbyes. After a moment, a friend whispered as she hugged me, "Be careful, Christina." I knew she was not referring to the slick street.

I was stunned. Was there something she knew that I didn't? I wanted to say, Can't you tell? Can't you see how he feels? How I feel? How happy we are? How long we've waited? How right this is?

"What?" I said, my face flushed.

She stopped herself. She knew him well. "Just be careful."

A cab pulled up, and John whisked me inside. "1040 Fifth," he said to the driver, before sinking back beside me and pushing his foot against the jump seat. "Mummy's away tonight." And we set off.

1040. His mother's home. The stone scallop shell of the Pilgrim above the taut green awning. The paperwhites in the vestibule at Christmas. The front gallery where everyone gathered at parties. The narrow hallway near the bedrooms that was lined with black-and-white photographs and collages of summers in Greece, the Cape, Montauk. His old room, with the captain's bed and the navy sheets and the old school paperbacks and the tall cabinet filled with his father's scrimshaw. I had been to 1040 many times, but this was the first time I would be alone with him there.

I don't know why we went there that night instead of to his apartment across the park or to mine in Brooklyn. As the cab drove off, I did not find it curious that we, at age twenty-five, would stay at his mother's, but rather I thought it was wonderful that there were so many possibilities. I remember a quickening of hope that maybe, with John, I could grow up and not grow up, I could have an adult life but not lose the girl, the *jeune fille* who was careless and wanted to dance and wore stockings with tears.

When I was twenty-five, I wanted freedom. I was afraid of being hemmed in, of having responsibilities and limits. None of the grown-up women I knew seemed happy. Not my mother or her friends or the few of mine who had begun to marry. When I was twenty-five, I cared passionately about two things: acting and love. With John, I thought I could have both. He was the first boyfriend I'd had who wore a suit and tie to work, but he also possessed the playfulness of a large dog.

The lights got brighter as we drove past the strip of triple-X theaters near Times Square, and I thought, *There'll be no relationship talks, no conflicts, no jealousy, no drama. None of the things that love has led to in the past.* I thought this only because these were things that hadn't happened yet and conflict was a level of intimacy I feared, one that tore at the gossamer skein of romance. In the cab, on that night, I felt hope.

As though he read my mind, he pulled me close, one fishnetted leg on his, and looked at me with what appeared to be wonder. "I can't remember being this happy. Why is that?"

"I don't know why. I don't know, it's strange. We're different—"

"But you know me, you *know* me."

"I know you."

"It's like we're simpatico." We both smiled when he said it.

"I keep trying to go slow, but I can't. I can't help myself." He pushed my hair back and kissed me. Then, pressing his forehead to mine, he said solemnly, "I can't imagine us fighting ever."

"Me either," I said back, as if it were a vow, a good thing, a thing of mystery and of promise. And with that, the words of caution were banished from my mind, and we sped off on the wet city streets to the latticed iron doors of his mother's apartment building.

Slowly I began to meet his family. A cousin here and there. Easter with his sister. And on the Saturday of Memorial Day weekend, after stopping for the night at Brown for Campus Dance, we were on our way to Red Gate Farm, his mother's 464-acre retreat on the southwestern end of Martha's Vineyard. I had been there once before, but it was in winter, and we had been alone. On a morning when the sky was bright, he had taken me to the cliffs and told me the Indian legends—how they buried their dead facing east to the sun. Ancient graves had been found over the years, he'd said, in the tangled briar of his mother's property.

This time I would meet his mother. There had been greetings and goodbyes at holiday parties, and polite conversation, but nothing that she would have recalled. And even if she did, this was different. I was the girl he'd done the play with. I was nervous and anxious, and I overpacked.

On the Steamship Authority ferry from Woods Hole, we inched across Nantucket Sound to Vineyard Haven. We'd rushed from Providence up Route 195 that morning to make an early boat. Friends he'd invited caravanned behind us. We rallied in the ferry parking lot, and the cars stayed on the Woods Hole side. It was that time in late spring that aches with possibility, the time when it's forever cold in the shade, sometimes warm in the sun, and hovering always is the errant promise that there will be more.

The *Islander* was clean and smelled of diesel. It was windy on board, but none of us stayed below. Excited for the weekend ahead, we planted ourselves on the upper deck looking for sun. Halfway across, John disappeared, and I lay sprawled on a bench in the center of the midsection—one leg bent, the other dangling out of a summer skirt, an arm propped over my eyes. Heat rose from the metal and wood, and my back was warm with it. I felt the engine's droning hum, the shift of pitch and drop over water.

A trickle of air buzzed in my ear. It stopped, started, then stopped again. I opened my eyes to find John crouched beside me, his face close to mine.

"You're sweet," he said loudly when I groaned. "Are you grumpy? Hmm? Just a little?"

I shook my head, and he watched me yawn.

"Oh, so sweet. Did anyone ever tell you you're sweet? Don't be *too* sweet, or I'll bite you. Come on, get up, get up. No breaks for you," he half-sang. "C'mon—I'm the boss of you."

I rubbed my eyes and tried not to smile. "You are *not* the boss of me," I insisted. But, laughing, I followed him around the pilot-house to the breezy side of the boat.

We were almost there. White houses and low green hills. He turned, his hair already salty from the air. "See—aren't you glad you're here?" It was my first ferry ride there, and the first time for anything is an occasion, he said. He pointed out the places. West Chop Light, the yacht club, the sails of the schooner *Shenandoah*—and that way, down and around, to Oak Bluffs and the storied gingerbread cottages.

"What do I call her?" I asked. I knew the answer but wanted to make sure. He didn't dismiss the question. He may have anticipated our meeting, just as I had, but for his own reasons. He considered it for a moment—eyes on the shore, on the busy wharf that was coming pristinely into view.

"Call her Mrs. Onassis. Call her Mrs. Onassis unless she says otherwise."

We were supposed to be met at the dock by Vassili, a short, wiry Greek from Levkás. He'd worked for years on Aristotle Onassis's yacht and was now in John's mother's employ. Instead, there was a rounded man in a striped shirt with a most engaging smile.

"Maurice, what are you doing here!" John looked pleased.

"I'm surprising you," the man said brightly. I liked him immediately. Maurice Tempelsman was a financier, a diamond trader, and Mrs. Onassis's last love. Rob, John's friend since college and current roommate, knew him, but for the rest of us, there were introductions all around. He had come by boat, he said, and thought it would be fun if, instead of driving the thirty minutes to Gay Head, we continued on by water, anchoring at Menemsha Pond, a stone's throw from Red Gate Farm.

After lunch at the Black Dog, we piled into the open Seacraft. As the waves kicked up, Maurice pointed out the landmarks. When he saw me shivering in a jean jacket, he gave me his windbreaker and had me sit in the captain's seat behind him. I caught sight of

John. He was perched up front as far as he could go—his face leaning hard into the wind.

Red Gate Farm was off an unmarked dirt and gravel road. If you continued on the main route as it swung north, you would come to the end of the island—the cliffs, the redbrick lighthouse, a small cluster of shops—and when the road wrapped back inland amid fieldstone fences and stunted sea-bent shrubs, there was a small library, a firehouse, and a town hall. But if you turned before the road curved and entered a weathered wooden gate that in those days was rarely locked, you would have found it. The land, a vast parcel of the old Hornblower estate, was wild with scrub oak, native grape, poison ivy, and deer ticks. It bordered Squibnocket Pond and a spectacular swath of private beach. Mrs. Onassis had bought the property in 1978, and the traditional cedar-shingled house—a series, really, of adjoining saltboxes with clean white trim—had been finished in 1981. There was a garage, a vegetable garden, the caretaker's lodgings, and tennis courts hidden by hedges. A short distance from the main house, there was a guest cottage, known as the Barn. Next to this, designed with John in mind, was an attached faux silo with a bedroom at the top that we called the Tower.

Wherever you looked you sensed proportion—a symmetry between what she had built and what had always been. It was there in the way the lawn ended and the wild grasses began, in the slant and angles of the saltbox roofs, in the cut trails that wound their way through dense brush to the beach, and in the pensive space between the fruit trees in the orchard. It was there in the wildness she left, there in the stillness. She had built her house in agreement with the land, and the Tower, where we stayed, stood sentry.

The years that I visited, she remained on the island for most of the summer, from Memorial Day to Labor Day, returning for meetings in the city only when she had to. With her were Efigenio Pinheiro, her elegant, earringed Portuguese butler, and Marta Sgubin, who had begun as a governess to John and Caroline and was now cook, confidante, and cherished part of the family.

On moonless nights, the sky there was so black, even with a riot of stars arched above. In August, when the grass was parched and the sea untroubled like green glass, we often went up with friends, staying in the Barn and cranking the stereo. But when we were there alone, it was quiet in the Tower—the wind, crickets, a bird's call, and the oblivious blanketing beat of the waves. At sunset, there was a ruffle of scarlet in the west before the shadows came.

Being there felt like you were in someone else's dream—one created for pleasure, not to impress. Everything was pleasing to the eye. Things were in their place, without fussiness or clutter. Rustic New England pieces mixed with comfortable chairs and couches, and the rooms unfolded like a story. In her house, the intangible quality of light and color conspired to shift you to yourself, and what you felt was peace.

I remember looking in the kitchen for a glass one morning. Instead, I found vases and, attached to the inside of the white cabinet door, an unlined index card in her hand—which flowers in which vase in which room. It surprised me. When I saw a small carafe of sweet peas or a clutch of dahlias in a room, it seemed unplanned— as though they had just happened there, as though they belonged. Or there'd be a path that appeared to go nowhere, but when you reached the meandering end, you felt its purpose. What seemed happenstance was crafted, chosen by her unerring artist's eye.

Dinners were announced in the Barn by a buzz on the intercom, and showered and changed, we'd gather in the main house. No matter how glorious the day had been, this was the time I loved best. The dining room was simple: a plank pine table with candles sheltered by hurricane glass, a framed schooner above the mantel, and Windsor chairs. She sat at one end, and Maurice, with his back to the window, sat at the other. Nothing was formal on those nights when her table was full—it was happy and festive, although she rang a small silver bell between courses and placed each of her guests with a seer's sense of how the conversation would flow.

She was curious about John's friends and could pry a witticism from even the most tongue-tied. Talk centered on the day's exploits, a bird that was spotted, current events, a book read, an exhibit or play someone had seen in New York. And woven through were the family stories. Stones of remembrance for his father laid at a friend's cattle ranch in Argentina; John's fall into a fire pit in Hawaii when he was five and his rescue by Agent Walsh; summers on Skorpios—the Molière plays directed by Marta that John and Caroline put on for their mother's July birthday. If the story warranted, she would mention with ease and fondness his father or Mr. Onassis, and I began to feel as if I knew them. When his cousin Anthony was there, they would tandem-tell their tales of a dreadful English camp in Plymouth and spar over who pushed whom down a glacier in the Alps when they were teenagers. One year, by force of argument, John would win. The next, it would be Anthony, winking over the candlelight when he had claimed the last word. At the end of each meal, after chocolate roll or berry pie, there was lavish praise for Marta, who appeared from the kitchen smiling.

After dinner, there might be a game—Bartlett's or charades, maybe. John and Caroline were both fierce players and in the spirit of fairness were often relegated to different teams. But always, we moved to the living room for mint tea or coffee. Waiting were the fluffed sofas and the cashmere throws, a wall of books, a fire if it was cool, and, in the dark distance, the far-off sound of the sea.

What she wore on those evenings I imagined belonged to this place, as if the fabric and metal existed only in her Up Island sphere. Large hoop earrings, a gold snake circling her wrist, an inexpensive necklace of silver and blue stones that John had brought from India and that she treasured, long-sleeved black T-shirts with jeweled necks, and slim printed skirts that fell to her sandaled feet. She was always radiant at dinner—hair pulled back, sun-kissed by the day.

The second summer, she lent me books. Some she had edited— I especially liked *The Search for Omm Sety: Reincarnation and Eternal Love* by Jonathan Cott—and others she picked from the shelf: a psychology study on family constellations, a collection of poems by Cavafy, Edith Hamilton's *The Greek Way*, Jean Rhys's *Wide Sargasso Sea*, and a first edition of Lesley Blanch's *The Wilder Shores of Love*, its cover somewhat crumpled. She smiled when she handed me the book of tales of Victorian adventuresses. "I think you will like this one."

The next summer, John and I lived in LA, near Venice Beach in a blue-gray house with a white picket fence. I was doing a play at the Tiffany Theater, and he was a summer associate at Manatt, Phelps, Rothenberg & Phillips, and we'd fly back whenever we could. John had become an uncle for the first time when Caroline's daughter Rose was born in late June. I was carting around *Timebends*, Arthur Miller's 599-page autobiography, and one afternoon while I was submerged in the McCarthy hearings and *The Crucible*, his mother asked if I liked the book. I did, I said. Had she read it? "No, I haven't." She beamed like a child stealing candy.

"But I've heard it's good—I just looked up the parts about Marilyn Monroe."

If I wanted to go off to the beach on my own, she would let me use her jeep. This incensed John, who, though a better driver, was relegated to one of the older vehicles. I had just gotten my license, but I still couldn't parallel park. (The driving lessons had been a prodding gift from John, and he'd written on the card, "Merry Christmas Baby! May the rest of us beware.") When he complained, she held firm. "She won't get my jeep stuck in the sand and you will."

On occasion, we'd venture off to the tamer parts of the island for Illumination Night or the Agricultural Fair, or for a concert at the gazebo in Oak Bluffs. One night, we went with his mother into Vineyard Haven for ice cream. We browsed the paperbacks at Bunch of Grapes, and caught an early showing of *Roxanne* at the Capawock. (I liked it, Mrs. Onassis didn't, and John was indifferent.) But as I recall, she rarely left the environs near Gay Head, and her life there had its own rhythm.

If I was up early, I'd see her biking along Moshup Trail— sometimes with Maurice, sometimes alone—her head kerchiefed, maybe stopping off with her binoculars to spot a warbler or a Cooper's hawk. Some days after lunch, if the water was flat, she'd water-ski at Menemsha or join us at the beach to swim laps in her cap and rubber fins. Other afternoons, she would read outside in the quiet, bricked corner behind the library. There she was sheltered from the wind and could look out over Squibnocket to the sea, with a view of the changing dunes and the empty island just off her shore called Nomans.

By then I knew not to disturb her.

. . .

On the second morning of Memorial Day weekend, there was a big breakfast, and afterward John and Rob set up a net in back of the house. With Ed Schlossberg, who would marry Caroline that July, they measured out the boundaries for the 1986 inaugural summer volleyball game. It was an especially sporty crowd that weekend, and Mrs. Onassis, Marta, and Maurice stood by and cheered. Even Efigenio came out in his trim, striped apron to watch.

John was big on "Do your best, win or lose," and that day I tried. Despite my lack of ability, he was my own private coach. When I sent the ball sailing into the net and it ricocheted back to our side, he called a time-out to clue me in on exactly what I'd done *right*. "Just aim a little higher." When my rusty underhanded girls' school serve made it over but landed in questionable territory, he argued fiercely with Ed at the net until the point was called. Swept up by his enthusiasm and the constant pep talks, I almost believed that if I just harnessed my inner jock, one day this might actually be fun. I kept my knees bent, like he said, and my hands prone, but I eyed with gratitude the skinny girl across the court who was as disinclined as I was. After several hours and heated rematches, most of us lost interest and returned to the Barn, but John wasn't done. He corralled whomever he could for water sports at Menemsha. I took off for the beach. Like sleep, sex, and food, time alone was a requirement.

There was a branched path that led to a set of silver canoes. From there you could paddle across to a break in the high dunes, slip the boat up on the sand, and walk to the ocean. He'd taken me there the day before. But first I had to find my book. I'd left it somewhere after breakfast.

When I reached the back of the house, I saw the volleyball net and a lunch tray pushed aside on a lone patio table. Nearby, on a cushioned chaise, Mrs. Onassis sat barefoot—a pencil in her hand

and a manuscript resting on her bent legs. I thought to leave, but she'd already looked up. She wore large-framed sunglasses that were nowhere near as grand as they appeared in photographs. The day before she had been polite—just shy of aloof—and I had been, too.

Rarely at a loss for words, I mumbled that John had gone waterskiing and I'd forgotten my book. Without getting up, she glanced, swanlike, to either side of the chaise, then shrugged. She seemed to me impenetrable. By then I'd found my battered copy of *A Sport and a Pastime* on a chair near the tray. I had it in my hand, but to leave I'd have to cross back in front of her. I could hear the stillness—that hot, dense three-o'clock kind—and I wanted to vanish, to be whisked off by some passing bird. But something kept me there. Then, softly and without smiling, she spoke, her eyes toward the water. "I was watching you earlier—you reminded me of me." As I clicked off the many things this could mean, we began talking—how beautiful the day was, the manuscript she was working on, ballet, our childhoods in New York. I knew, as we spoke, that she was still watching.

In the course of our conversation there was a gesture to sit, which I did, at the very edge of her chaise. She set down the pages, bringing herself cross-legged, while I fingered a loose button on the upholstery. Soon the pauses between us lessened. The glasses came off. She slid them high on the colored scarf that covered her hair and shaded her wide-apart eyes with her hand.

Later that summer, when we knew each other better, she would ask me to tell her all about the play the summer before. She wished she had seen it. And when I said how good, how funny John had been, she smiled with pride, pressing the tips of her fingers to her lips.

But on this day, we began, somehow, to talk about children—about babies and early bonding. Because I had no experience, I had strong ideas about the subject, and although the psychology of breast-feeding seemed a rather iffy topic, I risked it. No longer observing, she hugged her knees tight and leaned in with a quality of attention and empathy I'd rarely experienced. Things are *so* different now, and women have more choices, she confided. She told me that when she had her children, the baby nurses just swooped in and spirited them away. They'd fasten them by their layettes to their cribs with large pins, and there was nothing you could do. Really, I said, amazed, wanting to take her hand in comfort.

As she spoke, the years fell from her face. Like an actress, she could reach into the past, and with a shift of thought, her features would change, mirroring the emotions of another time. Beside me, at the back of the house with the sun still high, she was no longer in her mid-fifties, the poised chatelaine of Red Gate Farm and mother of the man I loved, but a young woman of twenty-six, her brow raised in wonder at all that would happen.

There was a lull. We smiled, relieved somehow. I stood to go. I could have talked with her all afternoon, but I had my book, what I'd come for, and I didn't want us to run out of things to say. I turned, but she spoke again, her eyes far away and remembering something. "Oh . . . about the volleyball—you don't have to."

As I walked across the grass, I felt changed. My step was lighter, and there was a tenuous catch at the back of my throat. Joy, maybe. I'd always assumed I would like his mother, but I hadn't guessed that it would be this much.

Later, when John got back, we traded stories. We were dressing for dinner in the large rounded closet on the second floor of the Tower, his clothes on one side, mine on the other. In between "did I like his shirt" and "this dress or that" and "shall I wear my hair up or down," I told him I'd canoed to the beach and that in the shallows of the pond near the old fishing shack, I'd seen two giant snapping turtles. "Oh, and I had a nice talk with your mother." Half-listening before, he now appeared alarmed, the pastel linen shirt he'd chosen trailing from his hand. "What were you doing there?" he scolded. "You never, never go there between lunch and dinner." He said it as though it was a canon I'd grown up with, adding that I should have known better. I felt my face grow hot. It was the first time he'd gotten angry with me; it didn't sound like him. And I felt terrible for committing a faux pas, for disappointing him when things were going so well and mostly for intruding on what was clearly his mother's private time.

When he left the closet, I wondered if there was more to it. If, in childhood, he'd been scolded often—before he'd committed to memory when to be around his mother and when to stay clear, before he'd learned to temper his boisterousness around her, before she'd built him the Tower. He'd told me that when he was younger, after his father died and before his mother remarried, she was a different person than she was now, and there were times that had been difficult for him, times when she would be away for too long. I could see that they adored each other, that they understood each other with an uncommon depth, but I knew from my relationship with my father that with such depth came complication. Perhaps, as I did, he just wanted the weekend to go smoothly. I saw clearly, if I hadn't known already, that if things were to last between us, I would need her approval. Without it, they would end—not right away, but they would end.

I was learning the rules, the unspoken codes, the secrets and agreements that make up the edifice of every family. And I was learning something else: that his anger, quick and rare, jumped to bright heat and was over.

. . .

That night I wore a dress he'd given me. (To learn my size but still surprise me, he'd asked for shoe size, hat size, and glove size as well.) Fancier than required, it was strapless, of fine, heavy, black Italian cotton, and in the right light, there was a sheen to the fabric. I loved that dress. It was his first real gift—something I might not have chosen, but when I put it on and felt the bodice snug around me, ran my hands along the folds of the full, flirtatious, tiered skirt, I thought he knew me better than I knew myself. As we walked across to the main house, fog had come in off the pond. Suddenly, he turned and took me in his arms. He was sorry about the closet, he murmured to my neck.

After dinner, we moved to the living room, and Mrs. Onassis had me sit beside her on the sofa as she poured the mint tea into fine china cups. She sat erect like a dancer. John was by the window, telling a story about some boat mishap earlier, and the dim room shimmered with laughter. He was across the room, and I missed him. Through the picture window, I could see that the rain had started. After everyone else had been served, she handed me a cup; it trembled for a second against the blue and white bone saucer. I looked down, trying to think of something intriguing or smart to say. But she began, her voice a low infectious whisper. My dress was lovely. And how had I done my hair, she wanted to know, drawing me out like a cat.

I looked up—his mother's face, so open in the soft, broken light.

When the summer was over, John told me that his mother had given him some advice: Now that you are with Christina, you must be a man. She'd counseled that in the past, it had been different, but now he needed to grow up, to take charge and protect me. I was, she told him, very feminine. We were twenty-six then, but neither of us talked about what that meant. It hung like a treasure map between us. Inside, I smiled. *This must be a good thing.* That she had said it. That he had told me.

For years after that first weekend, even when my romance with him was over, there would be a letter from her now and then. On occasion, she would call—she'd seen me in a play or on television, or there was a book of hers she wanted me to have. It would arrive by messenger, and slipped inside the fresh pages would be an oblong cream card with the decorous Doubleday anchor at the top: *Thought you'd like this, love Jackie.*

The letters—on pale-blue stationery in blue pen, or on heavy lapis correspondence cards embossed with a white scallop (and one black-and-white postcard of Pierrot)—I kept tied with a red ribbon in a shoe box. The last arrived a month and a half before she died, before I flew back from Los Angeles to attend her funeral Mass at St. Ignatius Loyola—police barricades outside the baroque church and a slew of perfect white flowers blanketing her coffin.

"I hope all goes well," she wrote in the last letter in her artful, tended script.

And whenever she called—there would be her voice, more like music than speech, and I would feel a small thrill, like the kind you get from a cloak-and-dagger crush you want always to stay secret.

In the spring of 1991, five months after it had ended with John, I came home to a message on my answering machine. Excited and flustered, as though an idea had just come to her, she said, "I think I have someone to help you with your career. Call me, bye . . . It's Jackie."

The truth was, I didn't know what to call her. She was more

than Jackie by then, more than John's mother, more than Mrs. Onassis. But there had never been a word for it, never the right word. I thought back to that first summer—how we'd gone from wary shyness, to approval, to enjoyment. And now I just missed her.

I remembered how she giggled when she ate ice cream in August and how her walk at times had a kind of slow swagger. I remembered a party early on when I'd failed to greet her as soon as we arrived. She had been standing by the windows in her living room with what I thought of as Important New York People, and I didn't want to interrupt. But a few days later, in the limo on the way to see a play for John's birthday, she made sure to correct me. Maurice, Caroline, and Ed were there as well, but she did it so gracefully, marking her displeasure in such a way that no one else knew, and I never made the mistake again.

And there was a windy ride one summer on Mr. Tempelsman's boat. I was alone with her on the back deck; we were on our way to pick up John, who was spearfishing off Gay Head. The whole way, she told me stories, the ones I wanted—not of the White House, but of her adventures in Greece and India and of the balls and parties she'd gone to in Newport and Southampton before she was married, when she was a girl in New York.

I smiled, thinking of a spring evening a year later, when I'd run into her at the theater, a production of *Macbeth* with Christopher Plummer and Glenda Jackson. John was studying for finals that night, and I went alone. Afterward, she and Mr. Tempelsman offered me a lift in their Town Car, and when we passed the marquee for *Speed-the-Plow*, she lit up. Had I seen it? I hadn't. The play, she said, was good, but Madonna was terrible. She drew out the last word, each sparkling ounce of syllable brimming with glee. The tabloids had been rife with stories about them that spring, stories he scoffed at. I leaned closer. "I think you should go," his mother said, smiling. "I think you should go next week—and have John take you. And go backstage!"

I remembered also how she always made a point of complimenting me—my hair or some detail of what I wore. At first, because of who she was, it stunned me. But what may have been good manners or the desire to nurture confidence in a young woman became for me a lesson in feminine grace and the poise of acceptance. She required that. And I learned, in the end, to simply thank her.

I replayed the message before I called her back, listening once more to the glide of her voice. Then I dialed the office number. It was the first time we'd spoken since Christmas, since I was no longer her son's girlfriend, and if I expected awkwardness, there was none. We caught up. We spoke of other things.

Then she explained why she had called. There was someone she thought I should meet, an author who was also a producer. Should she give him my number? Yes, that would be fine, Mrs. Onassis, I said, and thanked her.

"Oh," she said, stopping me, and for a rich moment I could almost hear her mind whirring before she landed. "Call me Jackie."

Whether it was an earned intimacy or an acknowledgment of the shift between us, I didn't know. But the following year, when I ran into her at a production of *The Eumenides* at the Brooklyn Armory and she greeted me with the same delight she always had and gave me a ride home in the Town Car, I called her Mrs. Onassis, as I always had.

O n July 18, 1986, the day before Caroline's wedding, I took three cabs, a train, and a plane in my eight-and-a-half-hour journey to Hyannis Port from the wilds of northwestern Connecticut, where I was in rehearsals for a summer stock production of Wendy Wasserstein's *Isn't It Romantic*. We were six days from the opening at the Sharon Playhouse, and Robin Saex, the director, had shuffled and juggled so that I could attend the wedding. When the flight, delayed several hours by fog, finally landed at Barnstable Municipal Airport, the rehearsal dinner was long over, and there was a note waiting at the Provincetown–Boston Airline ticket desk: "Gone home, take cab, Come quick baby!"

I couldn't wait to see him, and as the cabdriver began to load my luggage into the trunk, I smiled, knowing that John would tease me when he saw what I'd brought for the thirty-six-hour stay.

I had tried to pare down, putting clothes in piles of importance—yes, maybe, what are you thinking?—and shifting them back and forth, until finally, the agony of decision became too much, and I stuffed everything in. My dress, thankfully, had been decided. It was borrowed from Stanley Platos, a society designer. An ex-boyfriend's mother worked for Halston and knew Stanley well, and she thought he would have just the thing. It wasn't low-cut or short or tight, the way I tended to lean. It was sophisticated, a "lady dress"—the first I'd ever worn—and I worried that it would be right.

It was still early in our relationship—I was just beginning to get to know his family—and with the invitation came the understanding that along with performing a host of best man duties, John would be his mother's official escort. He'd be seated with her at the dinner, and although Maurice would also be there, she would require John's attention. She was concerned about how I would feel, he said, but when I reassured him that I would be fine on my own and had friends who were going, I received the thick envelope with the engraved response card in the mail. I had a reservation at Dunfey's, the hotel in Hyannis where many of the guests were staying, but a few days before the wedding, I was invited to stay at the house. As the cab got closer, I was afraid I would be intruding.

I'd been to the Cape house twice before, but on that night, everything looked different. The Compound, as the press and locals called it, was really a cluster of three houses, the largest bought by Joseph P. Kennedy in 1929 and the two adjacent "cottages" acquired later by John's father and his uncle Bobby. The Shriver family had a house nearby. There was a large pool and tennis courts, and at the main house, a circular drive and a towering flagpole. As we approached Irving Avenue and the sea, there were detours and barricades, along with a smattering of onlookers milling about on the road—the next day at the church there would be thousands. It was still foggy, and the streetlamps cast an eerie light. Suddenly, the cars ahead came to a dead stop, and police began directing vehicles without clearance to turn back. As an officer approached, I rolled down the window.

"I'm a friend of John's."

"I'm sorry, miss, but we can't let you through."

"Could you at least call the house? They're expecting me."

"I'm sorry, miss. We can't disturb the family. You'll have to move along."

The driver grew impatient and began swerving up a driveway to turn around. "I'm dropping you at a pay phone in town, lady."

"Wait!" I implored. There was a screech of tires, and the driver threw me a look.

Just then, through the haze, John appeared, barefoot and shirtless, an orange sarong tied low at his waist.

"It's all right, Officer, she's with me."

The policeman's gruff demeanor dropped at once. "Mr. Kennedy, I had no idea. Our orders were to—"

"No harm done," John said, exchanging enough small talk to put the man at ease.

He took a bag in each hand, and I carried the dress, safe in its plastic sheath, and the wide-brimmed black hat I planned to wear the next day. "Nice," he said. "Going down the Nile, are we?" Then he led me past the small crowd at Scudder and Irving, through a high hedge, and down the walkway to the back door of his father's house.

Before we went in, he pulled me from the porch light and held me tight. "Where've you been? I missed you." He smelled of sun and Eau Sauvage.

I expected everyone to be asleep, but they were all gathered around the kitchen table, laughing. In keeping with tradition, Ed was about to leave to spend the night at a house nearby. Maurice was staying elsewhere, too. Caroline smiled. She was tanned and relaxed, more serene than I could ever imagine being. She greeted me warmly, and his mother turned and rose from the table.

"We're so glad you're here! You poor thing, you've come so far."

"It's been an adventure."

"Well, you're here now. Are you hungry? Marta, Efigenio, heat up some of those lovely leftovers from the rehearsal dinner."

I sat down at the table, and as Marta fussed over a plate, John began teasing his sister—one last grand ribbing before she was a married lady. He kept trying to get a rise, but each time she bested him. Even he couldn't faze her.

His mother always seemed beguilingly girlish to me, and that night even more so. She spoke excitedly of preparations, of how well the rehearsal had gone, how delightful the dinner had been, and who would be in what car on the way to Our Lady of Victory Church in Centerville the next morning. Then her face brightened.

"Oh, John," she said, as if it were Christmas morning, "show Christina the tent!"

And so, close to midnight, we made our way through dark hedges and down the dip in the hill by the main house—John's grandmother's house—which stood watch over Nantucket Sound. As if she couldn't help herself, she followed us through the wet grass to the lawn, where a huge white tent stood billowing. It was lit up and filled with people. And when we reached the entrance, she walked in ahead.

There were actually two tents, she explained, one for cocktails and the receiving line, and a bigger one for dancing and the seated dinner. In the main tent, waiters from Glorious Food moved by us with the swift grace of dancers as they set up the large round tables and the white wooden folding chairs. Florists from New York were hanging lanterns and filling buckets and grapevine baskets with the simple summer flowers she loved.

She introduced us to the man in charge and lavished compliments on the staff. John hung back, wandering at the edges; he'd seen it earlier. She stood at the center of the tent under the highest peak, a bower of blossoms suspended above her, and surveyed the world of her making. She stretched out her arms. "Isn't it wonderful?" she said, her face glowing.

And it was, to see the magic before the magic, the event before the event. I watched her then and thought, *This is a woman who does not take life for granted. This is a woman who knows her luck and lives it, who grasps that beauty is transformative and transient.* Even in a wedding tent.

The next day, there was football in the morning and a laughing bride. Tears at the church and cheering from the crowd. There were champagne toasts and dancing. After the receiving line and before the dinner, the wedding party gathered near the dunes in the russet afternoon light, and pictures were taken: the bridesmaids in easy elegance, their hair wreathed and their silk dresses fluttering; the groomsmen with blue bachelor's buttons in the lapels of their periwinkle jackets. All wore breezy smiles. And when a wind came off the water, Caroline's veil got tangled behind her.

The guests stood on the lawn and watched from a distance, the women holding on to their hats and smiling. The clink of glasses. High above, in front of Rose Kennedy's wraparound porch, the flag that was lowered for tragedies whipped about, furiously dancing over the old lions of the Kennedy administration and Manhattan's literary and media elite. Later in the main tent, John and his uncle Teddy gave their toasts, Carly Simon sang, and the mother of the bride danced in her pistachio dress, a gloved hand on her son's shoulder. George Plimpton's anticipated fireworks were applauded but impotent, done in by a bank of fog. As the night went on, the traditional standards shifted to the bluesy funk of an R & B band, replete with a horn section and Marc Cohn on vocals.

I was seated at a table diagonally across the dance floor from the wedding party. It was lodged in a corner near an opening in the tent and came to be known that night as the "John's friends' table." Kissy was there, along with Rob and his girlfriend Frannie, and Billy Noonan, a wag from Boston who told salty jokes most of the night, his eyes narrowed and needful of your response.

To my right was Jeffrey Ledbetter. He was seeing John's cousin Kerry but wasn't seated with her either. I knew him but not well. He'd also gone to Brown, and there had been no missing him on campus. Heads above anyone else, he was always bounding somewhere, with his Irish setter at his side. Radiant and fearless, he wore his hair long, and I saw him as a kind of Daniel Boone, rallying others over the mountain. He was from Arkansas, from a politically active family, and he let you know about both right away. John had visited him in Little Rock, and there had been some famous camping fiasco in the Ozarks, each of them telling the tale with a different twist. "Our boy did well," Jeffrey whispered after John gave his toast. He told me he was glad I was with John, glad I made his friend happy, and we talked of love that night.

Months after the wedding, Jeffrey would die of an aneurysm. When John found out, he wept through the night, inconsolable. He had lost a close friend, one who was so young, but I knew that it was more. "We were simpatico, you know," he said, as I held him, the boy whom death had touched many times, who made friends easily, and for whom life, in some ways, opened like a parting sea, but for whom intimacy and trust were rare. He'd had that with Jeffrey. When he returned from the memorial service, his grief had settled, and he spoke philosophically. Jeffrey had died in the middle of a snowball fight. There was poetry in that, right? And the autopsy had revealed a congenital heart defect that, if known, would have meant an entirely different life for him—a life that his twin/friend sensed would not have matched his spirit.

The wedding was studded with beautiful women. On the other side of the tent, before the toasts, as John busied himself with best man duties, I saw him laughing with an attractive bridesmaid he'd once had a dalliance with. He'd told me about it, and although he'd brushed it aside and said it was nothing to be jealous of, I was. I remember because it was the first time I had felt that with him— not the seething sort, but an opening, a soft sinking recognition of how deeply I'd fallen, how much I adored him, and how well I could be hurt.

John sent his cousins by the table to check up on me and make sure I was amused. Willie Smith was courtly, with sad eyes, and he delivered messages in a muffled voice. Timmy Shriver took it upon himself to relay all the weaknesses of his younger cousin's character and each and every childhood failing. John was skinny, he wasn't a good athlete, he dressed like a sissy. "Why are you with this guy?" he prodded. I noted the code of the beloved cousins: The more you love, the more you tease. The band had begun "Our Love Is Here to Stay," and like a white knight, Anthony Radziwill interrupted Timmy's spiel and asked me to dance.

Anthony, son of Jackie's sister, Lee, had grown up in England and looked proper in his groomsman's jacket. Through his father,

Stanislas Radziwill, he was a Polish prince, although the title was now a courtesy and he never used it. Of all the cousins, he ribbed John with the greatest élan and the most pleasure. He was less aggressive than some of the other cousins, but his words had a certain spur. In the middle of the Gershwin tune, John appeared on the dance floor and tapped Anthony on the shoulder, asking to cut in. Anthony ignored him and, grinning, spun me repeatedly out of reach as the song continued. *Not for a year / But ever and a day.* John followed, darting around us. "Cutting in, Anthony . . . I said, cutting!"

I laughed as they tussled. Finally, he elbowed Anthony out. "Sorry, Prince, find your own girl. I'm stealing her away."

His hand was warm on my back. "Where've you been all this time?" he whispered in my hair, and told me I looked pretty. Then he made me repeat everything the cousins had said about him. "Jerks!" he bellowed, but I thought he seemed quite pleased.

I loved dancing with him to the old songs. He did well with the box step, and I coached him on the fox-trot and Lindy. Like any private school boy, he knew the steps and could dip and spin with the best of them, but he didn't like to lead. It wasn't his forte. He was better doing his own thing, solo but connected, and so was I.

When it grew dark, after dinner and the cake and the fireworks, he found me again. The second band had come on. His pink tie was loosened, the jacket was off, and his shirtsleeves rolled. He pulled me onto the dance floor, and soon I kicked my sandals into the wet grass.

On the night before the wedding, after we returned from the late-night tour of the tent, Mrs. Onassis showed me to the room where I would stay. It was small, near the top of the stairs, with sewing supplies and an ironing board ready for morning. As she held the door open, she said she hoped I wouldn't mind, the guest rooms were full. My bags were already there, placed neatly inside the door by Marta. In the back of the room, suspended from the eaves, was Caroline's wedding dress, low-waisted with a shamrock appliqué and a twenty-foot train stretched out in sweeping dips.

"Oh," I gasped. The dress was stunning.

Mrs. Onassis smiled, watching. "Well . . . good night." She stood there a moment before she closed the door, her voice a caress that lingered.

Maybe, I thought as I undressed, the bridal custom extended to all the women in the house, that we all must sleep alone the night before a wedding. Maybe, like Aphrodite, purity could be renewed by ritual. As much as I wanted to sneak across the floorboards to my man in the sarong across the way, I didn't dare. Not that night. She had shown me to the room.

I sat on the edge of the single bed. The dress hung in front of the small window, backlit by a streetlamp on Irving. When I was little, I hadn't always played at being a bride—it was more harems and intrigue, more ballerinas and Indian princesses, torch singers and Mata Hari. But that night was different. Under a thin coverlet, I tried to sleep, but the dress, consuming and fragile, moved in and out of my dreams, like a beautiful ghost.

In the years that I was with him, and the many nights I was a guest in his mother's homes, this was the only time I was shown to a separate bedroom. I asked him once if his mother was all right with us sleeping together under her roof. I knew there were rules to be followed with her, and I didn't want to misstep, but he assured me that this was not one of them. His girlfriends had always stayed over. "She's cool with it," he said with a measure of pride. "Since high school." I thought of my parents and the byzantine double standards of those years that never seemed to include my brothers. Even at the age of twenty-six, having a boyfriend sleep over was an iffy prospect. "No, she's not like that. Not at all." His mother had a theory, he went on, that his grandmother Rose's attitude toward sex had created problems for his father, and she didn't want that for him. I didn't ask about the problems. I nodded.

The day after the wedding, before I left to begin the trip back to Connecticut and the long push of rehearsals before opening, John took me to meet his grandmother. She would be ninety-six that Tuesday. Two years before, she'd suffered a major stroke and couldn't attend the wedding ceremony, but after morning Mass in her living room, the house was alive with children, grandchildren, and great-grandchildren, who'd gathered to say hello.

Two of the Lawford girls stepped aside, and it was our turn.

"Happy Birthday, Grandma. It's me, John." She didn't speak and kept nodding her head.

"It's John, Grandma."

The nurse told him to speak louder.

"There's someone I want you to meet."

I knelt down by her wheelchair. She was so frail, so small, it surprised me. And I remember pink all around her. A dress, a blanket maybe. Her hair was done just so, and she wore lipstick. The desire to look pretty had not left her. I took one of her soft blue-veined hands, and she smiled. Her grasp was strong. John held her other hand. He spoke about me, how we had met and the play I was doing, and that he would start law school in the fall. With a gleam in her clouded eyes, she motioned as if she wanted to tell him something. He leaned in. "Why, yes, Grandma," he said with a wary smile. "You're right—that's true."

As we walked back across the lawn, I asked him what she had said.

"Nothing," he answered. "I just pretend I understand her. She likes that."

"Really . . ."

He thought for a moment. "She said it's time I settle down and you seem like a lovely girl." He squeezed my hand hard and kept walking. "I'm glad you came. I'm glad you were here for all this."

I would see him in a week, after the play opened, but I began missing him right then.

We reached the corner of Scudder and Irving, and as he loaded my bags into the waiting Town Car, I asked if he wouldn't mind taking my dress and dropping it at the designer's showroom when he returned to New York in a few days. I wouldn't be back in the city for weeks. "No problem," he said. I learned never to do that again. He would leave it on a wire hanger, out of the hanging bag, in the back of his Honda with the window down at LaGuardia short-term parking. The dress wasn't stolen, but a rainstorm bled the dye of the fragile silk. No dry cleaner would touch it. My boyfriend, I learned that weekend, was the man of the hour in a striped sarong, a toastmaster par excellence, and a dancer who made my knees weak. He was not, however, one to trust with prosaic errands involving couture.

He'd been lukewarm about the dress to begin with, I could tell. He was always complimentary about what I wore, always noticing small details, but this dress, he said, was "fine." Maybe it was the bone and black pattern or the sheer organza ruffle at the neck, but I suspected it wasn't sexy enough for him. It was a dress other women liked. At the reception, even his aunt Lee, a frequent fixture on the best-dressed lists, had asked who the designer was. Ever politic, he did say, "Mummy loved your dress. She thought you looked very pretty." Any praise from his mother I took in tenfold; I wanted to please him, but I wanted to be accepted by her.

As the plane lifted off the runway in Hyannis, I pulled out my script to run lines. I glanced down for a moment, then turned it on its spine. The last two days had been exciting. I was glad I had come, glad I had danced into the small hours, glad I had seen his sister get married. Mostly, I was happy to have been a part of something that meant so much to him.

In time the Rockies may crumble, Gibraltar may tumble, / They're only made of clay. The lyric from the night before wouldn't leave my head, and I turned to look out over the arm of the Cape, the territory that was his. I tried to make out the white tent or the flagpole or the many-gabled house, but there was only a puzzle of shoreline. Just then, the plane banked, and the sun bounced off the silver wing and blinded me.

I lowered the shade. I felt lucky. And my dress, I decided, had been right. It had been just right.

Holding

Come quickly—as soon as
these blossoms open,
they fall.
This world exists
as a sheen of dew on flowers.

—IZUMI SHIKIBU

When you fly over the coast of Georgia, press your face to the glass. The land below is flat, emerald green, and cut with water. Creeks and rivers meander in tight switchbacks, snaking their way through mudflats to the sea. Above the trees, smokestacks of paper mills rise like watchful gods. Before you land, you're already in a different world. There is something in the air, something ancient that makes you move more slowly. You turn a corner, you catch your breath, and the pale color of the sky reflects back the sheer measure of your soul.

In the dead of summer, three weeks after Caroline's wedding, we flew to Jacksonville, Florida, and after a side trip to Disney World and a VIP tour of rockets at Cape Canaveral, we caught the last boat of the day, the *R. W. Ferguson* from Fernandina Beach, and set off for a nearby barrier island. It would be our first real vacation together.

"You want to take a trip, madam?"

His asking had been both shy and nonchalant. We were sitting by a cornfield in Connecticut, and he was fiddling with the laces of his red Converse high-tops. The field was near the Sharon Play-house, where I was doing *Isn't It Romantic*. The day before, he'd looked at me quizzically and said he'd never been with someone whose career was so important. My eyes opened wide. Was that bad? "No," he said. "It's attractive. I think that's what makes us work, that we're equals."

He had driven up the Taconic the night before to surprise me, announcing himself in lipstick on my dressing room mirror. I'd dashed off the stage, changed quickly, and found him in the July night, smoking a cigarette near the parked cars with one of the crew.

We'd had long weekends alone or with friends at the Cape, Martha's Vineyard, my parents' country house on Long Island, and his mother's in New Jersey. And there had been a rafting trip with his cousins that June in Maine, where we'd spied a moose up close. This would be different. Ten days in close quarters, testing mystery, the mainstay of romance—with no possibility of retreat for a night or an hour.

"Someplace neither of us has been. Someplace we can discover together."

It touched me that he thought of it like that, as a way for us to grow closer. A place that would be ours. It felt grown-up.

I knew at once where we should go.

"How about Alaska? Or Taos!" he said. "I've always wanted to go there, and you'd look sweet on a horse."

"Too hot," I countered. And I told him about a place I'd known about for years—Cumberland Island, off the coast of Georgia.

I'd first heard of Cumberland in college, when friends camped there over spring break and brought back tales of an island as large as Manhattan, with ruined mansions and feral horses roaming on white sand beaches. I was hooked, then promptly forgot about it. In 1983, I read an article in *The New York Times* travel section, a paean to the island by Lucinda Franks. I clipped it, and for three years, it had followed me, dog-eared, from sublet to sublet. Without having set foot on Cumberland, I was already in its thrall.

There are places one falls for as deeply and as devotedly as for a lover. For reasons you can't quantify, the alchemy of air, light, and smell call to the most primal part of you and conspire to make you theirs. I've been moved by Santa Fe, Paris, and Seville. I've reveled in Rome, Telluride, and Guadalajara. I've been awed by the deserts of Morocco, the spires of Wyoming's Wind River Range, and the painted depths of the Grand Canyon. But it wasn't love I felt.

Sometimes it's the place where you grew up that says, *You belong to me.* No matter how long I've been away, when I come back to New York City in a taxi over the Triborough Bridge and the afternoon sun shifts off the steel skyline and blinds me, I feel it. In the heavy July of privet tinged with sea salt on the East End of Long Island, where I spent nearly every summer until I was twenty and many since, I know it. And in an empty theater, with the ghost light on and the darkness, warm and velvet like a dinner jacket my father once wore, it's mine.

But it can also be without history—sudden, violent, a *coup de foudre.* I've felt the sharp jolt of recognition in my throat, the pull in my chest, standing at the humble stone huts in Dingle, walking up the winding path to the Cave of the Apocalypse in Patmos, and, most profoundly, in Big Sur, where I'm reminded that I'm not all human, not just heart and flesh but soil, sea, and sky. Big Sur is a place that lives in me, a place that does not let me go. Another is an island off the coast of Georgia.

Cumberland, the largest and most southerly of the Sea Islands, stretches north from St. Marys Inlet to St. Andrew Sound. It is eighteen miles long and three miles across at its widest. There are no paved roads, no bridges, no stores. The double dunes of the barrier beach, the mudflats and maritime forest of oak, pine, and palmetto, are home to loggerhead sea turtles, armadillos, white-tailed deer, bobcats, feral horses and hogs, and more than 277 species of land and sea birds whose bones litter the sand.

Arrowheads and oyster middens attest to the presence of the Timucua people, who called the island Missoe. French corsairs landed there, British and Spanish flags flew over forts on the north and south ends of the island, and James Oglethorpe, founder of the new colony of Georgia, established a hunting lodge he called Dungeness near the Indian burial grounds at the south end. In 1803, the widow of Revolutionary War hero Nathanael Greene built another Dungeness close by. Within its thick walls, Light-Horse Harry Lee died, and legend has it that Eli Whitney invented the cotton gin there. In antebellum times, Cumberland, with its temperate climate and marsh-fed soil, thrived. The harvest of timber, indigo, figs, cotton, and sugarcane made the plantation owners rich. After the Civil War, the island's mansions were burned and abandoned, and the freed slaves who remained built a community on the north end near Half Moon Bluff called the Settlement.

But it is the Carnegie legacy that looms largest. Through a stone and iron gate at the end of a wide sandy road, you can still see the crumbling façade of the Gilded Age mansion. In 1959, after years of neglect, it was set on fire by a poacher after a hunting dispute. Wild turkeys scurry about the rubble, and crows gather on the spire of a skeletal brick wall. But it was not always so.

In 1882, at the site of the old Greene mansion, steel magnate Thomas M. Carnegie began construction of a winter retreat for his family. In its heyday, this Dungeness—visited by Astors, Vanderbilts, and Rockefellers—rivaled the fabled mansions of Newport and Southampton. A turreted Victorian affair, it boasted fifty-nine rooms, a carriage house, an indoor swimming pool, squash courts, manicured gardens, a golf course, a working farm, and accommodations for a staff of two hundred. After Thomas's death, his wife, Lucy, went on to acquire 90 percent of the island and built homes for her children, notably the Cottage, Plum Orchard, Stafford House, and Greyfield, now an inn run by her descendants.

In the 1960s, in an effort to protect the island from development, family members began selling tracts to the U.S. government, and in 1972 Cumberland became part of the National Seashore, with parts of the north end later designated as a Wilderness Area. So unless you know someone who lives there or come with tent in hand, Greyfield Inn is where you stay.

The air was thick and salted when we landed. Someone from the inn met us at the dock. Bearded, he had a smile like Bacchus, deeply tanned feet in worn sandals, and black curls that fell over a wide, seaworthy face. "Hey, I'm Pat," he greeted us in a Coastal drawl, then threw our bags in the back of a jeep.

"Where's the inn?" John asked. "Can we walk?" After an hour and twenty minutes on the slow ferry, he was itching to move.

Pat cocked his head to the right. Amid looping dirt paths and horses nibbling at the scrub of what was once a grand lawn, Greyfield rose like Tara through a stand of live oak trees shrouded in silver moss.

Built in 1900 as a wedding gift for Margaret Ricketson by her mother, Lucy Coleman Carnegie, Greyfield has white columns, a red tin roof, gabled attic windows, and a large front veranda with potted ferns and a cushioned porch swing on each end. The steps that lead up to the main entrance are low and wide—"for long skirts," we were told later. In the style of many old southern houses, the kitchen and dining room are situated on the ground floor because of the summer heat. On the main floor, there is a library, a drawing room, and a small self-service bar. A ledge near the ceiling in the bar is lined with every size and color of sea bottle, and a sign above the mixers reads, HONEST JOHN SYSTEM. In the dark-paneled drawing room, a chesterfield sofa done in velvet, wingback chairs, and a red leather bench are arranged by the stone fireplace. On two of the walls, portraits of women who lived here long ago face each other—one a waif in white, the other a warrior in a head scarf and dagger, both sad-eyed and beguiling. There are tattered globes and Audubon prints, a child's rocker, whale bones and sea turtle shells, and a tiny pair of wedding slippers, as thin as parchment, enshrined in a tall china cabinet. Nearby is a black-and-white photograph of a dashing man in a loincloth—part Errol Flynn, part Ernest Hemingway—his rifle gracefully poised to shoot into the surf. It is a house filled with stories.

We left our bags in the hall by the grandfather clock with a moon sailing by on its face, and took off on bikes to find the beach before dinner. The fat tires of the rusted cruisers were slow on the main road, a sandy lane that stretches from Dungeness to the north end, but when we turned east by the sign TO GREYFIELD BEACH, they rolled faster. The branches of the live oaks on either side bent toward one another, canopying the narrow path of dirt, leaves, and crushed shells. All around was the hum of cicadas. Then we saw it—the rise where the dune began. And at the end of the tunnel of trees, a patch of blue appeared. John got there first and hollered to me. I dropped my bike and sprinted up the embankment. When I ran past him, he caught me, wrapping me in his arms and rocking me side to side.

Spread out before us was a beach unbroken for miles, as white and bleached as bone. In the distance, by the low-tide mark, stood a spotted stallion and his herd.

We fell easily into the rhythm of the island. Morning bike rides to the ruins or hiking the trails. Afternoons on the veranda with our books and pink lemonade. Cocktails before dinner. The days too hot, we swam at night, with the moon heavy on us—and searched the sand for the tracks of giant sea turtles, which pulled themselves ashore to lay their eggs in the dunes. We also spent time in the large, pine-paneled kitchen, scavenging for cookies and SunChips and hanging out with the inn staff rather than the other guests. There was an inviting camaraderie among those who lived on the island full-time, and you wanted to be around it. John had deemed Pat "especially cool."

One morning after breakfast, we stopped by the kitchen to pick up tall, plaid thermoses of sweet tea and lunches packed in wicker hampers—supplies for our tour of the north end that day. Through the screen door, white sheets billowed on a line, and a man in Way-farers and a faded pink button-down propped himself against a rusted jeep. The naturalist was on vacation, and Andy Ferguson, a great-great-grandson of Thomas Carnegie, would be our guide for the day. A few years older than us, he had a sly smile and a shock of white-blond hair that fell in his face. He didn't look di-rectly at you; he observed, as if there were a story he might or might not tell depending on his mood, as if there were a secret that hung on his lips. I liked him. He also had a great love and knowledge of the island, and he shared it with us that day. The next year, in the bloom of his youth, Andy would shoot himself with a rifle and be buried in the Carnegie plot near Dungeness.

We climbed into the open jeep and took off down the main road. I sat next to Andy, and John rode in back. We were going on a picnic, and I'd worn my picnic dress, or at least my idea of what that would be in the wilds of southern Georgia when you're in love. The fiercer the sun got and the farther we went, the more I wished I'd worn long pants and a long-sleeved shirt, like Andy, and a wide-billed cap instead of the braided straw hat that rested on my knees.

We were quiet for a stretch as the jeep lumbered along the rutted road. On either side was a forest of loblolly pine, wax myrtle, red bay, and oak trees draped in the trailing vines of muscadine. Below the trees, thickets of skunk cabbage and fan palmetto grew low and sturdy.

"You sure picked the hottest time of the year to come," Andy announced.

"Well, one of us wanted to go to Taos, but the other someone thought it wouldn't be as hot here, and that somebody won out, didn't they?" John reached around the seat and gave me a sharp pinch.

"Oh yeah?" Andy looked over to me, then back to the sandy road, slowing for a fawn that happened to cross in front of the jeep. "Next time, you might want to skip August."

"Can we see an alligator?" John wanted to know. He'd been talking about it all morning.

"We'll try. It might even be too hot for them." He pointed to some frizzled brown growth in the crevice of an oak. "That's resurrection fern. It's an epiphyte. It looks dead now, but when it rains—and it will—that fern will burst into green."

"What's an epiphyte?" I asked.

"It lives off the air."

At Stafford, after the road split and then joined again, the forest cleared and there was sky. On the right, across from where the plantation house once stood, was a field that served as an airstrip. "You have to buzz the horses a couple of times before you land," Andy confided. "Even then they're stubborn. They think it's theirs."

The forest grew denser the farther north we went. Andy took us to the Chimneys, the charred ruins of the slave quarters at Stafford; to Plum Orchard, a Georgian revival mansion, where we peered into huge windows at the wide, vacant rooms; and to an old hunting lodge, the wood grayed and overcome by giant sand dunes. We waited without luck by a marshy creek for alligators, but spotted ospreys and ibises near Lake Whitney. We rambled over trails with names like Roller Coaster, Duck House, and North Cut. And when we reached the tip of the island near Christmas Creek, we saw the giant shell mounds where, a thousand years before, the Timucua had held their banquets. Then, through a tangle of trees and winding paths, we came to the Settlement—the abandoned homes of ex-slaves near Half Moon Bluff. There was an old church there that Andy wanted to show us after we had our picnic in the graveyard nearby.

It was during that lunch, perhaps, as we sat in the shadows of the trees feasting on chicken salad, oatmeal cookies, and sweet tea, that John brought up one of the hypotheticals he'd sometimes play with: If you could choose—excluding being old and happy and in your own bed—how would you want to go? He said he wanted it to be quick. I disagreed. I didn't *want* illness, I told him, but at least it had consciousness. You knew what was going on. Being hit by a car, you're just gone. Boom. Exactly, he said blithely.

The small, clapboard chapel that Andy took us to after lunch stood by a grove of longleaf pines. Pale grass snuck from the edges of the stone foundation, and I remember that the paint on the sills of the First African Baptist Church where he would one day marry was a worn, flaking red.

John and I went inside, but Andy did not. He waited for us by a barbed wire fence, arms crossed, one leg hitched over the other. Behind the wooden doors, the chapel had a musty, shut-in smell. There was a dirty green runner and eleven pews—five pairs and one on its own. In the center of the room was a stand with an open Bible. We sat in a back pew and said a prayer, and before we left, John placed a pinecone on the makeshift altar.

We took the beach route back, a straight shot of packed sand all the way. I sat in the back of the jeep next to the empty wicker baskets, a stray thermos rattling at my feet, while John rode up front with Andy. They were compadres—eyes narrowed by the glare and wind on their young faces.

"Hold on!" Andy shouted as he gunned the engine.

"Faster!" John rallied him. With one hand braced against the dashboard, he stood up and let out a war cry. He almost fell but, laughing, steadied himself. Andy floored it, and we zigzagged in and out of the waves. John turned back to me, alive from the speed. He put out his hand.

"You try!" The sound of his voice was lost to the wind and the roar of the engine. I shook my head vehemently—I didn't need to do this, the things he did—and I gripped the back of the seat. But he wouldn't give up.

"Don't be afraid. I've got you!" he yelled to me. I began to stand up, shaky at first, without commitment, one hand still glued to the seat, the other clutching his wrist on my waist. I believed in his hands. He stayed on me until I yelled back, until he saw on my face the same exhilaration he felt and knew that my fear was gone. *I've got you!*

Andy dropped us at the beach near Stafford and took off. We would walk back. By then, the sun was blinding. I tossed my hat on the sand. John doffed his clothes, leaped into the flat water, and swam out as far as he could. I tied the long skirt of my dress on one hip and waded in, thigh-high, to wash off the dust of the day. The water was clear and there was no wind. I turned back to the land. There was no one there, and I could almost see the whole island, end to end—from Christmas Creek in the north to the jetties near the Pelican Banks in the south. Behind me, I could hear his strong, even strokes cutting the water, a sound of safety, of constancy. "This is the widest beach I've ever seen," I said aloud. It was low tide, and the sand was bare, dressed only by coquinas, slipper shells, and bits of jellyfish—a string of tiny cabochon moonstones laid out like a necklace on the broad lip of the shore.

John came back and dressed, drying himself with his T-shirt.

"Brown as a berry." He kissed my shoulders. "Let's make it back for cocktails."

I laughed. "More like a salmon." I knew I was getting burned.

"Look." He pointed up as we walked. From the west, a bank of black clouds raced toward us. Then—a deafening rumble.

"What do we do?"

"What do you mean what do we do? We keep walking."

The rain started, lightly at first, in patches, as we moved south to the break in the dunes at Greyfield. But then the sky darkened, the rain kicked in, and, as hot as it had been minutes ago, I was suddenly shivering, my hat bedraggled and my flowered dress soaked through.

Out of nowhere, a red truck appeared. It was Pat. He reached over and rolled down the passenger's side window. "You folks want a ride?"

His devil grin was a welcome sight. Relieved, I moved toward the truck.

"Thanks, I'm gonna walk," I heard John say behind me.

"Why?"

"It's just rain."

I was stumped. Why would anyone choose a downpour over a dry truck? When my efforts at persuasion fell flat and it was clear this was a nonnegotiable, I knew I had to choose—John or the truck. I didn't want to get any wetter than I already was and I hated the rain, but the truth was, at that moment, twenty minutes away from him seemed unbearable to me.

I hemmed and hawed. Pat revved the engine.

"For Christ's sake, make up your mind!" John barked. "It's only rain."

The pickup won, and I jumped in. I was not, to my dismay, the girl who walked in the rain. I was the girl who chose the truck. I smiled at Pat, a little embarrassed that he knew this. As he smiled back, my hat slid to the truck floor, and I saw that my dress was stuck to my thighs. I began to shake it. "Don't worry, you'll be warm soon," Pat said, turning on the heater. Just then, the sky lit up. The storm hit full-tilt, and the rain came down in a crackling roar. Instinctively, I ducked.

When I lifted my head. I could barely see out the window. "They don't call it a barrier beach for nothing," I said.

"What?"

"I said, they don't call it a barrier beach for nothing!"

Whether he heard me or not, Pat nodded. Windshield wipers beating furiously, we made our way up the roll of the double dune. Maybe John had changed his mind. Maybe he was running to the truck. I looked back. The glass was fogged, but I saw him. He was walking slowly—head down, hands deep in the pockets of his windbreaker. I was safe, out of the rain, but he was infinitely cooler; he was getting drenched, and he was happy.

The night before we left, we went to a party in a small A-frame in the woods—a roof raising for Mouse McDowell, one of Andy's cousins. We danced barefoot in the small hours to Little Feat and the Band with the inn staff and various Carnegie descendants—McDowells, Fergusons, Fosters. The virgin house throbbed to the beat and reeked of bourbon, weed, and sawdust. The heavy night air wafted through the glassless windows, and when Prince's *Dirty Mind* came on, John pulled me in, mouthing the words on the back of my neck. We danced like there was no one else in the room, his arms over my shoulders, mine on his back.

On our way back to the inn through an open field, with horses and armadillos rustling unseen in the dark, he told me he loved me for the first time, though I already knew. And as the night began to deepen, we made love on one of the porch swings at Greyfield, a fan overhead ticking time.

Afterward, I thought I heard someone. "There's no one there," he said. But moments later, below the high porch, Andy walked by, his blond head aglow in the darkness.

That fall, John switched apartments and began law school. He left the shared two-bedroom in a doorman building off West End Avenue where he'd lived for almost two years and moved to the top floor of a renovated town house on West Ninety-first Street. The building, more spruced up than those on the rest of the block, had a red door with globe lighting. Steps from the entrance was a community mural depicting people of all races in harmony, but if you left your bike outside overnight or neglected to pop the car radio, it was likely to be stolen. The apartment was a block from the park, around the corner from a D'Agostino market, and across from the PS 84 schoolyard, and afternoons, the sounds of children playing fell lightly over the street.

Before our trip to Cumberland Island, he took me to see the

apartment, and we walked through the empty rooms on a summer night. We stood in the largest one discussing the pros and cons. "What do you think?" He spoke softly, leaning in to nudge me. "Should I take it?" He wasn't sure; there was another place closer to NYU. If there was a choice of trails up a mountain or where to set up camp for the night, instinct served him, but with less corporeal decisions, he'd check himself and weigh what others thought. Maurice thinks this, he'd tell me, or Mummy and Caroline said that. As the amber light deepened in the room, I saw, in a way I hadn't before, how much he trusted my counsel, desired my guidance, and, more than simply wanting my approval, needed me to be happy here, too.

I touched his cheek. "I think it's grown-up. I like it," I said, before asking if he would leave his water bed behind.

While we were away, the bare rooms were outfitted with sturdy essentials—comfortable furnishings you could kick about. A nap-inducing canvas-covered couch, a leather recliner, a plain coffee table, a small dining set. Simple lamps and mirrors. The masks he collected peered from the walls. I opened a kitchen cupboard. It was stocked with matching dishes and oversize mugs. In the linen closet, new sheets and towels had been stripped of their plastic and folded squarely by someone who knew how. "You must have a fairy godmother," I teased. He winked, aware this wasn't the norm. "Well, Mummy did what she does best and called up Bloomingdale's and Conran's. Nice, huh?"

At the back, down a dark skinny hall, there were two small rooms. In the one that would become his study, there was a saw-horse desk and a pine bookshelf. Spider plants crowded the window. The bedroom was furnished with an antique highboy, a new brass bed with an art deco lamp of his mother's on the side where I would sleep, and, in a corner, one of his father's padded rockers. It didn't quite fit, and whenever he passed it, he grazed the arm.

I moved as well, from Brooklyn back to Manhattan, and after a series of ill-fated and illegal sublets, I found a studio in a converted brownstone on West Eighty-third Street—a front apartment with tons of light and little floor space. The stairwell was shabby— a torn carpet and the perpetual tang of Chinese food—and when the couple upstairs argued, as they did weekly, I could hear every word. But I was in heaven. A vanity, my grandmother's bed, and a green velvet love seat fit snugly, and there were high ceilings and a working fireplace. It was a perfect artist's garret. Plus, I had a lease, and in New York, where geography is destiny, it was eight blocks from John's.

The apartment had a terrace that jutted over the parlor floor below, and whether he remembered his key or not, John preferred to enter through my window. He'd give a whistle—soft, two-toned, and flirty—and with a foot on the stone planter and his hand on the iron rail, he'd hoist himself up the side of the brownstone. I liked it, and the neighbors got used to his Romeo act, but one night when we were in bed, we heard a voice through a bullhorn.

"This is NYPD. Come to the window."

We burst out laughing. Then a spotlight froze the room.

"You go to the window," he hissed.

"No, you!"

"Come on . . . the papers."

I did what he asked and lifted the sash. Everything's fine, I explained. Just my boyfriend crawling through the window. Below, three officers stood in front of a double-parked squad car, the cherry lights whirling like mad. One of them aimed a bright beam on my face.

"Ma'am, I'm sorry. We need to confirm you're all right."

"Really, Officer, I'm fine."

"Ma'am, whoever's in there needs to come to the window at once, or we *will* enter the apartment."

John stepped beside me, and they turned the light on him. He spoke with an easy, self-effacing charm, the same way he did with reporters and people he didn't know well. He didn't press the point or pull rank; he simply wondered if this might stay off the record. Even two flights down, they recognized him—not right away, but when the officer in charge began to apologize at length without blinking, it was apparent. Before they got back in the squad car, the junior guy, slow on the uptake, suddenly began shaking his head. "Sir, I think . . . Was that JFK Jr.?"

I closed the window and pulled the lock shut. John was back in bed, hands behind his head and ankles crossed. He looked pleased. "I'd say we gave them their story for the night, don't you?"

There were times when he could go unnoticed, slipping through the streets without heads turning or his name being repeated sotto voce as he passed. But after the fall of 1988, when he appeared on the cover of *People* as the Sexiest Man Alive, that happened less often. From then on, whenever a picture was published in the *Post* or the *Star*, it was more likely that strangers would approach to tell him what his father/mother/uncle meant to them. He would be cordial, graceful, and sometimes, depending on his mood, he'd thank them. Most of the time, he would just let them talk. And when they left, it would be with the sense that they knew him, that the words they had said had not been said before.

There would be a shift in him then, effortless and imperceptible to whoever was walking away, but I'd notice. It was as though a measure of spirit would leave him and then, as easy as breath, would slip back in. He had found something that had not quite been realized when the woman in the ice-cream shop near Sheridan Square thought she recognized him years before—a necessary removal that allowed him to walk this world and keep his kindness intact. Conscious of it or not, he had found a persona.

Mornings, if he didn't take the subway, he would ride his bike the eighty-odd blocks to Vanderbilt Hall, a large redbrick building at the south end of Washington Square. He had been away from school for more than two years, and law school was a challenge, especially that first semester. But he kept at it.

On weekends, we'd drive out alone to his mother's house in New Jersey. We'd take walks in the fields behind the house, visit the barn cats next door, and, if the weather was good, head down to the stables for a ride. But afternoons, he'd hit the books. I was just beginning to drive and didn't have my license, and while he worked, he'd send me out to practice in his mother's racing-green BMW, a birthday gift one year from Mr. Onassis that she kept at the Peapack house. "Go on. She won't mind," he'd say, opening the door and scooting me in. So I'd go off on the winding, wooded roads, past horse farms and mansions, past fields of autumn green, sometimes stopping at a small lake I knew. We'd gone there the summer before with Robin, the day after he'd kissed me by the horse barn. There was an old boathouse, whose floorboards were sunken. A river had been dammed at the turn of the century by a wealthy banker, and if you rowed out far enough, you could hear the rush of water.

When I'd return, he would be where I had left him—head in his hands, books open. Looking up, he'd sigh. "You have no idea. It's like another language."

. . .

We had been together more than a year, and there were things I had learned. He was chivalric and competitive, puritan and sensual. He wore Vetiver and Eau Sauvage, and when he didn't, his skin was like warm sun. He loved to cook but burned his food, and he slept with the windows open. I wore his sweaters, he ate off my plate, and we spent most nights at his apartment on Ninety-first Street. And if he was in a mood and I wanted something, a small thing—a light turned on, a fan turned off—I found that if I said the opposite, it worked like a charm. When I smiled and told him this, it made no difference. Like a reflex, he was helpless to it. He had a theory, he said, that what he called his occasional contrariness was due to being "bossed by so many women" when he was young.

One evening in New Jersey, he announced, somewhat nervously, that he had something to discuss. He had me sit on the peach-colored sofa while he settled on one of the hard-back chairs near the fire. He took a breath. By his look, all seemed dire. You must ski, he began. Now that we're together. It was one of the things he loved best in life and, by his own admission, excelled at. It was so important, so much a part of him, that if I didn't share it, he was worried about our future. I bit my lip, trying not to smile at his gravity. I did, in fact, ski, but in a haphazard, here-and-there sort of way, and he knew this. After consulting a cousin or two, he'd even chosen the place to begin. Sun Valley, he was sure, would be the spot where I would fall for his passion. He'd observed relationships—the ones he admired, the ones that were lasting—and believed that their success was due in part to shared hobbies. As an example, he mentioned his aunt Eunice's marriage to Sargent

Shriver. His pragmatism, of which I had none, both surprised and touched me. I felt happy.

So I skied more than I ever had. I camped and I climbed. That January, he gave me my first scuba lesson off Lyford Cay and the next year, in Baja, we kayaked among the gray whales. These forays into his world never felt like conforming. Instead, I felt as if I was spreading new wings, ones I hadn't known were there. And when I saw the sunrise out of the flap of a tent in the Green Mountains, or felt my skis cut the slope, or learned to feather a kayak paddle so it sliced the air with precision, in these small ways I knew him.

One December, we took a weekend trip to the Adirondacks. We stayed at the Point, a fancy, seventy-five-acre lodge that had once been a Rockefeller summer retreat. Animal heads hung in the Great Hall, jackets were required at dinner, and a sumptuous breakfast was brought to the cabins each morning. Ours was called Trappers, and it resembled a Ralph Lauren photo shoot. The other guests that weekend were older, and they weren't about to go hiking. They stayed in the Great Hall playing backgammon and reading by the enormous fire, biding their time until cocktails. But we set off, although the forecast was for snow. It might not happen, he reasoned, and when we left, the ground was dry and the sun bright.

The trail was flat at first, through a hardwood forest with a noisy brook, but the last mile was straight up. Flurries had begun to fall, and we kept losing the trail. He pushed me up the last bit, and when we reached the bare summit, there was a spectacular view of the lakes and the High Peaks region to the north. "Worth it, right?" he said. He loved a mountaintop more than anyone I knew. We stayed for a while, out of the wind, by the hollowed stump of a dead tree, and ate chocolate and apples until without question the storm had arrived. As we descended, it roared around us. The trail, hard to spot on the way up, was now treacherous. So he wouldn't lose me, he had me walk just ahead of him, and when the path grew icy, he found a length of rope in his pack and tied it around my waist to keep me from falling. We also traded gloves; his were warmer. I was afraid, but I knew he would get us down the mountain.

After several hours, the trees got thicker, and we began to hear the brook. And when we made it to the flat stretch at the bottom, everything was white. By a stand of aspens, we lay down in the new snow and made angels, and he kept laughing as the snow fell on his face and on mine. I looked up. The trees, still leaved, towered above us, and suddenly the wind quieted. *I will remember this,* I thought. And on my back, on the snow that was no one's but ours, I could see a slip of silver sky. I turned to him, to tell him, but he was already there—arms wide like a prayer—looking at me.

Later, when I asked why, on that night in New Jersey by the fire, he had been so nervous, he replied, "You might have said no."

As he made his way with civil procedure and torts, I was discovering life as an actor. Halfway through my time at Juilliard, I'd longed to be out. After rehearsals, we'd gather at McGlades and talk knowingly of the real world. Now that I had graduated, I was finding out what that meant. Along with the thrill I felt running to appointments, with headshot and highlighted mimeographed sides in hand, at the casting directors' offices that dotted Fifty-seventh Street, and the sleeker ones at Paramount and CBS—or, if it was a Broadway play, to the illustrious theaters farther south, there was also rejection, downtime, and the harrowing phrase "They went with a name." And I began to learn that the loss of certain parts, for no reason I could fathom, was far more painful than others. It cut and bruised, something like heartbreak.

I rode the zigzag of energy and time, keen to find balance but not knowing how. Days of nothing were succeeded by others so full I could hardly see straight. And doubt was lifted by a single message from my agents on my Bells Are Ringing answering service.

I wanted everything to go faster.

"Patience," the agents said. "It's going well."

"Maybe you need a persona," John suggested after a particularly crushing audition.

But it was my friend Kate Burton who counseled best. She was three years ahead of me in all this, a graduate of the Yale School of Drama, and genetically wise about the ups and downs. "In a minute," she promised in her sunny way, "everything can change."

At the end of January 1987, I was cast in a one-act festival on Theatre Row, and before the run ended, I had a job at the Shakespeare Theatre in Washington, D.C. *Love's Labour's Lost* was the play, and the contract was for fifteen weeks. With it came a ground-floor apartment on Capitol Hill, blocks from the Folger Shakespeare Library, where the theater was then housed; a round-trip ticket on the Metroliner; and a weekly check of $375. It seemed like a fortune. The company of actors became instant family, bound by out-of-town necessity and the rigor and joy of saying words that remained alive centuries after they were written. After performances, chatty and awake, we'd spend our paychecks on charcuterie and wine at a small brasserie near Constitution Avenue.

"It'll be an adventure," John said when he put me on the train at Penn Station. And it was. He'd fly down on the shuttle; I'd go up on the Metroliner. I sent long letters; he sent postcards of howling dogs with a list of days until we'd meet. He spent his term break in my small apartment on the Hill, studying at the Library of Congress while I was in rehearsal. "I've never been faithful this long," he told me on one of those quiet streets behind the Capitol. And when I had an unexpected five days off during the load-in of the set, he sent me a ticket to meet him in Palm Beach at the house on North Ocean Boulevard that his grandfather had bought in 1933.

The sixteen-room estate, once the Winter White House, was secluded behind high hedges. Designed by Addison Mizner, famous for the Mediterranean Revival style of many of Palm Beach's grand homes, the house had been christened La Guerida by the previous owners. At the entrance, a pair of espaliered trees hugged the pale stucco wall. A wooden door, Spanish-style and studded, led to a covered walkway through a courtyard to the main house. We rarely used it; John preferred the side door by the kitchen.

Most of the bedrooms were upstairs, but on the first floor the main rooms opened to one another and the sea. There were floor-to-ceiling windows with pinch-pleated draperies, the flowered chintz faded. Outside were tennis courts, a terraced pool, a well-trimmed lawn, and the patio where his father had announced his cabinet in 1961. By the seawall, tall, lean palms swayed, one of them deeply bowed by wind and age. To juggle the visits of so many children and grandchildren, the house was booked in advance through Joseph P. Kennedy Enterprises, the family trust offices in New York.

It was a cavernous place, neglected but clearly loved, and unlike his mother's homes, it reeked of the past. When I walked through the rooms, it was as if there was music of another time playing. John agreed. Ghosts, he said. Good ones. And on that first trip, we found a wing of the house he'd never been in before. We explored the musty rooms—some draped with sheets, others empty—and he told me that one night many years after Joe Kennedy died, he had the sense that his grandfather was there with him. He smelled the acrid sweet of his pipe. Did I think it was crazy, he asked, to feel the presence of someone after death?

We had spent the first night of our trip at the Breakers. John's aunt Ethel was scheduled to leave but had asked him for one more day, and he didn't want to intrude on her time. When we arrived at the house, we were greeted by Nelly, the Irish housekeeper, who inquired where our bags should go. Mrs. Kennedy, she said, was playing tennis. And Mrs. Kennedy was staying in the room near the pool, the one John had requested, the one that had been his father's. He seemed surprised that she was still there but shrugged it off. Perhaps, Nelly suggested with a knowing sigh, the bags should go to the Ambassador's room until Mrs. Kennedy departed later in the day. We followed her up the stone staircase, and when she opened the door to the room where his grandfather had slept almost twenty years before, I thought, *The house is still his.*

Later, after we returned from the beach, my suitcase was missing. John found it down the hall in his grandmother's suite. Nelly confessed that Ethel, on a tear because we were unmarried and sharing a room, had ordered the move. The bags went back and forth a number of times before she gave up. It was clear that she saw women as falling into one of two categories, and with a beady-eyed harrumph, she had cast me as the fallen sort. Perhaps I reminded her of someone? No, John said. She was just like that. He'd seen it with his cousins. Privately, he was incensed, but he opted to steer clear. "She's difficult, but she's still my aunt." One of his mottoes was "Choose your battles," and this wasn't one of them. Nor was the fact that Ethel stayed put for the rest of our stay without a word about it to him.

But one morning in the kitchen, when she pointedly refused to speak to me and I left the room in tears, John defended me. His sense of fairness, always acute, was inflamed, and she had crossed a line. This was our time at the house, he said, his voice raised but steady. He wouldn't ask her to leave, although he could, but if she chose to stay, she would treat me with respect. Like most bullies when confronted, she was speechless, and she retreated red-faced to the tennis courts for the rest of the day.

Afterward, he was shaken but relieved to have spoken up. He smiled when I told him that law school had come in handy. He'd been firm but not rude, and I was proud of him. What I didn't say was that there was something undeniably sexy about him coming to my rescue.

That summer in Hyannis, it seemed all the cousins knew the story of how John had stood up to Ethel. They knew about the bags and they knew about the rooms. I smiled, somewhat embarrassed, until I realized that nothing was private in his family and everyone had an opinion. It was a rite of passage, his cousin Willie explained. "We've all had our run-ins with Ethel." And what was initiation for me was a badge of courage for John. The cousins admired him, and there were backslaps and high fives. In private his mother especially appreciated the story. She clapped her hands and made us retell it, then divulged one of her own. Even his beloved aunt Eunice, while not condoning the premarital sharing of rooms, weighed in during a morning sail on his uncle's boat. Her behavior was inexcusable, she said, as we lowered our heads for the boom. And when it came around again, she touched my arm, adding, "You remind me of Jackie, you know."

. . .

"Did you always know?" he asked me.

It was our last night in Palm Beach. The casement windows were open wide, and the moon was on our faces. I lay in his arms watching the shadows on the vaulted ceiling.

He asked again. "With other people? Did you know how it would end?"

9½ Weeks had come out that year, and there was a line about it, about knowing the end at the beginning and waiting for it to happen.

I told him I had. It didn't keep me from falling; it didn't keep me from anything. But I had. And when I knew from the start, that made it all the more poignant. Like fighting fate.

Earlier, he'd kicked the sheet off, and now I pulled it close.

"Cold?" he asked.

"No—keep talking."

He told me the times he knew it wouldn't work. When and how. The sadness he felt. The difficulty of parting. "But with you, I can't imagine how it would end. And I don't want it to."

"Me neither," I whispered back. It wasn't a real lie. But earlier that day, as I had walked alone on the beach, I had sensed something I'd never sensed before. It was the distinct impression that I had two lives and I would have to choose.

As if he knew my thoughts, he began to talk about what he called our lifestyle, choosing each word carefully.

"My career, you mean?" I said wryly. "I miss you so much when I'm away. I wonder, could I give it up?"

"No." He shook his head. "I don't want that. That's not why I'm saying it. It's part of you."

I knew there was more, but we listened to the waves.

"Only, sometimes—I'm afraid to open up, afraid you'll go away, and that when you come back, you won't speak my language anymore."

"Never," I said, my voice quiet and bright because then I knew. "I promise that won't ever happen."

He pulled me closer and took my face in his hands.

"I love your hair. I love your neck. I love that other people see how much we love each other. I love when they tell me."

When we spoke of these things, we were almost shy, as if the feelings might drown us, and at times it was safer for him not to look at me. But not that night. That night he looked in my eyes. That night we spoke of family and marriage, how he never wanted to get divorced and that he believed in what he called his family's way of family. He wanted that, he said, and it was more important than success. For the first time, I told him, I could see having a child, and in the rain one night, walking home from the theater, I'd imagined a tiny hand in mine. I wasn't going to tell him; I thought it might make him afraid, but he gathered me in his arms and told me how happy that made him.

What we were talking about then, although we didn't use the word, was equilibrium, and I wonder now, more than twenty years later, if the house that knew secrets made us speak. That night, for the first time, I thought I could be both a wife and a lover; and I knew what kind of father he would be. And in that room, I saw myself growing old with him.

In April, John accepted a summer internship with the Justice Department. Since our time in Washington would overlap, he suggested that I stay on after the play ended. New York and auditions were only a train ride away, and he missed me. I looked at places.

There was a small house I loved on the Hill and an elegant but expensive apartment in a Georgetown row house near his cousin Timmy and his wife, Linda, and their new baby. But Myer Feldman, an adviser in his father's administration and a family friend, had graciously offered us a vacant duplex condo. It was across the river in Rosslyn, one stop north of Arlington on the Blue Line— a high-rise, the kind where you get lost in the corridors and all the doors look the same. Inside, everything was white and glass— pristine white carpet, white baby grand, and a small balcony that overlooked a highway and the Iwo Jima Memorial.

I pushed against it, but John's mind was made up. "It's free!" he argued. But the real enticement, I knew, was behind the building near the parking lot: the Olympic-size pool he'd spotted before we'd even set foot in the apartment.

On my day off in New York at the end of May, weeks before he moved to Washington, I went to a fortune-teller. I had been there before, and she read the numbers and cards with a green-eyed cat sleeping on her lap.

"With this one, you've had lives," she said, glancing up to check my face. "The first was happy, then tragic. He lost you near water, and when you died, he never recovered. The next was a great passion. Forbidden. Undiscovered. Powerful families."

She's read her *Romeo and Juliet*, I surmised, trying not to wrinkle my nose.

His Venus. My Sun. A Grand Trine and the Sun/Moon midpoint. Challenge would come later. This summer, she continued, the feelings would deepen, but I would discover things about him I wouldn't like.

"What things?" I leaned in, the backs of my knees pressed against the frayed fabric of the chair.

"Minor things. Irritations."

. . .

On the train back to Washington and a performance that night, I
had a red Mead notebook on my lap, and I was thinking about "the
things." Some of his more jocklike friends irked me (if there were
too many on a Vineyard weekend, I gravitated toward Caroline
and her friends); he didn't always tell me his plans; he was often
late and sometimes messy; and when he lost something, he expected me to find it. But these were slight grievances, and even
they had dissipated these past months with the comings and goings
and the romance of distance. "I can't imagine how it would end,"
he had said, and I felt that way, too. I was eager for the summer,
and yet a part of me wondered whether in living with him, I might
lose something.

The week before, he had told me a story. He'd seen a Karmann
Ghia on the street with a For Sale sign in the window and bought it
on a whim. He called his mother and Marta to say that he had a surprise and would tell them all about it that weekend in New Jersey.
When he drove up, proud in his vintage orange sports car, it was
his mother who had a surprise for him.

"She . . . got some things out of the safe." He looked nervous.

"What things?" I said dimly.

"Her engagement ring."

His mother, he said, wasn't surprised. She'd expected it, although it had happened quicker than she thought it would. Since
his call, she'd been adjusting herself to the idea. Then he began to
laugh. Marta, it seemed, anticipating an engagement party, had
bought a $1,300 Ungaro dress that couldn't be returned. Funny,
huh? He laughed again, an elbow in my side.

I opened the notebook. At the top of the page, I had jotted
phone numbers, what I'd spent that week, and a line from the play.
Yet swear not, lest you be forsworn again. I smiled. On the next page,

John had drawn a Picasso face for me to find. All unruly lips and eyes. Beside it, a mushy note. "I kiss your faults," I scribbled with abandon beside the face, the ink staining my fingers. I closed the notebook and pressed it deep into the bag on the seat beside me and settled into the familiar rhythm of the train.

It was the end of his first year of law school. Exams were starting, and I wouldn't see him for fifteen days. Outside the window, the houses turned to woods, and I waited for the dreamy stretch of green that came somewhere before Baltimore. *Make time count, Don't count time*, I told myself. But I didn't. I numbered the days until I would see him again, until we would move into the mammoth white apartment across from the Key Bridge, the one so close to Arlington.

He remembered things about his father, but those recollections came with the uncertainty as to whether they were his own or someone else's telling enfolded in his memory. Sometimes, if we were lying in the grass, he'd graze a buttercup against my chin to prove I liked butter. "My father did that," he'd say. Or he'd whisper nothing in my ear—*Pss, Pss, Pss*—until I laughed. *My father did that.* There was his hiding place in the desk; the helicopter's roar; his father calling him Sam and that making him mad; and nine days before Dallas, the performance of the pipers of the Black Watch on the South Lawn of the White House. The last memory he knew was his: the drums, the marching, and how he'd squirmed off his father's lap to get closer.

There was a park nearby we'd bike to after work. On the way, we'd pass the entrance at Memorial Drive, but we never went in. That summer, while careful of his reticence, I urged him to go. Some mornings, before the heat was too much, he'd run the trails, past the flags and the military graves—it calmed him, he said—but never to where his father was. We visited his cousins in Georgetown and mine in Maryland. He took me to meet Provi, his mother's personal maid at the White House and someone whom he considered family. So it felt strange to me to be so close and not to go. It was a visit waiting to happen. But he'd put it off or we'd forget. Something would come up. Until the last day. With the Karmann Ghia gassed up for New York and packed to the hilt, and everything else shipped, we stopped for a moment to say a prayer by the flame on the hillside.

It was to be a grand tour, a trip to end all trips. "We've spent weeks sweltering in DC," he said. "We deserve it!" First, Aspen and white-water rafting on the Colorado River. Then five days in Cora, Wyoming, at his friend John Barlow's ranch. He had worked there the summer he was seventeen and was anxious for me to see it. And after that—Venice. He'd asked his mother where he should take me. Well, she'd replied, Venice is the most romantic city. Marta, who'd lived there, concurred. We would stay a few days at the Gritti Palace, then a week at the Cipriani.

There's an old adage in theater: Plan a vacation, get a job. (In the years since, I've found it's best also to buy the tickets.) And so it was that when we got back to New York a week before the trip, I was cast as Ophelia at Baltimore Centerstage—a great theater, a part I'd longed to play, and Boyd Gaines, a few years shy of the first of his four Tony Awards, as Hamlet. I paused, imagining the Grand Canal, but it was impossible to turn the part down.

When I called John to tell him, he was disappointed about our trip but excited for me. "I'm proud of you. Come over—we'll celebrate," he said. But when I got to his apartment, the lights were out.

I found him in the back on the small terrace off the bedroom. It was August, but the night was cool. He was smoking a cigarette in one of the metal deck chairs, and his feet were bare. He didn't look at me. His eyes were fixed straight ahead, on the bricked backs of the brownstones. Slowly, I knelt beside him. I saw it was not the trip.

"You will always be leaving me," he said at last. And I said some things, trying to break the spell. The part—how I wanted it. A month less than Washington. Two train stops closer. Over before you know it.

His voice didn't change. "You don't understand. This is how it will be. You'll always be leaving me." I wanted to cajole him from the darkness, lift him from his mood, but I knew it was an old sorrow, one nameless to him, and whatever I said or did would be powerless against it. But I said it anyway. "I'm not leaving you." And it was then that he looked at me, saw me, and lowered his head to mine.

In the morning, it was over. We went to the Greek coffee shop on Eighty-sixth Street, where he ate two breakfasts. "I'll get used to it," he promised over Belgian waffles and a big plate of scrambled eggs.

I left the next week, and we fell into the back-and-forth and the drill of the trains. He saw the play twice, the one about the prince who mourns his father; and he liked my mad scene. After the curtain, we kicked around the bars and fish restaurants near Fell's Point. On an October night, we went to hear an Irish band at the Cat's Eye. He sang along to "The Black Velvet Band" and "The Skye Boat Song." His nanny Maud Shaw had taught him when he was little, and he remembered all the words.

Speed bonnie boat like a bird on the wing
Onward, the sailors cry
Carry the lad that's born to be king
Over the sea to Skye.

Though the waves leap, soft shall ye sleep,
Ocean's a royal bed.
Rocked in the deep, Flora will keep
Watch by your weary head.

On the late-night streets, we walked back to the actors' housing near North Calvert, and he taught me the songs. By the courthouse steps, deserted and grand, he asked if I would come to Los Angeles with him after his second year of law school. He'd been offered a summer associate position at a firm there. "You don't have to tell me now, but think about it," he said, hunched on a step. "And if you won't come, I'll stick with one of the firms in the city. I've thought about it, and I don't want us to be apart."

A few weeks later, I decided. My agents had an office in L.A., and by spring I was cast in a play at the Tiffany Theater on Sunset Boulevard. That's one thing about being an actor—you may spoil vacations, but you can also pick up and go.

Before, in Washington, living together had just happened. This time he asked me, and he had me pick the house. It was by the beach, a clapboard cottage on Thornton Court, with roses in the garden and a low picket fence. I'd finally gotten my driver's license, and he bought me an old powder blue Buick Skylark Custom with a black interior.

Santa Monica Airport was close, and that summer he took up

flying again. He went up with an instructor most Saturdays and always came back happy. When he was ready to do a solo landing on Catalina Island, he pressed me to come along. A tricky descent, he said, excited—downdrafts and a slim, pitted runway on top of a 1,602-foot mesa.

"Don't worry, Puppy," he said. "The instructor will be there."

It was a cloudless LA morning, and he buzzed us around the basin—John in the pilot's seat, the instructor next to him. They talked over the headphones, pointing to the colored lights on the instrument panel. I was in the back, peering down at the tight squares of neighborhoods snaked through with gray highway. He turned the plane, and soon we were over water. Near a sheer cliff with the runway in sight, the plane began to shake. He was afraid of stalling, but when the instructor reminded him of something, John leveled the wings and the landing was easy.

Before we flew back, we wandered across the tarmac to the Airport in the Sky Café and celebrated with buffalo burgers. The instructor was pleased, John was elated, and even I, who knew nothing about planes, could tell how well he had done.

It was in this way I knew he was jealous.

He was never controlling in the tethering way some men can be, but there'd be a gibe or a tease if I flirted too long at a party or if the calls from a particular matinee idol or ex-flame were too frequent. He didn't like my screen kisses, no matter how chaste they were, and he'd scold, "Do you have to kiss *everyone?*" Plays were a different story, perhaps because he knew that world, and the space between audience and proscenium made it palatable.

There was one exception—an especially torrid clinch in a Naked Angels production of *Chelsea Walls,* where the theater was tiny, I was in a slip, and the bad-boy actor in question, clad only in boxers, threw me on the bed with Method gusto. Later that night, John refused to speak to me and insisted on walking around the block alone. To cool off, he said. But he never forbade me to do anything. He gave me freedom, and I believed it was because he trusted me.

In November, after I'd returned to New York from playing Ophelia in Baltimore, we went to a dinner his aunt Jean gave at her town house for Roger Stevens, the veteran theater producer and founding chairman of the Kennedy Center. I was seated next to Jane Alexander, an actress I had always admired. Over the toasts, we spoke of her long-cherished project, a film about Alfred Stieglitz and Georgia O'Keeffe, which she would both produce and star in. Maximilian Schell, newly signed to play the famed photographer, would direct. And, she added, with palpable excitement, he was flying in next week from Munich. I hadn't seen his Academy Award–winning performance in *Judgment at Nuremberg*, but I knew his film *Marlene* and thought it was genius. After dessert, she handed me her card and said that I bore an uncanny resemblance to Dorothy Norman, Stieglitz's much younger, married lover and protégée of almost twenty years.

Five days later, I was on my way to meet Jane, the screenwriter, and Maximilian Schell in his rented suite at the Warwick Hotel. I'd been out of drama school a year, and although I'd come close on film and television roles, I had been doing plays since I'd graduated. The script was unfinished, my agents said, so over the weekend I rushed down to the Gotham Book Mart to find a copy of *Encounters*, Dorothy Norman's newly published memoir, in an effort to glean what I could.

At fifty-six, the Viennese-born actor was still handsome—his eyes bright, his thick hair peppered with silver—and the nubby black scarf thrown about his neck gave him the air of an old-time impresario. As I entered the room, he appeared to smolder, impatient perhaps with the long day of meeting young actresses who, he would later confide, were "too American." I sat in the chair opposite him, and after the initial chitchat and a perfunctory glance at my résumé, he leaned forward.

"Are you Jewish?" he said, searching my face.

"No," I answered, then quickly remembered that Norman was. "But I am a New Yorker. And my friends say I was Jewish in a past life."

He frowned. "My friends say I was Peter the Great in a past life, but I'm *not*. Still . . . there is *something* Jewish about you."

Instinctively, I knew not to appear cowed by him and began to assume what I imagined were Norman's qualities: passion and an alluring, penetrating smarts. He loosened up and so did I, and soon he had us laughing with his stories. He didn't look like Stieglitz, but when he spoke, I could picture the legendary black cape over his shoulders. Finally, Jane rose. It was late, and she had to beat the traffic to her house upstate. "Why don't you stay," she suggested, placing a soft hand on my shoulder, and the screenwriter followed her out the door.

Hours had passed, and I was still there. It was dark by the time she called. There was only the light from the street and the glow from the table lamp between the two couches. Though by no means an assurance of getting the part, a heavy whiff of flirtation wasn't uncommon in auditions, but this was beyond anything I'd experienced. Perhaps it was European, I told myself, and when he offered me a glass of wine, I moved closer, to the empty couch nearby. Tossing my head back, I sat with my feet curled under me, and although I could see a wedge of bed through the half-opened door to the next room, I didn't leave.

"Are you all right?" Jane asked when he handed me the phone. "You can go now, you know."

We had talked about everything, about painting and philosophy, our childhoods and religion, and certainly the theater. He had played Hamlet and I had played Ophelia, and we'd both been in Pinter's *Old Times*. We talked of plays as if they were real worlds, but when I asked what he would see while he was in New York, he said, "Why watch when you can do." His gaze was intense, and at one point I moved to the window, touching my wineglass absently. "Does the tension make you nervous?" he asked, adding that for him it was a rare thing. "No," I replied. But I had dropped mentions of a boyfriend and how I was meeting him later. He smiled, cat-like, but scoffed when I used the word *boyfriend* again. It was, he said, so American.

Then we began to talk about the film—how he would shoot it and what did I think of this or that idea, and if I had the role, how would I respond, how would I wear my hair, how would I move. Together we conspired over the story, sliding easily into the roles of acolyte and mentor. It was, after all, the point of our meeting, to test the thread of chemistry, and when I stood to leave, he stood as well, offering to get me a cab. Once in the lobby, he wanted to show me a mural in the Time-Life Building a few blocks south. He knew the painter, Josef Albers, and collected his work, as well as the paintings of Klee, Rothko, and Dubuffet.

I was eager to learn, and I went with him.

After the murals, we kept walking. To show my daring, I took him not up Columbus, but through the park, until finally we stood under a streetlamp outside John's apartment building on West Ninety-first Street.

"Farewell," I said.

"Adieu," he corrected. "I will see you again." With that, he kissed my hand and backed off into the cold night.

Upstairs, the apartment was empty. I sat at the dining table savoring the moment. I was giddy, seduced not so much by the still-chiseled movie-star profile or the quality of attentiveness an older man can give to a much younger woman—although I was flattered by the fact that he'd followed me thirty-odd blocks in the cold—but by the spark I'd felt. The talk of Art and artists. The ebullient sense of what it would be like to work with him. This was what was powerful to me, and though relieved to have escaped, I wanted the part and thought, as I waited for John to come up the stairs, that this might be the break I'd been waiting for, the role that would change everything.

I heard the key in the door. John wheeled his bike in, dropped it by the bench, and, grinning, turned on the hall light. "How'd it go?" he said, whipping off his headphones. He had been as excited as I had about the meeting. I began to tell him everything—the walk through the park, the murals, the questions. Then, with my eyes fixed on the middle distance, I sighed and said, "He's the most powerful man I've ever met."

His smile dropped. As soon as I said it, I wanted to take it back. Speechless at first, he began to berate me. I was foolish, naïve, and, more than that, silly. How could I not see that? "I can't *believe* you!" he bellowed. "He's playing you." When I protested, he waved me off. There'd be a lull and he'd go off into another room, but soon he'd stomp around the apartment and it would start again. He carried on so much that night that I began to doubt what had happened. Until the next morning, when my agents called. He's smitten, they said. *Nice work.*

To my embarrassment, John began to tell the story every chance he got. I didn't like it, but when I heard him act it out for Anthony, I had to admit he had me down pat.

At his mother's holiday party two weeks later, we were greeted at the door by a smiling Maurice. When John left with our coats, Maurice lowered his voice and shook his head, concerned. "My dear, I heard about Maximilian Schell." Ed's reaction was similar, only more dismissive, and by the time I reached his mother at the center of the gallery, I was prepared to take my lumps. But she surprised me. She beamed.

"Oh," she said, kissing my cheek. "It's so exciting about Maximilian Schell! John told us all about it at Thanksgiving dinner. He seemed to be making fun, but you just knew he was *so* jealous." The thing was, until that moment, I hadn't known. I smiled, grateful she'd let the secret slip. That he was jealous seemed in some way to delight her. She wanted to know more. After all, though she was his mother, she was also a woman who knew and appreciated power in men and, without question, valued her effect on them.

Not long after that, I had a second meeting in the suite at the Warwick. This time I was more confident, buoyed in part by Mrs. Onassis's enthusiasm, and before I was out the door, he offered me the part. I did end up playing Dorothy Norman, but it was years later and with a different actor, in a different time altogether. Due to a writers' strike, Maximilian Schell was no longer attached to the project.

When I saw Max again, it was at an opera opening in Los Angeles in 2005. By then, I'd long abandoned the thought that a role might change my life—the sanguine belief that all actors hold close. He was seventy-five. His eyes were still bright, and tossed around his neck was what appeared to be the same black scarf. When we spoke, his face lit up, and I knew he remembered everything.

On that night years before, as we'd walked past his hotel to John's apartment, he'd turned to me with an abrupt tenderness and said, "Whatever happens with the film, whether we work together or not, when you pass by the Warwick, I hope you will think of me and this night." Strange thing is, I do.

The waves licked the sides of the kayak as we set out from Great Pedro Bay on the remote southern coast of Jamaica. We pushed past the barefoot children on the shore and the brightly colored fishing boats to have our adventure. It was why we had come.

The day before, we'd left the more predictable resort scene in Negril and headed southeast, not knowing where we would land. We traveled well together from day one. John was the spontaneous pied piper, the one who'd swerve the car over, saying, *Let's go— let's get out and do this.* I was the navigator, riding shotgun with a variety of guidebooks, reading aloud historical and cultural tidbits as he drove. He loved that, being a team. He called me Chief, and I called him King.

After we were no longer together, he'd send a postcard now and then from his travels. A riverboat in Asia. A midsummer bonfire in Finland. And from Costa Rica, a card covered with golden toads that said, "It's a beautiful country, but I must confess to feeling ignorant about the place without you."

At this point in our lives, we were like a puzzle and our different pieces fit; I held him back a bit, and he pushed me to go further. And we both relished the idea of taking off without a plan and seeing where the day would take us. We loved the possibility that something could happen, something we could tell a story about later on. Stories were the golden treasure, shiny bits that brought us closer.

In February, a few months back, I'd broken my foot horseback riding in Virginia. The jump was low; it was a fluke, really. But the break was serious. I'd be on crutches for four months, and the doctors wouldn't know until then if the bone had died and would need to be fused to my heel, the result being a permanent limp.

John's cousin Anthony was with me when I fell. After I underwent a six-hour operation, he spent the night beside my bed at Fauquier hospital. As I went in and out of a morphine daze, he read aloud to keep me company. Anthony had a habit of teasing everyone he liked. Otherwise, he could appear quite formal. He goaded me once at a gym, saying his aunt Jackie could lift heavier weights than I could. In a baby voice, he loved to imitate the pet names John had for me—Christmas Mouse, Puppy, Sweet Frog. But that night, he showed his true and tender colors by keeping vigil, not wanting me to wake up and find myself alone hooked up to an IV.

The next morning, when I opened my eyes, the room was filled with flowers—from my family, from John's mother and his aunt Lee. Red roses from John in New York, along with a card: "Let's go dancing, Baby!" In the chair beside me, Anthony, the night watchman, was dozing, a *Newsweek* sprawled on his lap.

When I returned to New York, I was treated at the Institute for Sports Medicine at Lenox Hill Hospital. The institute had been founded by Dr. James Nicholas, one of President Kennedy's doctors and a good friend of Mrs. Onassis. She was kind and supportive, and gave me the use of her car service for months while I was laid up. She told me stories of when she was engaged to John's father and broke her ankle playing touch football. "That was the last time," she said. *You don't have to keep up with him,* her eyes seemed to confide. *He wants you* because *you're feminine.* She smiled, recounting the effort it took to hobble across the room for a book or a cashmere sweater. I didn't have a drawerful of cashmere, but I nodded as if I did.

After three weeks, the cast was taken off, and in its stead I was given a lightweight removable brace—a blue plastic miracle. I wouldn't be able to walk without crutches for another three months, but now, with the brace, I could swim in a pool, receive ultrasound treatments, and take a bath. John would gallantly carry me up the five flights of stairs to his brownstone apartment, but he wasn't able to look at my cadaver-like foot. Nor could he bear to hear how painful it was or of the fears I had. He wanted me to be a trooper, a sport, but for all his exploits, he was squeamish about blood and weakness of any kind.

Around Easter, he had a break from school and decided a vacation was in order. His aunt Lee invited us to join her and her husband, Herbert Ross, at a rented villa in Acapulco, and it was tempting. But we chose the less cushy alternative.

We landed in Montego Bay. Waiting for our delayed luggage at a roadside hut, John drank the manroot drink to be manlier and bought me a wooden cane carved by a Rasta with wild eyes.

On a side road to Negril, we saw a handwritten sign—HOLY

CAVE—and pulled over. When the men there caught sight of my crutches, they began waving their arms and shouting, insisting I go to the healing spring deep within the cave. I smiled at John, and he smiled back; it was the beginning of adventure.

A price was settled on, torches were lit, and my crutches were laid at the entrance. With three men as our guides and one tagging along, John flung me over his shoulder he-man-style, and we entered the cave. Soon any trace of sunlight was gone, and we were enveloped by rock. Bats flew by us. I swallowed my fear and tried to breathe the dank, dead air. Against my stomach, I could feel his heart beating fast. As we went deeper, the rock walls narrowed, and when the ceiling got so low that his knees shook, one of the younger guides took over carrying me. He moved quickly in a deep squat until we heard the roar of the spring.

The passage opened suddenly into a wide cavern. Without speaking, the men began to form a half circle around the spring, as John and the young guide lowered me into the cold water—the force of it so strong, I had to grip the rocks or be swept into the deeper darkness. The gush of water and the men's voices echoed off the rock walls. Because of the dialect, no words were discernible; it was like a chant, louder and more insistent, until finally I cried out. By the whites of eyes lit by fire and the black smoke of the kerosene, I cried and prayed. I prayed to the divinity of the dark that I would be healed and walk again.

We drove away invigorated by my baptism in the cave spring. We sang old songs as the rental car hugged the coast. Then he said he had a surprise, a temporary but genius solution for my inability to walk, at least in Jamaica. He'd secretly brought his Klepper kayak, a fancy collapsible kind. I didn't tell him that I would have been happy to lie on the beach reading while he explored solo to his heart's content. He wanted us to do things together and he wouldn't have believed me anyway. His sense of well-being was so tied to his ability to move and do that he thought everyone was like that. He had also packed something else—a book on Tantric sex a friend from Andover had given him after returning from Thailand. "It comes highly recommended," he said with a wink, and assured me that walking was not a requirement.

Treasure Beach is made up of a string of sleepy fishing villages and farm communities in St. Elizabeth Parish, between Negril and Kingston. There are no big resorts on the four bays—Billy's Bay, Frenchman's Bay, Calabash Bay, and Great Pedro Bay—and the people who live there are friendly and laid-back. The feel is offbeat and authentic. Pirate Billy Rackham had headquartered there, hence the name Treasure Beach, and legend has it that in 1492, Columbus came ashore after the *Niña* sank nearby. The locals of Treasure Beach are called "red men" by other Jamaicans, and indeed there is a prevalence of blue and green eyes, blond and red hair, and freckles. They're said to be descended in part from seventeenth-century Scottish sailors who survived the wreck of their ship and stayed to fish and work the fields.

We checked into the Treasure Beach Hotel, built in the 1930s. It was charming, un-renovated, and relatively devoid of tourists. We dropped our bags and went down to Great Pedro Bay to catch the sunset. The last cove of Treasure Beach dead-ended into Pedro Bluff, a promontory more than a hundred feet high and jutting more than a mile out to sea. In the waning light, it loomed above us.

As John tinkered with the kayak, he realized he'd left the spray skirts and life jackets back in New York. Spray skirts are made of neoprene and keep water from getting in the boat. You wear them around your waist and fasten the edges to the round opening of the

kayak, and if you're hit by a large wave, they keep you from sinking. In the bay, we would be in protected water, so not having them
didn't seem all that important.

After the boat was ready, we sat on the beach and drank a little
of the magic mushroom tea we'd brought from Negril, a requisite
purchase there and, we were assured, "da real ting." The effect was
mild and relaxing, the pace of Treasure Beach just right, and we
paddled around in the smooth waters of the bay. But soon John
began to steer the boat toward the current at the end of the bluff.
The unknown beyond was referred to by locals as "back seaside,"
miles of undeveloped land and cliffs that rose up 1,750 feet. One of
the highest points was a spot called Lover's Leap, where two slaves
had jumped rather than be separated. Or, as another tale told, a
woman had watched as her lover sailed away and then leaped from
the cliff in an effort to join him.

"Just a little farther, Chief. It'll be fun."

The sun had gone down, and the silver waves grew higher.

"I promise. Just around the point and we'll come back."

He always wanted to see what he couldn't see. Like an itch, like
longing, it was out of his control. I was dizzy from the tea, but I
wanted to overcome my fear and push through it. When I did, I
felt powerful, more alive—and with John, I'd found an inkling of
my risk-taking self. I wanted to keep going, to show him I could,
but I looked up at the darkening sky and remembered the rudi-
mentary map in the Lonely Planet guide that showed no towns, no
roads for miles on the other side of the bluff that led east to Spanish Town and Kingston. No one and nothing.

Maybe it was the mushroom tea. Maybe it was common sense
or my busted foot. Maybe it was just plain old fear kicking in—not

the self-created, insecure kind I was prone to and he wasn't, but the necessary fear that keeps you alive by alerting you to danger. But when I asked him to turn back, he didn't argue, bargain, or cajole with the battle cry he often used: *Couragio, Christina!* He seemed relieved and kissed me lightly. He was also hungry, an urge as strong for him as conquering the unknown. "Tomorrow, tomorrow is another day," he sang in a soft voice, and I knew we would be back in the morning.

That night we ate at a thatched place a fisherman had told us about. We were happy. John ordered the goat curry—he told me that in Indonesia he had once eaten monkey brains—and I had conch. There were hardly any lights in Treasure Beach, not where we were, and the stars were huge in the moonless sky. We stopped the car on the way back to the hotel and got out—to stand in what seemed to us the rarity of utter quiet.

We kissed for a long time in the open field, until goats encircled us, nudging greedily at the backs of our knees and gnawing on his sneaker laces. The moon rose. Then, in the distance, we heard faint chanting. Moving toward the voices, we saw a whitewashed building—a Pentecostal church. It was the night before Palm Sunday. We listened outside as people spoke in tongues, sang, and testified, their voices rising into the midnight sky. The enchantment of Treasure Beach began to show itself as more potent and primal, more mysterious and subtle, than the magic of the mushroom tea, the cave spring, the manroot drink, or the Rasta's cane.

The next morning, we set out in the two-man Klepper with three sandwiches, a mango, and a liter of water. A Klepper is a folding kayak, an elegant version of the Plexiglas kind, with a frame of blond wood and a hull of heavy canvas. They have circled Cape

Horn, crossed the English Channel and the Atlantic Ocean, and served on expeditions to the North and South Poles. You can also pack one in two duffel bags and travel with it. John had fallen in love with them, so much so that he and Michael Berman, the friend with whom he would later start *George* magazine, founded Random Ventures to invest in similar handmade boats.

In the daylight, Pedro Bluff was transformed, no longer ominous or shadowy, but a thing alive with seabirds, brush, and cactus flowers. We paddled hard and made it through the heady current at the end of the bluff around to back seaside. It was beautiful and wild and seemed to go on forever—miles of high cliffs, jungle, and deserted beach.

"You see, nothing to be afraid of." He leaned in, nuzzling my neck. "Good job, Sport." He was right. We were together, the water was turquoise, the sun was shining, and we were far enough out so that the swells beneath us were only a murmur of what they would become. We stopped, ate our sandwiches, and watched the dolphins nearby. A good omen, we said.

Then he wanted to go a little farther. And once we did that, he wanted to land. I refused. I had agreed only to come past the point. We had no spray skirts, I argued, and we hadn't seen another boat since we'd left Great Pedro Bay more than an hour before. But he was seductive—the water was calm, we didn't need spray skirts—and he wanted what he wanted. He also knew more than I did about the sea, about anything outdoors. He had opened these worlds to me. But more to the point, in Negril I had glanced at the book John had brought, and the idea of landing on one of those beaches and enacting our very own desert island Tantric sex fantasy was alluring.

We moved in for reconnaissance, staying behind the break, but the same swells that had seemed so gentle farther out were now larger. They were also breaking on something well before land. We drew closer, and I saw it—darkness in the water. Danger between paradise and us.

"It's a reef—turn back, King," I heard myself saying in a voice much higher-pitched than my own. We paddled back out and conferred.

"You're first mate and I'm captain, but we're a team and I need you behind me," he said. "If we pull in and you say no for any reason—any reason at all—I'll turn back." He kept his eyes on me and waited. There were the bits of dried salt on his large brown shoulders.

I wanted that desert island fantasy, sand and all. I also wanted to feel powerful, as afraid as I was. And somewhere in the mix, I wanted to please him.

"Okay. But you *promise?*"

"Don't worry, I promise."

We advanced again. A reef. We went back out, paddled farther down the coast, and pushed in once more. Another reef. By now I was tired and ready to give up, but he pleaded. As we got closer, he spotted a break in the coral just wide enough for the kayak. Risky but not impossible.

"If we're going to do this, I need you with me. And I need you to paddle hard, so we can pull ahead of the break. I can't do it alone. What do you say, are you game?"

I nodded. And as captain and first mate, paddle we did. John steered us expertly through the chute with the waves rumbling beneath us. At some point, I was frightened and wanted to stop, but he shouted above the roar, "Too late. No turning back, Baby. Paddle. Now!" He was laughing. We were going to make it. We were almost there, a stone's throw from the beach, when suddenly the tide pulled back to reveal what had been hidden—a large boulder blocking the narrow entrance to dry land.

We were going to wreck. No way around it or through it. I was in front. Beneath the bow, my broken limb lay immobile from knee to foot in its shiny blue brace. My leg and the boat were sure to shatter. I closed my eyes and waited, too afraid to cry.

Then there was a whoosh of sand against the canvas bottom. Not rock—sand. Just as we were about to hit, a wave came, just high enough to carry us over the rock. We—and our craft—arrived without a scratch. John hauled the kayak up. I hobbled out with my soggy crutch, the day pack, and the mango. We caught our breath, unable to speak.

I know now we were in shock. I thought it was just me who was terrified, but then I saw John, my captain, John, who was never afraid. Unable to be still, he paced the beach muttering something, his eyes wide and to the ground. "Don't tell Mummy, don't tell Mummy," he repeated like a mantra to no one. Mummy wasn't there, and he wasn't talking to me. I could have passed my hand in front of his eyes, and he would not have blinked. It was then that the danger we had been in really hit me. *John* was afraid. I had never seen him like this—not skiing down a chute in a whiteout in Jackson Hole or nearly colliding with a gray whale in Baja. There was an exhilaration about him, a high. He was almost smiling. Then he noticed that his hand was shaking. He held it out to show me, and we marveled that it continued to shake for the next fifteen minutes.

We didn't speak as we set up camp on the small beach. The mangroves on either side grew down to the water and made it impossible to walk to the next beach over.

I took the brace off my leg and left it leaning on the kayak with the crutch. Then I hopped to the towel he had laid out and sat down with the book, the damp copy of Mantak Chia's *Taoist Secrets of Love*. John planned to explore the reef. Broken and mottled, it stretched out from the beach for about half a mile, but lengthwise it seemed to go on forever. Close in, the water was shallow—in some places, no more than ankle-deep—and he tightened the laces of his sneakers so that he could walk on the sharp, dead coral to the deeper spots to dive.

Neither of us broached the question of how we were going to get back. But I knew John, and it was best to let him go off on his own. Physical activity calmed him. As he walked away, swim goggles draped over his shoulder, he turned back to me. "Don't eat my mango, Baby," he yelled.

I smiled and watched him disappear behind the mangroves. I wanted him—his tanned body, his jones for adventure. Even his mango hoarding. I wanted all of it. We'd been together a long time, but desire was always there. It ebbed and flowed, but the current stayed strong between us.

I took off my white bikini and lay back. The sound of the waves grew faint, broken by the reef. The sun felt good on my body. *For this moment, we are safe.* We would find our way back. It would be okay. It always was with John. I believed that when I was with him, nothing could happen to me. I believed it, even on that remote beach with the reef out there waiting.

I woke to the sound of voices. There were no roads that we knew of on the high cliffs above, just jungle and goat paths, but through the leafy green, I saw five men making their way down to the beach. Red men—our deserted beach, no longer deserted. Had they seen me? I called for John, but there was no answer.

When they reached a large pile of wood near the rocks on the far side of the beach, they began to place the branches that they were carrying on top. I was sure I smelled smoke. Then one of them saw me and began moving down the beach, stick in hand. As I scrambled for my sarong, I saw the headlines—NAKED ROMP: JFK GAL PAL RAPED, ROASTED AND EATEN.

John was nowhere to be seen, and my crutch was too far away to hop to. My hands trembled. I gave up on the bikini top, shoving it under the towel with the book, and pulled my sarong up over me, knotting it tightly under my arm. Before the men approached, I succeeded in getting the suit bottom somewhere in the vicinity of my thighs. My first thought was to keep the men talking until John got back.

The largest one sat near me, and the rest towered above. With his red hair and freckles, he looked like one of the locals from Treasure Beach, but his patois was harder for me to understand. How had I gotten here, he asked. I pointed to the boat, then realized they would see the crutch and know I couldn't walk. The youngest sat on his haunches. Was I alone? Married? Oh, yes, I said, and my husband will be back any minute. The leader lit up a joint and offered me a hit off the enormous spliff. Jamaican hospitality and impossible to refuse. In return, I gave him the mango.

As we shared the fruit, they told me they were childhood friends and had fished off this reef as boys. The one who'd spotted me had gone to the north of England for work and had just returned after twenty years away. There would be a full moon that night, and they were here to fish and celebrate. They didn't have poles, they said, but they showed me the small nets, sharp sticks, and tin cans rigged with string.

Finally, John arrived. He was happy and relaxed, greeting the men and handing me a present—a colored shell he'd found while diving off the reef. When he smiled, saying something to the effect that he'd found a way off Paradise, I pointed to the trail the men had come from. Dismayed to find that his mango had been eaten, he stretched out on the sand and finished what was left of the joint. Then he got a lesson in tin can fishing. As they stood in the shallows of the reef casting their lines, John was especially intrigued by the youngest, who easily skewered the small reef fish with his stick.

He inquired about the goat path. Steep, they said. A thousand feet up. We would have to abandon the kayak, that was clear, and I would need to be carried. He asked for their help, offering to pay them at the hotel, but the men didn't want to leave before morning. Instead, they invited us to spend the night with them roasting fish under the stars. We stayed on the beach for hours but nixed the idea of sleeping there. As eager as we had been to arrive, we now wanted to leave.

Arguing for the devil we knew, I said we should return the way we had come, through the break in the reef.

"Not an option," John said, shaking his head.

"But we made it the first time."

"Yes, but even if we got to the end of the channel, even if we made it that far, we'd be slammed where the surf meets the reef."

I looked out. He was right. In the distance, the waves hit the submerged coral with such force that they were tossed sky-high.

"My way," he said, "we steer clear of the reef altogether."

"How?" I asked. "It's everywhere."

"That's what I thought. But when I was diving off the side, I saw it, I was in it. In front of the other beach, no reef, no coral—it's clear."

I tried to stall. "Can we walk there, so I can at least see it?"

Again he shook his head. "Mangroves. And rock. The beach

there is lower, set farther back than this one. We'd have to climb down—you wouldn't make it with your foot. I'll take you in the kayak and you can see from there. The coral makes a ledge, and if we drop down, we're home free."

I looked away from him, my eyes catching sight of the crutch by the boat.

"Just check it out," he said. "You can always say no."

After we said goodbye to the fishermen, he picked me up and set me in the front of the kayak and began to pull the boat through the shallow water. Whatever haze we may have felt from the red men's joint was gone, and we were clearheaded, invigorated by decision. The side of the reef ran perpendicular to the shore and, along with the mangroves, divided the two beaches and their waters. It also created, as he had described, a shelf with a drop of about six feet into the waves on the other side.

We reached the edge. He stood waist-deep in the calm reef waters, one hand steadying the stern. We were silent as we surveyed what lay before us. To the right, there was the wider beach, with jungle behind it and white surf pounding the shore. To the left, the Caribbean, the horizon, and a straight shot back to Treasure Beach. But below, huge swells rolled by, unbroken by reef and rock. That was where we were headed. John would drag the kayak farther out, but where he could still stand. This would place us as far past the wave break as possible once we dropped down. Then he would jump in behind me, in the steering position, and push the kayak off the reef. We'd be parallel to the swells when we landed, but he'd time it between sets and quickly steer the boat a quarter turn out to sea.

I bit my lip and watched the water rise and unfurl until it

crashed on the sand of the larger beach. Then I remembered my leg.

"But what if a wave hits us? What if we capsize? I can't swim in that." My doctors had said yes to pool swimming only. And by the looks of it, I wasn't even sure John could make it in that surf.

"That's not going to happen." He sounded more confident about his plan now that we were actually here. "We're sneaking in from the side, not head-on. And look how evenly they're breaking."

It was true. The waves weren't wild; they were rolling straight. And from our perch on the reef, there was nothing sideways about them.

"It's our best shot. There's no reef below. No way we'll wreck. I know I can turn the 'yak. I can time it right. I'll get us past the break. You just paddle and I'll steer."

It was a risk, I knew—a roll of the dice. But it did look less harrowing than our arrival earlier through the channel in the reef. And we'd survived that, hadn't we? I looked at John. He was counting under his breath, as serious as I'd ever seen him, marking the time between wave sets. His brow was furrowed, his jaw set. I squeezed his hand, took the leap, and nodded yes.

He pulled the boat out a little farther and hoisted himself in back. Then, with his oar, he pushed us off the reef. Once we dropped down, the tip righted itself—just as he had said it would—and we began to make the turn out to sea before the next swell. But he had misjudged; the waves were much larger and the current stronger than they had appeared from the shelf above, and we soon realized that we were being dragged sideways to the shore, the prow in danger of heading toward the surf. If we were caught in the break, we'd be tumbled in white water and slammed against the sand. To avoid the danger of the reef, we had put our-selves at the mercy of the sea.

I heard his voice. He was shouting for me to keep paddling as he tried furiously to keep the tiny boat away from the shore.

Then, without warning, we were underwater, inside an enor-mous swell. Like a hurricane's eye, like its very own world, it was silent and still. Time stopped. My eyes opened to unending pale blue. I was amazed that I could see everything. I looked to what I thought was above. My eyes widened: Ten feet, fifteen feet up, I saw a trail of light filtering down. Not white water—just the small-est ridge of curl. It meant we were beneath the crest, in its thick-ness, but it hadn't broken. Not yet. It meant the boat was still righted and we hadn't flipped. It meant hope.

Suddenly, there was pressure on every part of my body. We were surging toward the break somewhere to our right. I didn't know if I could hold my breath much longer—the wall of water was endless. I panicked and began to push myself out of the boat, to swim toward the light, when I felt a hand on my back pulling me down. I turned; his eyes were open. He was shaking his head as forcefully as he could against the weight of the water. I had for-gotten that he was there, that he was caught in the wave with me.

Air hit, and we gasped. But the next swell came, rough and hard, and we were under again. I watched as the paddle was lifted from my hand. I watched as my fingers let go of the wood. I wanted to breathe but reminded myself I couldn't. My head was light, so light. I thought, *This is it. This is how it ends. We are going to die together. This is what it means to drown.*

But the sky broke through. In the air, the sound was deafening. My lungs hurt, and as we crested a steep wave, I coughed, spat water, and clung to the edge of the boat with my head down. I waited, fully expecting to be flung backward out of the boat, but we made it over. I looked back at him, amazed, and saw that he had never stopped. He'd never given up, and he was beginning to shepherd us over the waves, not under them. He had turned us out to sea, just as he'd promised, and we were coursing past the break to safety. Then I heard him yell.

"Bail!"

"What?"

"Bail. Find the bailer. Now!" he ordered.

I looked down. Water to my waist. No spray skirts; they were somewhere in a closet in New York. I rummaged frantically around the bottom of the boat. My crutch, like the paddle, was gone, and there was nothing to bail with. I started to cry, but I was furious.

"There is no bailer, John! How could you not pack a bailer?" I shouted. "We're in the goddamn ocean!"

"Fuck, use anything, use your hands! We're sinking."

"The hell we are."

Resolute, I scooped the water overboard with both hands, until he found a cotton baseball cap wedged under his thigh. And when the danger had finally passed, when we were far enough out so that there was barely a ripple in the surface of the sea, I remember thinking how beautiful the day was, how clear the sky. And that it was all so incongruous with what had nearly happened to us three times that day. A jeer almost.

We had gone into the open sea without consulting anyone who knew the waters, without spray skirts, life jackets, or a bailer. And here we were, surviving, on our way to Treasure Beach with a single paddle and a soggy baseball cap. Fate had smiled on us.

As we passed the high part of the cliff, I looked up. Hawks were circling. I remembered the woman who had jumped to join her lover, the water, and death, and I thought, *No, that is not me. That will not be me.* I repeated it to myself like a promise I would not betray. But I knew, in some small way, it was. That April morning, whether I admitted it or not, I had followed him every step of the way.

When we pulled into Great Pedro Bay an hour later, I was still shaken. John seemed fine, oblivious. As he pulled the kayak past the fishing skiffs to a fence near some old bikes, he whistled. Unlike me, he had left it all behind and was fully in the present—although he did make me promise not to tell his mother.

"But John, we could have died."

I was angry and frightened, and I wanted him to know. I wanted him to hold me, to tell me that he was sorry, that it would never happen again, that he had been afraid, too. I wanted him to say something. Something to acknowledge that it was more than just a story or a jam we'd gotten out of. He was puttering around the boat, securing it for the night, and a group of children had gathered to watch. Setting down the rope, he glanced up at me for a moment before returning to his bowline knot.

"Yeah, Chief, but what a way to go."

He gave me a card the first year we were together, a black-and-white drawing of lovers kissing, with the words "Girl's Eye View / Boy's Eye View" etched above their heads. The girl's eyes are open, filled with doubt and excitement and the fevered anticipation of what comes next. In the tangle of her hair are a myriad of thoughts, wishes, and fears. The boy's eyes are shut; he's smack in the present. He has only one thought: "Who the hell knows?"

There were things he would say like mantras. They might have been passed along by someone wiser, someone who knew, his uncle, or his mother maybe. He'd say them to remind himself of human nature and the way of the world; that struggle wasn't always the best path, but sometimes it was; and that whatever Fortune brought, it wasn't because he thought himself superior. He had faults, like anyone, but never arrogance, never meanness, never snobbery. What he aimed for, and succeeded some days in attaining, was the remarkable equipoise of humility and confidence that is grace.

It goes with the territory, he would say. This applied, I learned, to the small scrutinies he faced daily—to the press, stories true and untrue, to people's behavior at times glassy-eyed or grasping. To good tables in restaurants, exciting parties, great vacations, velvet ropes parting, and the occasional bump to first class. It also applied, I would learn, to the attentions of other women.

Once we were alone in a room and a girl came in. It was one of the last performances of *Winners,* and we were on the top floor of the Irish Arts Center in the room where we'd meet to run lines before the stage manager called places. That night, we stood close to the brick wall talking, the old floorboards washed in the honeyed push of light before sunset. The girl came in, beautiful in chinos and sneakers. Later, when we asked, no one seemed to know her or how she'd gotten past the lobby. The audience was invitation-only, and it seemed she had talked her way in and snuck up the stairs. With pale, thin hair, she looked like a young Jessica Lange, but there was something in her eyes, tilted and feral, that made her strange. She'd seen his picture in the paper, she said, the skin at her collarbone flushed magenta. And she just had to meet him.

He tried to be polite. When that didn't work, he kept moving his back to her. But she stood—waiting, circling, rapt—with no acknowledgment that I was there, in the room, not two feet from her. I watched, fascinated. "Excuse me," he said, with his eyes locked on me as if that would make her go. She touched his hip, and he startled. Her voice was soft. "You have a hole in your pocket. I can sew that for you." Gently at first, she began to pull at the lining until it became a mission. That's when he turned. He was angry. He told her to leave—this was a private conversation, he said, and she was being rude.

Before she reached the door, she looked back, and I saw that there was something satisfied about her. And the heat that had begun on her chest had risen like wildfire to her face.

"Can you believe that?" he said after the door closed.

"Do you know her?" I asked.

"Never seen her before in my life."

So I knew from the start that this happened, that this also went with the territory. But it hardly mattered then. It was the beginning—the time when you're sure, when you know by the way he looks at you across the room, by the way he stands or says your name, that he is yours.

More than a year later, I asked him to make me a promise. We'd been away for the weekend at a resort, and a girl had followed him around—thrown herself at him, we called it then. She wasn't a movie star or a model. She was tall and plain, someone I'd known vaguely in grade school. He showed no interest, and I don't know why it bothered me so much, but it did. There were other things: numbers pressed into his hand whether my head was turned or not, items in gossip columns. Some we'd laugh over; others I wondered about.

After that trip, I knew I didn't like what it did to me. I didn't want to be looking over my shoulder, to be always guessing what was true and what wasn't. I wanted to trust unless there was some reason not to. One afternoon in his kitchen, I asked him to tell me if he was ever unfaithful, if there was ever anyone else. He agreed. He understood, he said, but he wanted me to promise something as well: that if there was ever anyone for me, someone who meant nothing—a tryst—I not tell him. Other girlfriends had, and he didn't like it.

"You want me *not* to tell you?" I almost laughed, amazed at the difference between us.

"Yes," he said quietly. "I wouldn't want to know. I know you like me better than anyone, and I wouldn't want to know. If you cheated, I would take you back."

On a December night, long after that conversation in the kitchen, he asked for time.

It was after the summer we lived in LA, in the house by the beach with the shutters and the roses. When we returned to New York, John started his last year of law school, and I was cast in *A Matter of Degrees,* an independent film that was being shot in Providence. I played a seductress torn between two men—one dark and brooding, the other adoring—and made a lifelong friend out of Arye Gross, the talented actor who was playing the adoring one. While I was away in Providence, there was a phone call— a slight pulling back, which I attributed to distance. I knew all would be right, as it always was, once we were back in the same city.

Now I was wedged in a corner of the couch in his living room, and he was on the floor at my feet, the glare from the table lamp on his troubled face. His back was curved, his hair shorter than usual, and when he spoke, I thought I'd never seen him look so young. He was happy with me, with us—*the summer had been so happy*— but he wanted to see other people. Not forever. For a time. He knew where we were headed, and that was part of it.

I couldn't look away from him, and I wanted to, and though the couch was deep and the cushions sank, I tried to sit straight, as if the effort would mean something. I tried to reason, to argue, but when he reached for me, I cried. Was it someone . . . ? He stopped me before I could finish. "No, it's nothing like that. I love you." He couldn't imagine spending his life with anyone else, he confessed tearfully, as though it pained him to say it. And there was a connection in his mind with this time apart—this freedom of months—and the future he said we had.

Every good man goes down fighting. It was one of the things he said, and I'd never liked it. He would toss it off, breezy and knowing, when a friend got married or a roguish compadre settled down. Or whisper it loudly, as he held me down and tickled me. But that night, he said it the way you'd admit to a secret. Once, under his breath with his head bowed, and then as he looked up at me, his ankles crossed in front of him. I told him I wasn't going to fight him or trick him or make him do anything. If we got married, it would be because we both wanted to, and he would have to ask me.

I refused to believe it then—that saying of his. And for a long time after. But he was, of course, partly right. Some men, good or otherwise, do go down fighting. They are won without knowing how they've been taken.

At this point in the story, it's best if the girl storms off in a fury or, better yet, takes a lover. I did neither. He had his sayings, and I had mine, and "Love conquers all" was hardwired in me then like catechism.

A gay friend who knew us both suggested that I try the time-honored tradition of getting pregnant. "Don't be shocked," he said, smirking. "People do it all the time. He's crazy about you. He just needs a push." The fortune-teller pored over his chart. "It's Neptune," she said. "Delusion is heavily aspected for some time."

I confided in a worldly older friend. Though married to her second husband, with a Park Avenue life, she still carried a torch for

her first. Years had passed, but she still loved him. "Give him
rope," she advised. "Let him get it out of his system now." By that
time, he'd met Daryl Hannah. By that time, there had been an item
in the columns that he had called to refute—something he never
did. When I asked him, he was evasive. "We're just friends. She
doesn't even live here. And anyway, she has a boyfriend."

Whatever time we had decided on in December, it lasted six weeks.
By the end of January, he said he was desperate to see me, and I realized I wasn't inclined toward sharing. That winter, there were
passionate reunions and love letters left on balconies. We fought
like we never had, and in ways we were closer. But by spring, confusion returned. I had found things—a bent pair of cat-eye
glasses, a Filofax, an earring—and in May, after he graduated, we
said once again we would take time apart. We still saw each other,
but that's what we said.

There were distractions. A dreamy actor who took me to
French restaurants in the West Fifties and kept his Marlboros
tucked in the sleeve of his T-shirt. A musician who saw auras and
sent notes with wildflowers pressed in the pages. An older, upbeat
Wall Street hotshot who kept saying, *What do you see in him, anyway? He's not strong enough for you.* And when I was offered a part
in a new translation of *The Misanthrope*, one that would take me
out of town for four months—first to the La Jolla Playhouse in
California and then to the Goodman Theatre in Chicago—
I jumped at it. The production, updated to Hollywood, was to be
directed by Robert Falls. The set, inspired by a *Vogue* photo shoot
at Madonna's mansion in the Hollywood Hills, would feature gym
equipment and a vast closet filled with identical black lace-up
boots. Kim Cattrall was cast as the temptress Célimène, and this
time I was Éliante, the adoring one.

We met for dinner before I left. I chose a dress, black with small roses and a pencil skirt, that I knew he would remember, and when he whistled up at my balcony, a straw hat in his hand, I smiled. "You look like Huck Finn," I called down. We were on our way to Café des Artistes but ended up at the All State instead. At dinner, he ran his hand down my back, and closed his eyes. "What are you doing to me," he murmured. "You still make me melt." I had changed the outgoing message on my phone machine recently, and when he said it was needlessly provocative, I smiled like a cat. He told me about studying for the bar, "a mother beyond belief," and that his days and nights were like a monk's. He wasn't seeing anyone, he offered. *Why then, were we apart?* I didn't say this. I blinked. The spell of the evening was too potent.

We walked up Broadway in the soft June rain, we kissed in doorways, and he bought me irises pressed in damp paper.

I took that night with me, one he later called pure pleasure. I took it with me that summer, through phone calls of back-and-forth and misunderstanding and possibility. Through distance, through rumor.

I took it with me, until frayed and worn, it no longer was enough.

"Are you still there?"

Before I answered, I held the phone against my chest, trying not to imagine him where he was—on the white couch in his living room in New York, with his feet braced against the coffee table and all the lights out. I was in Chicago, in a short-term rental on North LaSalle that the Goodman had leased, boxes all around and Levolor blinds open. It was early evening at the beginning of November, and there'd been a strange bout of heat. But when I think of it now, the whole fall had been like that, bright, hot days one after another. The play had just closed, but I'd stayed on. I'd been cast in an independent film that was being shot in Chicago. Arye was in it, too, along with Courtney Cox.

I had seen John sporadically that summer and fall—at the Four Seasons in LA after he took the bar exam, a long weekend at the La Valencia in La Jolla, a smattering of days in New York between the California and Chicago runs, and then, in October, a night at the Drake, when we'd both tried to end things for good but couldn't.

"I'm here," I said finally, playing with the phone cord.

He told me I sounded different, distant, but really I had cried all day. And if I sounded distant—if I managed any sangfroid—it was practiced. I'd talked to two friends in New York before he called, and they had coached me: black or white, yes or no, fish or cut bait. On the yellow pad near the phone were words to remind me of what I'd already resolved, what I knew. But it wasn't only his presence that had a hypnotic effect on me; it was his voice as well.

"Are you still going to California?" he asked warily. After the night at the Drake that had been so painful, I was finally able to risk losing him. I'd flown to New York on my day off, and we met in Battery Park. We walked by the river, and I told him he was free to choose whatever he wanted, but I needed things to change, to move forward. I could no longer be in this limbo; he meant too much to me. And if they didn't change, if he couldn't—I was moving to LA when the movie was done.

He'd called that night not to tell me what he'd decided. He wanted me to meet him in Virginia three days later, while the weather was still good, to hike in Shenandoah National Park. He knew I had a break in filming, and he would bring everything, even boots. I just needed to show up. The friends in New York who gave advice would have said he was buying time.

"Can I ask you something?" I said.

"You can ask me anything."

"Why do you want to see me?"

"It helps me to see you," he said slowly. "I don't know . . . I think of you. I walk by your old apartment, and I think of you. I can't imagine you not being here. Or you being here without me. You're my best friend. I'm closer to you than anyone."

He pushed a while longer for the trip to the mountains, then changed his tack. "Just promise you'll sleep on it. You can even decide when you wake up that morning. There'll be a ticket for you at the airport and I'll be there regardless. I won't count on it, but I'll be glad if you come."

He knew me well. When pressed, I was stubborn. But if I felt like there was a choice, chances were I would acquiesce. In that way, we were alike.

I told him I would think about it.

"Wait. Don't get off," he said.

"What is it?"

I was lying on the floor, the phone now cradled against my shoulder. The white cord was coiled around my wrist, and the shadows from the traffic made a slide show on the low, laminated ceiling. I knew that, miles away in New York, he had not gotten up from the couch but was leaning forward, his head dropped, his elbows pressed on his knees.

"Just . . . don't get off," he repeated. "Not yet."

When I arrived at the small airport in Weyers Cave, Virginia, he'd been in town for hours, buying supplies and maps and organizing the gear. We were shy with each other at first, puttering about the car. My eyes adjusted; I hadn't seen him in weeks. In the parking lot of the Super Save, we poured nuts and dried fruit into baggies and transferred the apples, oranges, chocolate, sausage, and hard cheese into food sacks. He opened the trunk and pulled out two boxes of boots he'd bought in New York, unsure of which would fit me better. There were two frame backs, two water bottles, two sleeping bags. By early afternoon, we were on one of the feeder roads that lead to the Skyline Drive. He passed me the map with several trails circled. The higher peaks were farther north, but he thought I would like the one at the bottom best—the less crowded backcountry south of Loft Mountain.

For three days, there were hawks, streams, mud, and yellow leaves. It was a final gasp of warmth in what had been the longest Indian summer I could remember.

The last night, we had a fire. It was illegal, but we did it anyway. We were too far for the rangers, too far for anyone to care, and by our tent there was an already blackened circle of stones. My job was to gather twigs, and his was to start the fire and keep it going. We always brought poetry books when we camped to read aloud to each other, and before I left Chicago, he reminded me of that. He packed Seamus Heaney, and I brought Edna St. Vincent Millay, along with the one I always carried, my blue clothbound book of sonnets from the Yale series. I read number 129, the one about lust. I'd discovered it over the summer, and it had become my new favorite.

The night was clear. We drank Constant Comment spiked with whiskey, and I lay with my head in his lap while he told me stories of the stars. It didn't matter that I'd heard them before.

I asked him which of the seasons reminded him of us.

"The first snow. I don't know why, though. You?"

The truth was, it was all of them.

"The September part of summer," I said. "When it's still hot, but you know the next day it might be gone, and the leaves at Gay Head have bits of red in them."

He took me by the shoulders and pulled me to him, my hair in the way of his mouth. He brushed it back, and with his hands tangled there, I heard him say he had missed the end of summer with me. I heard him say that he was still mine.

In the morning, we smelled of smoke. He was up before me and had the water started on the tiny camp stove. He was crouched over what was left of the fire from the night before, stirring the ashes intently with a charred broken stick. When he saw me through the tent flap, he called me a sleepyhead and handed me a mug of tea.

We didn't talk about reuniting then, or about any of the things we said we would. Not that day. We packed up the camp after breakfast, and we walked. And when we crossed over the small river, the trail began to veer straight up from the valley.

I can almost see him now, just above me, scrambling on the granite ledge, pointing out the best handholds, the surest footholds. The sky was overcast when he turned back, and I squinted to look up. He asked what I thought my best and worst qualities were and the same for him. And he wanted to know what three things I loved best about him. "You're fishing," I teased. He frowned, but because it was his question, he went first. "Your hands. The place where your collarbone meets your neck. The curve of your hip when you lie on your side. When you read to me at night. And your letters, I love your letters."

"That's more than three."

"I know," he said, and kept climbing.

They weren't the things I'd imagined he would say. They were sweeter, more considered. The letters especially surprised me. I'd always written to him, and there were many that year—cajoling, seducing, longing, analyzing, pleading, scolding. Long letters that I'd thought had no effect. He shook his head. I save them, he said. They make me think.

Right then, I couldn't go any farther. The new boots he'd bought had given me blisters. He propped me on a flat rock, threw down his pack, dug out the first aid kit, and covered my foot with moleskin and white tape. It'll last, he said, handing me the canteen. We sat for a while looking over the narrow valley, and when we were ready, he took up my pack as well as his. I watched for a moment as he made it over the crest, the rolled neon sleeping bags bobbing off the metal frames.

That is what I love, I will think later, *remembering you with both our packs easy on your shoulders. That and the animal way you move on rocks. Your arm around me as we sleep. When you point to the constant stars—Orion, your favorite: hero and hunter. That you ask me this question. And that the mystery of the cord that ties us—even through this last year, through pain and heartache and the attentions of a beautiful woman—remains, whatever we choose when we leave this trail.*

It is what I would say to him now.

On the drive to the airport and our flights in opposite directions, I asked him about Daryl, if it was over. He didn't answer right away. His eyes were on the country road, his hands on the wheel of the white convertible he'd rented for the weekend. It had been a fantasy, he said, a way to deal with his fears of commitment. "She took on the fears of us." He'd begun therapy a few months before, and it had changed the way he spoke. "I was enamored, but not any longer."

I both believed and doubted him. We had decided nothing in

the Blue Ridge wilderness, but at the gate, before my flight to Chicago, we agreed to keep talking.

The film wrapped two weeks later. I went to LA but didn't stay long, and when I returned to New York, John took me to a benefit at the Plaza. We left early, and as we stood outside on the red-carpeted landing, the fog was so dense, we thought a cloud had descended on Fifth Avenue. He loosened his tie and slipped his tuxedo jacket over my bare shoulders, and I held the silk gown to one side as we walked. By the Saint-Gaudens statue, a row of hansom cabs waited. "Let's do it," he said. I was glad to see him happy. He'd found out he'd failed the bar exam weeks before, and the effects were defeating. With the press, he showed his game face, but alone he had cried in my arms.

He took my hand, and we ran across Central Park South to choose the horse we liked best. When the carriage entered the park, it was quiet, and the fog rolled beside us. It wasn't cold, but we huddled, cocooned under thick wool blankets. A sliver of moon, and all around, familiar shadows of the old limestone buildings that framed the park, the shapes and turrets we'd known since childhood.

He spoke first. He was intrigued by the way the last year and the time apart might have changed us. Our relationship would be different and, he believed, stronger. His voice sounded sad, but he said that he wasn't.

"Few people are so lucky to have what we do. I have a lot of hope."

I had hope too. My trust was frayed, but I had hope.

"Can you forgive me?" His head fell so that it rested on mine, the weight I'd longed for somehow painful, and we passed that way through the dark trees. "This is the first time . . ."

I waited, listening to hooves on pavement, listening to his breath.

"Yes," I began.

"It's the first time I thought I might lose you."

Before Christmas, on our way to stay with friends in Vermont, we drove upstate and looked at land near Albany. It hadn't snowed, but the ground crunched under our feet without give. What did I think, he asked, while the real estate agent waited in the car.

I hadn't wanted to go, I think now, because I knew what "land in Albany" meant. That he was thinking about it somewhere down the line, a life I feared might subsume me. I thought of his cousins' wives, one in particular. She was ten years older than I was, smart and elegant, and although I didn't know her well, she had always been kind to me. It was nothing she said, but her face held such sadness, even as she smiled. Like a memory of pleasure but no longer.

Before we left, he told the agent no. He agreed it wasn't right. And he asked me then, in that cold field toward the beginning of a new year, whether I could see myself living up here someday, and whether I thought I'd always be an actress.

I said yes to both.

We're in a field in New Jersey not far from his mother's house. We wear jackets and the sun is out. October bright. That night, we'll have a fire. At the far end of the field, there's a bank of trees near a brook, and the leaves are a shudder of pale gold. I'm on Frank, and he's on the new horse, the black one, and as he leans down to pat the glossy neck, I think how gentle he can be.

We've warmed them up and take one quick canter around the ring. I rub my thumb along the rein. I know what comes next. It's what he's thinking of, has been all along. As we drove and talked of other things. In the stable with the saddles and the leads. And without question, once the barn door opens.

I see it in his face, a certain widening of the eyes. The way his jaw gets tight but he could be smiling. He's thinking of the feeling—the flying flat-out run across the field. The feeling where your heart beats against your throat and you know you are alive.

I'm thinking of it, too. How I'll dig my heels down this time, knot my fingers halfway up the mane if I'm afraid. How I'll hold the horse close like a lover. I won't think about the rest: the pocket holes that pit the field, a slip, a break, a twig. That I'm an average rider at best. I'll keep my eyes burrowed on those trees ahead and pray I hold my seat. I'll find the part in me like him that craves the rush of speed.

I don't know why it is, but I feel safe. It may be because he believes in me. Or the way I know we'll laugh when we reach the other side. Out of breath, relieved, sated. And after a break, when the horses are ready, we'll go again. Each time, it will be easier, faster. Longer. Until I say no. I can always say no. He won't go without me. He's told me this, and I believe him.

There's something in this jeweled day. A thrill. A grace. That I am with him before the leaves fall. That we share this like a secret, this pushing back at fear, at death, on the backs of his mother's horses.

He turns to me and waits. I shorten the rein. I smell the dry earth, the leather.

"Ready?" he says. He's certain.

I look across at the trees and see how close they really are.

Ending

If we do not burn
How will these shadows turn to light?

—NAZIM HIKMET

On a November night, when the tops of the trees were bare, John came home from dinner with his mother. It was the time of the year he called "difficult." I met him by the door of his apartment where I had been waiting, and undid the chain in the brass lock. He was quiet, troubled by something. We sat on the couch in the living room, and he said that that night they had spoken of his father. In the course of the meal, his mother told him that if his father were to come back to her now, she wondered if she might say no. Hesitating, as she had, he showed me. He held up his hand, palm pressed out, and with his eyes closed, he began to shake his head slowly.

When he did this, I saw her in him. Her eyes, her mouth, her long neck, her tender, wise face clouded. I knew the weight he felt hearing this—I held my father's secrets—but the strength required for her to lift her hand, that I did not know. It was something I could only imagine. I did not know then that there are those you love no matter how much they hurt you, no matter how many years have passed since you felt them in the morning. I did not know how long it took to get over such a love, and that even when you did, when you loved again, you would always carry a sliver of it in your stitched-together heart. I did not know that you could love them in death, and that if one day they returned to you in a dream or half sleep, you might hold up your hand as she had done, because life and time had changed you.

Timing is the short answer. There was no single fight, no dramatic flourish, no black and white of tabloid scribes. We ended the way things do with most people when it's long and complicated, when there's love and desire and much that works and some that doesn't. We ended slowly.

Romances, like stories, have endings. In a restaurant overlooking Mulholland, a legendary but reformed lothario once told me that marriage is an ongoing conversation, but romance is something different altogether. "It's from the French word for story," he said, "and by definition it has a beginning, a middle, and an end." And if this were a story and I had to choose a dénouement, just one, it would be a night in early December 1990.

As the elevator inched its way to the top floor of a redbrick building on Hudson Street, one of two on that block with a crowned cornice, I rehearsed what I would say. John was waiting for me in the loft he'd moved to six months before. We both knew there would be a fight. He was better in an argument than I, but tonight, armed with facts, I would not back down. My anger was rare, but when ignited, it was the smoldering Old Testament sort—of I am right and you are wrong and I have ocular proof. That night, it felt like strength. The truth was more fragile; I could no longer continue as we were. We'd reunited the year before to see if things would move forward, but they hadn't. We hadn't. He'd warned me long ago never to give him an ultimatum, as they didn't work with him, but in October I had.

I can't remember now what it was that had set me off that night. It could have been any number of things—a phone number, a postcard left out, rumors of him with a raven-haired beauty, to which he responded, She's just a stupid model. Or the specter of Daryl, once receded, now hovering.

Or it could simply have been the wearing distance that had grown between us. I no longer remember, and it no longer matters. But what is burned in my mind is his face as the elevator door slid wide and how seeing him, I was instantly disarmed. It was a face not of fight, deception, or denial. It was a boy's face, open and marked by sorrow.

Still, I began my list of grievances. To each, he replied, "You're right." And when I had no more words, he murmured, "It's bigger than this. Don't be afraid." But I was.

He took me in his arms and carried me up the slotted pine steps, like a bride over a threshold, to his bedroom. The room upstairs was dark, save for the silver city falling through a tall window. The loft was a sublet. Some of the trappings in the room were his the masks he'd collected, a valet stand, a lap desk with a secret compartment I'd given him one Christmas, his father's padded rocker, a carved Indonesian sylph with wings and a painted smile. But others were foreign, heavy with someone else's stories, someone else's desires.

He sat on the bed, and I went to the bench under the skylight. I knew if I sat close to him, I would not hear what he was going to say—the nearness of scent and skin would make words and understanding impossible and I wanted to hear him. I placed my hands on the lacquered wood on either side of me, and he reached for the lamp on the table beside his bed. As he turned the knob, I saw that his face had changed.

In the half-light, his head down, he spoke of trials and tests, of soldiers, Green Berets, Greek legends, and failure. Sometimes he wept. There were things he had to tell me, things that only now had become clear to him. He confessed that he was not a man yet; maybe in a different time, one of warriors and rituals, he would have been. The words pained him. "I haven't gone through the fire," he kept saying. "It's like I haven't gone through the fire."

On another night, I would have bolstered him, held him, convinced him otherwise, believed that anything was possible, but that night, I stayed on the wooden bench and I listened.

"How can I reach out my hand to you? How can I ask you to join my life when I don't know what it is yet?" he cried. "You're lucky, you have a calling. You know what your life is."

"You don't want to be a lawyer?" He had started working for the Manhattan district attorney's office that fall, but as soon as I said it, I knew how foolish the words sounded. Of course, he didn't. Torts and voir dire were antithetical to his natural gifts. But he'd worked hard, and because he had, I'd assumed it was what he wanted, for a time at least.

He began to speak about the theater with such tender loss—grief even—as if it were a paramour he would always carry a torch for, one he could not part with but would never fully possess. I'd known his passion and his talent for acting. I had stood on a stage with him and looked into his eyes. But until that night, I hadn't fully known his regret.

"If that's what you want, you can do it. Just decide. You're a wonderful actor—you can do anything you want." I still believed that.

"No, I can't," he said, wincing slightly.

I didn't ask, but I knew by the way he spoke that it was not his mother, as the papers so often opined, that stood between him and an actor's life. It was the knowledge that deep within, no matter how much he loved it, it was not his path to follow, something Professor Barnhill had intuited long ago.

We talked about politics and, as he had at other times, he called it the family business. Was that what he wanted? I reminded him of the associates and friends, true or otherwise, who waited in the wings for him to say the word. He knew this but lowered his head. "I haven't done anything yet to earn it. I need to know what I believe."

The room had darkened, and the city was almost quiet, only the odd car rumbling up Hudson Street like a wave rolling. I moved to the bed and sat close to him.

"I've only told three people in my life that I loved them," he confessed. "You, Sally, my sister."

"And your mother."

"Yes, my mother."

He stroked my face. "You're my compass," he whispered, the lamplight hitting him golden from behind.

Compass? But he was the fearless one, the one who knew the seas and trails.

"You've always been my compass," he said, as if I should have known. "I'll be lost without you. I think of the time ahead and it's like a desert."

I said nothing. I closed my eyes and held him. He had imagined it, this desert, but I hadn't. I couldn't.

I stayed with him that night, and in the morning when I asked, he agreed not to call me for a while. We both needed time to think.

Four months earlier, we had sat on the steps of one of the row houses on East Tenth Street, across from St. Mark's Church. It was hot that July, and we'd just had Indian food. John was studying for the bar for the third time, and I'd finished a run of *All's Well That Ends Well*. In the spring, he'd decided to move downtown to Tribeca, and when I returned from Los Angeles, where I was doing a movie of the week, we looked at lofts with his real estate agent. We had decided to live together, but then, when he didn't pass the bar for the second time, he asked if we could hold off. "It's important. It's for our future," he'd said. I knew his anxiety about passing was not the entire reason, but I didn't push it. I relished my freedom almost as much as he did, and like all romantics, I wanted "Will you marry me?" to come freely.

In front of the iron gates of the old stone church, sweat on the backs of our knees, he told me he never wanted to get divorced. For him, that would be the biggest failure, and if it ever came to that, he'd go off to the mountains alone for a spell. I told him I had realized something, too, that summer. Although there were marriages where infidelity was understood, even agreed to, and many of them worked, I knew it was not something I could do, no matter how much I loved him, and I wanted him to know this.

"I don't want that either."

"You don't? Then what happens?"

He was staring at my hands.

"I don't know . . . It's like I fall off the wagon."

Before Christmas, we met at my apartment to exchange gifts. We'd spoken but hadn't seen each other since the night at his loft. I wore a short navy kilt with black tights and high boots, the fashion then, but when I caught my reflection in the glass, I looked like a child. I promised myself that, no matter what, while he was here I would not cry. The reality of what we'd spoken about was beginning to define itself. I'd arranged a time to get my things from his apartment, I'd returned his key, and tonight he would give me mine. I'd asked him to have an item placed in the columns after Christmas saying that we'd split up and, if he could, not to be photographed with anyone for a month. One month, I thought, would be enough. I was trying to figure out how to move on, but in my heart, I hadn't. And when I heard his steps heavy on the stairs, I couldn't wait until he walked through the door.

I'd bought him mother-of-pearl cuff links, a painted kite from Chinatown, and a Dalvey pocket compass. I was uncertain about the last gift, weighted as it was with meaning, but I wrapped it anyway. He gave me a down comforter and diamond drop earrings. "One a necessity, the other most certainly an ornament," he said. With the gifts, there was a card with a photograph of a forlorn dog on the front. He asked me not to read it until he left. In the firelight, colored paper all around, he suddenly grew tearful, and it surprised him. "I've missed you . . . Why aren't you crying, Puppy? You're always the one to cry."

Before he left, he handed me a shiny yellow box with a grosgrain ribbon and a tiny gift card. "Dear, Darling Christina—All my Love, Jackie," it said. Inside was a cream chiffon scarf, edged in black, as sheer as could be. I took it out of the tissue and draped it over my shoulders.

At the door, he stopped, then turned back. His voice was soft.

"I'm the boss of you always."

"Not true." I was trying to smile.

"No one will ever love you as I have." He got the words out and stood there a moment, then closed the door and slipped out into the night.

After he left, I opened the card. "Christina Christina Christina Christina I miss the name—I've started notes to you many times that could have burned holes through wood." Before I reached the end, I fell apart.

That's the thing about timing. It has nothing to do with love.

That January, the film about Stieglitz and O'Keeffe was finally happening. My part was smaller, but I was excited. No longer a feature, *An American Place* would air on PBS's *American Playhouse,* with Christopher Plummer as Stieglitz and Jane Alexander's husband, Ed Sherin, directing. In the interim, I discovered that Dorothy Norman was still alive and through friends was able to meet her. Oddly, I had grown up around the corner from her modern town house and had passed it on my way to school each morning. Glancing up at the strange, glass-block windows, I'd always wondered what it would be like to be on the inside looking out.

At the end of February, as soon as the love scenes with Mr. Plummer ended, I got on a plane to Cumberland Island. Behind, in my apartment, were red roses from John, now dried, that I hadn't managed to throw out, the comforter he'd given me at Christmas, and a letter asking me to wait for him. In it, he wrote how difficult the separation had been and how he might have done things differently.

He went on to describe the recent funeral of Murray McDonnell, outside of whose barn we'd had our first kiss. In the eulogy, one of Mr. McDonnell's sons had said that most of his father's life before he married was spent trying to capture the heart of his wife, Peggy. "I thought, that's me," he wrote. "I spent most of my teenage-adult years trying to capture the heart of the girl next door—you. I realize you can't be in contact, but it can't be that way forever. Let's wait a season or so and see what the times bring us. The stakes are different now and I understand what they are. In the meantime, I think about how cold it is outside and I hope you are warm warm warm."

On Cumberland, I stayed with friends. I slept and I read. I walked the soft paths. I rode horses on the north end and gathered clams and oysters for midnight feasts. I played with my friends' towheaded children, and we hunted for arrowheads in the marshes near Dungeness. Gogo Ferguson, Andy's sister, had invited me. "Come, I'll take care of you," she'd said. And she did. Slowly, in a place that held memory, I began to shake the sadness. I tried not to think of his letter. There were shards of hope in it, hope that pulled at me, hope that had become what was most painful.

The day before I left the island, I walked the wide beach alone and wondered if my heart would ever heal, if I would ever fall in love again. I spoke aloud as if the air would answer. At the lip of the shore, pipers, oystercatchers, and gulls stood as silent witnesses facing the sea and a bruised sky. It had been warm for February, but now the wind was picking up, and thick clouds rolled in from the west. The winter beach was different from when I'd walked here with John almost five years before. It was littered with moon shells and the broken backs of horseshoe crabs. Soon it began to rain, spotting the pale sand gray.

A red truck drove up alongside me. It was Pat from the Inn. His hair, once wild, was short. He leaned over the passenger's seat, and we caught up. He was married now with daughters. He asked if I wanted a ride back to Greyfield.

"Thanks, I'm going to walk."

"Looks to be a downpour."

"I'll take my chances."

He stared at me, bemused. "You've changed."

"How's that?"

"You don't remember?" He grinned as if it were an answer. "You don't, do you?"

I shook my head.

"When you first came here years ago, you *really* didn't like the rain."

It took me a moment. A dry truck. A flowered dress. August heat. A boy I loved. I began to smile, remembering. "No . . . No, I didn't. But I like it now, I like the rain."

I watched as the truck pulled away. It turned inland, got smaller, and disappeared over the high dunes on the path to Greyfield. I dug my hands into my pockets and kept walking. I walked past the Rockefeller gazebo and the Nightingale Trail. I walked past a herd of horses at Sea Camp and the salt marshes near Dungeness. I walked as far as I could on the empty beach in the cool winter rain.

I had bought him a compass, but I never gave it to him that night. It was there in the pocket of my jacket as I walked, my fingers warm on the metal. I kept it with me for a time—in a drawer or on my bureau; sometimes I held it. Until one day, without knowing how, I could no longer find it.

He had called me his compass, but he was wrong in that.

He had been mine.

After

Remembrance is a form of meeting.

—KAHLIL GIBRAN

There is a land of the living and a land of the dead
and the bridge is love, the only survival,
the only meaning.

—THORNTON WILDER

It was early June 2000, almost a year to the anniversary of his death, and I was driving across the country with a man I was in love with, afraid of the grief I would feel the closer we got to New York and July 16. We'd been in the Grand Canyon for two nights, and John had been present in my mind. He loved this place. Ten years before, we'd planned to go, but a play had kept me in New York, and he had gone without me. I got a postcard from him, telling me how much he loved it, how hot it was, and how he would have much preferred me in the sleeping bag next to him rather than his friend Dan, aka Pinky. "Ha! Ha, Baby!" he wrote.

There's a picture he gave me: John in a tank top, green-and-black nylon shorts, mirrored glasses, and hiking boots, dancing the funky chicken in celebration of the seven-thousand-foot descent on the Bright Angel Trail. The light is failing, and there are shadows on his face.

On the drive northeast to Durango the next day, we stopped at the Navajo National Monument to see the ancient cliff dwellings. We paid the fee and walked through the small museum. My friend went on ahead while I lingered by the headdresses and the labeled pottery shards. When I was done, I stepped into the open-air courtyard and began to cross toward the turnstile entrance to the dwellings across the gorge. Out of the corner of my eye, I noticed a small girl, maybe five, twirling like a dervish for an older couple, who sat with folded hands, watching. You couldn't help but watch. Half-wild in a dirty T-shirt—with hair in her mouth and her arms spread wide—she lifted her face to the sky, as if she was pivoting from the very center of her heart.

What freedom, I thought. I used to be that girl: asking people in airports if they wanted to see me dance, singing songs in kindergarten I made up on the spot instead of bringing a favorite toy to show-and-tell. I had a dispensation from Miss Mellion and even a title, "Make-Up-Song Girl." I used to be that girl and I wasn't anymore.

I smiled, dazzled by the heat. Then, at the turnstile, with my eyes on the ruins ahead, I heard her say something to her grandparents, to the bright sky, and to no one in particular. "Do you know where John Kennedy is?"

How odd, that I should pass by just now. Maybe she meant his father. Maybe I hadn't heard right. The heat.

She kept spinning. "Do you *know* where he is!" she insisted in singsong. "In the ocean? . . . Noooo. In heaven? . . . Noooo. In the Indian spirit world?" She paused briefly, then answered herself, "Yes! Yes! He's in the Indian spirit world!"

Laughing, sibyl-like, she spun faster.

I stood for a moment, half-expecting her to disappear. When she didn't, I lowered my hands to the shiny metal bar in front of me and pushed until it clicked. I didn't look back until I'd reached the bench where my friend was waiting. I sat near him, unable to grasp what I had just heard. Across the gorge, shadows began to dart like swallows from the ancient portals in the rocks, and finally, when I could speak, I told him the story.

It was only later that I knew, on a trip I took alone to Gay Head and the lighthouse, to the wild grasses and the smooth road near his mother's house called Moshup Trail and the view of the sea where the plane had fallen. I stayed at a bed-and-breakfast nearby, an old whaling captain's house, with sand on the floor and a ball-and-claw bathtub in the small room. It had been eight years since he'd died. I needed to go back, but on the ferry from Woods Hole, I argued with myself. *What are you doing, you don't need to come here; you've already said your goodbyes.*

At dusk, on the day before I was to leave, I walked back from the beach through the thick dune to the road. It was September and warm, and for some reason I thought of the girl. I'd remembered her from time to time, as if she were a piece of a puzzle. Her spinning; her words; the laughing. And the precarious fact that my lingering over a particular shard of pottery had made me a witness.

By then, the sun had fallen fully, vanishing into the water at the end of the cliffs, and I knew, in that violet light, miles and years from where it had happened, that I had been given a gift among the rocks and the wide sky of the Anasazi. One of acceptance.

I believe God speaks through others. Maybe John's spirit is at peace in the places he loved. Dancing in a canyon. Swimming off the Vineyard. Flying in the clouds. In all the wild places, where he was free.

On May 3, 2004, I was driving north on Highway One thinking about silence. When the car began its climb up the narrow coast road, passing the sign that divides Monterey and San Luis Obispo counties, I opened the windows and let the sea breeze in. It was the heat of the day, and the sky was cloudless. On the passenger's seat beside me was a white cowboy hat with a blue jay feather tucked in its brim, a present from my friend Rebecca. Tomorrow was my birthday. I would turn forty-four, and I had just been diagnosed with breast cancer.

I had seen the heavy wooden cross sunk into the side of the road at Lucia many times in my sojourns to the Central Coast over the past fifteen years, but I'd never stopped. Like a pilgrim to the sexy stuff, I kept moving on to the heart of Big Sur, to the places whose names were chants—Deetjen's, Nepenthe, Esalen, Ventana. But less than two weeks before, when I heard my surgeon, Nora Hansen, say the words that left me with none, when she held her blue eyes steady on me as I cried, I knew this was where I had to come. I knew that somehow, in this place I'd never been, I would be changed. Against the advice of doctors and family, I delayed the second surgery and booked six days of silent retreat at the Hermitage, a Camaldolese Benedictine monastery high in the Santa Lucia Mountains.

At Ragged Point, I stopped for gas and to stretch my legs. I had driven more than 250 miles from LA with only the radio for company, and for the last hour or so, it was static. Harleys in caravan roared by on their way to San Francisco. *Silence. A silent retreat.* What was I thinking? Was I crazy? I'd been baptized, and my bloodlines stretched back to the peat of Galway, Cork, and Kerry, but I wasn't sure I was still a Catholic.

And how could I be silent? In the past month, my mind had become like an unruly child, chattering, wandering, obsessing over details, ever since the mammogram report came back "Birad IV: Suspicious Finding." Sleep meant nothing; stillness was a memory. I spent hours on the computer memorizing medical studies, percentages, risk factors. I stared at the ghostly pattern of calcifications, a crescent of moondust on a negative. To the handful of people I told, I talked of nothing else. I was gripped by fear—fear of death, fear of change. I had no script for what was happening to me. And at that moment in the parking lot at Ragged Point, I was terrified of silence. I pulled the top strap of the seat belt under my chest so it wouldn't hit the stitches, and started the car anyway.

At Lucia, I came to the cross I had passed before and took a hard right. The long afternoon light had begun and rabbits darted on either side of the car. I downshifted and drove up the two-mile dirt switchback. At the top was a simple church built in 1959, the flax-colored paint faded. A bookstore stood alongside it, with the monks' enclosure behind. The smell of chaparral was everywhere.

"We've been waiting for you. Welcome." Father Isaiah was a slender man, bearded, in a white robe and Tevas. We had spoken on the phone two days before, and as he led me to the retreat house, a semicircle of nine rooms that faced the Pacific, he explained the rules. Silence was to be observed except in the bookstore. Meals were to be taken alone in one's room. Food and showers could be found in the common area at the center of the house. A hot lunch was prepared daily. If I wished, I could join the monks for the Liturgy of the Hours, but it wasn't required. Nothing was.

"Vigils begin at 5:30 A.M. And Lauds are at 7:00."

I didn't know what Lauds were, but I nodded as if I did.

We reached the retreat house. Each of the doors had a small metal plaque with the name of a saint on it, except for those at either end. Father Isaiah stood by a saintless one. It had an emblem of the Sacred Heart and my name on a slip of paper tucked into the edge of the rusted metal. Before I had time to wonder at the synchronicity, he opened the door. The room was clean and small: a narrow captain's bed with a wool blanket, a desk and chair, and a pine rocker. A large picture window opened on a tiny private garden, where at dawn and dusk, deer, fox, and quail would pass.

"The monks are available for spiritual direction. If that's something you want, just ask and I'll arrange it."

I dropped my bags and took a breath.

"If you feel like talking, come find me in the bookstore," he said brightly, and set off for Vespers before I could answer.

I didn't make it to Vespers that night. Or to Lauds the next morning. I don't know how long I stayed in the simple room with the hard bed and the window on the world. There was no one to come get me, no one to answer to, no one to buck up for. The bare walls were a comfort, and the silence I had feared, a relief. I ate the monks' food. I slept. I read. I wept until there was nothing left. Pain broke me open. In the darkness, I let it cradle me; I let it fall all around me.

On the second morning, lulled by the bells, I trudged to the church before dawn and joined the monks for Vigils. They sat, white-robed in the nave, facing not the altar but each other. I saw Father Isaiah, his clear voice leading the canticles and antiphons, the psalms and the Benedictus. I slipped into the back row. For the next four days, I fell into their rhythm—the rhythm of men on the mountain and the consecration of each hour of the day through prayer and contemplation. I didn't have faith, not then. But I followed theirs. The words I had heard before, somewhere in my childhood, but now they were rich with ancient meaning. Now they were words to rest in, and I chanted along with the monks. *Gloria Patri et Filio et Spiritui Sancto . . . et nunc et semper et in saecula saeculorum.*

After Lauds, I walked up a rise near the retreat house. Tangled in high grass by a large rock was a single wild iris, a small miracle. I climbed up the rock and wrapped my knees to my chest. On my back, I felt the beginnings of the sun's warmth, golden fingers that reached over the gray morning hills. I thought of those whom I had loved deeply, those who had loved me well and were no longer alive. My father, my grandmothers—the one with the medallion and the one who had married in red. My friend Christopher, who'd died of AIDS three year before, and Jonathan Larson, the young composer of *Rent,* whom I had known briefly. I thought of John's mother. They had believed in me, and their belief was like a hand that pushes you up the last part of the mountain or points you down a path, overgrown, you hadn't known was there, but once you're on it, your feet dusty with it, you find it was the way all along.

My father had been dead for almost twelve years, but sitting on that rock with the sun behind me, I missed him more than ever—the long lunches at a favorite Chinese restaurant on Third Avenue, his deep embrace, his dogged optimism, even his anger. Whatever his flaws, he was there for me in a crisis. He fought for me, and he relished the fight.

After his stroke in the spring of 1987, he began to regain his speech and the ability to walk, but this vital man, once the life of the party, called Fun Daddy by my friends in grade school, would lie in a darkened bedroom most of the day staring at the ceiling. "Just resting," he'd murmur. I was twenty-six and believed that everything improved, everything went forward if you just tried hard enough. It was what my father had taught me. I believed that with the right doctor, the right drug, the right diet, he would get better; he would become my father again.

During those days, Mrs. Onassis always asked after him. Even before he was sick, we would trade tales of our fathers, of their charm and panache, of how well they danced and how well they laughed. There was one story in particular she smiled over. Her parents had recently divorced, and Jack Bouvier would arrange to borrow dogs from a neighborhood pet store for his weekend visits—incurring the wrath of his ex-wife and the delight of his daughters.

One July morning on Martha's Vineyard after John had gone windsurfing, she asked how my father was. In the front foyer, with a wall of burnt orange leading up the staircase to her bedroom, I found myself crying in front of the one person I never thought I'd cry in front of. She guided me to a tufted chair nearby and let me talk. Her eyes grew moist. Sometimes she nodded, but her gaze never left me. Then she spoke.

"All will be well, I promise."

"Really?" I searched her face for clues.

How could she know? But then I thought, if anyone could discern the impossible, she would be able to—I endowed her with that much wisdom. Like Cassandra, through beauty and sorrow she had a gift, and somehow she knew that my father would come back to me. But that is not what happened. My father did not get well. For the next five years, there were ebbs and flows of health, a slew of operations, depression, painful physical therapy, the amputation of his right leg, until his death alone at Beth Abraham in the Bronx on a frigid November night in 1992.

All will be well. Seventeen years later, I knew her meaning. You will find the courage to walk with grace through whatever life gives you. It's what she had done, and I wanted to hear her say those words to me now, as I doubted my ability to walk through the next hour, to put even one foot in front of the other. A long relationship had ended almost three years before, and although I had good friends and family, cancer is isolating. Loved ones don't always know how to help you. It makes them afraid, and I felt bereft and alone.

John and I had once climbed the hills just north of here. As he often did when we hiked and I flagged near the top, he told me to keep going. He took my pack with his and walked behind, his free hand prodding me along. *Couragio.* As the second surgery drew closer, I wanted a hand to push me forward, a lover's arm draped around me, someone to carry my pack for just a few steps. I wanted someone who loved me to tell me not to be afraid. And it seemed, on that rock, I wanted to talk to the dead. In moments of great need, time becomes a trick, and the sky can open. And so it was. Perhaps it was mere longing, but I felt him there with me, his arm heavy on my shoulder, his head dipped toward mine.

We had come to Big Sur, both of us for the first time, for Easter in 1990. By the time the year was up, we would no longer be together. We stayed at the Ventana in a suite with pitched cedar ceilings and a hot pool that steamed at night in the spring rain. We hiked and bicycled and gathered giant pinecones on a mountaintop and talked about our future, a thing we didn't always do. At Nepenthe, we bought postcards we didn't send and books we didn't read and kept returning to the Henry Miller Library, which, regardless of the hours posted, was always closed. On Easter Sunday, we went to Mass at a chapel in the forest and stood in the back. We huddled on the windswept beach at Pfeiffer, the sand whipping our faces, a beach I would return to years later with another lover on a windier day.

The morning we drove to San Francisco to catch our flight back east, he pulled the rental car over at an outlook north of Partington Cove. We stood there on the cliffs, silent, breathing our last of the sea air before the drive north. The navy water below was studded with whitecaps and sea otters. Above, birds of prey circled.

"Look—red-tailed hawk." He took his hand from my waist and pointed up, not excited but pleased. He had an affinity for these birds, and because they are the most common of hawks— adaptive, with territory in desert and forest from Canada to Panama—he was always pointing them out. We'd stop a moment, watch them soar, pay homage. It seemed to calm him that wherever he was, red-tailed hawks were there, watching over him like wild kindred spirits.

I raised my head, following his gaze, and, squinting, tried to make out the buzzards from the hawk. He explained the differences as he always did. Head, belly, tail, wingspan. I'm not sure whether I could see them or not, or whether I just liked hearing him tell me. It was something that made me love him fiercely, this conviction of his that it was of utmost importance that I, as a member of the human race, know the difference between a red-tailed hawk and a turkey buzzard, and he wouldn't quit until I did.

As I scanned the sky, he told me that hawks bond beyond mating, some for life, and that when they court, the males make steep dives around the females until their talons lock and they spiral together to the ground.

"That's awful—you're making it up!" I cried.

Pleased by my response, he kept on.

"But you, Puppy, the way *you* will tell red-tailed hawks is by the way they *shriek* when they are hungry for rabbitsandsnakesandsquirrels, just like when you are hungry and you shriek and squeal."

"I do not. Stop it, John!"

"Oh, but you *are* right now."

"You're tickling me!" I yelled, and ran to the car. We were still laughing when we pulled up to the general store for sandwiches. We both knew, when he said I was hungry, that it was he who needed to eat.

Passing over Bixby Bridge with Big Sur fading behind us, I turned and touched his cheek. "King," I said to him, "let's come back next year."

The afternoon before I was to leave the Hermitage, I met with Father Daniel for spiritual direction. I walked to the chapel fingering a jade Buddha on a red string that my brother had brought back from China. He had given it to me the day before the biopsy, and now it hung, day and night, around my neck. The doors of the church were heavy. I opened them and met a round man in a white robe who looked like he had lived. He led me to a small room near the font of holy water, and when he quoted Jung and Robert Johnson, I liked him at once. For more than an hour, I told him about my life. I told him everything I could remember, the last failed love affair, guilts I had forgotten, anything that weighed on me. I even spoke of the pain I'd felt years before when I'd found out that John had gotten married on Cumberland. It surprised me. So much time had passed, but an inkling of it was there, deep within me.

I told him how afraid I was. I said that now, when I needed it most, I could not pray. It was as though my knees would not bend. As I spoke, I realized I was ashamed I had cancer.

"Pray from where you are," he said.

"But I am so broken," I whispered back. The scar across my breast was in my heart as well.

"God loves you just as you are. Pray from where you are."

"But I don't know if I still believe. I doubt so much—I don't know why I'm here. I don't know if I'm still a Catholic. There's so much I question."

He smiled, leaning back in his chair, and folded his hands over his belly. "I imagine you are *because* you question."

"But, Father . . . I don't believe in sin."

He waited for me to go on, and when I didn't, he said, "Sin, in the Greek, means missing the mark. An archery term. That's all it is. That which has kept you from God."

He asked if I wanted to receive the sacrament of reconciliation, what I knew as confession. And although I'd sworn to myself that morning that I would not confess anything because I didn't believe in it; although it had been more than thirty years since I'd said my Hail Marys in the dark and leaned against the confessional grate in the cold hall outside the Sacred Heart chapel, trying to make out the priest's face through the crisscross of metal (wondering if he was the handsome one or the old one); although I hated the words *sinner, penance, unworthy* with the ire of a rebel, I said yes. And when I did, words fell and unburdened my heart of secrets I hadn't known were stones.

The monk's eyes looked deep into mine. His voice was gentle. "Your penance, and this will not be easy for you, on your walk today, when you see something pleasing—a flower unfurling, a cloud going by, anything—I want you to imagine that you are the only person on this earth and God has created this beauty just for you. Remember, it will be hard for you. Can you do this?" I nodded, wiping my face with the back of my hand. Father Daniel then took golden oil from a small glass cruet and with his fingers marked the sign of the cross on my forehead. "This is the sacrament of the sick," he said. "You may ask for it at this time."

I stepped outside the chapel. The heat had abated, and I began to walk west on the path that led to a wooden bench and a view of the Pacific crashing at the cliffs, a thousand feet below. With each step, I watched my life go past, like a film in my mind's eye—chances missed, risks taken, fears, pleasures, joys, loves. The ghosts. I let them pass, and they knit themselves together as stories, my stories.

How much longer do I have? I wondered. Three months, a year, two years, five? Would the story end now, in the middle? Or would I live as long as my great-grandmother, dying on her ninety-second birthday after breakfast and the paper. I did not know, but something in these hills had allowed my mind to quiet so that I could name my fears. And I felt the possibility that I might be able to navigate the challenges and choices of the months ahead and accept where I was—whatever happened.

When I reached the bench at the edge of the overlook, I stood and watched the sea. The cliffs here were higher, the sweep of sky grander, but I thought of Gay Head.

Then the monk's words came back to me. *This will be hard for you.* I smiled. I was a slow learner; things often were. Father Daniel had spoken of God's love, a greater love. He said that grace and forgiveness are there for us just as we are, in our vulnerability and in our humility, in our fear and in our frailty, when we are at our most human. That we are loved not for what we do or how we appear, but because each one of us is a child of God.

I looked up. A red hawk was soaring, its tail flamed and fanned to catch the wind. No sound. No effort. I closed my eyes. Far below, waves were breaking. I could hear my own breath. I could feel my heart beating.

February 1986

It's our first weekend away together, a February long weekend. The day we leave, I buy a new coat on impulse—a camel-hair coat, long and belted at the waist. It's soft and it drapes. I get it on the last day of the Bergdorf 70 percent off sale, and though I'm a four and it's an eight, I must have it. The back has a deep vent, and it swishes when I walk. And in the store mirror, I don't see a flushed-faced girl in a too-big coat; I see Katharine Hepburn. I hand over my "for emergencies" credit card. The saleswoman cuts off the tags and packs my old coat in the lavender shopping bag. I slip the new one on and walk out onto Fifty-eighth Street near the Paris Theatre and the drained stone fountain by the Plaza.

On the way up to the Vineyard, we hit a winter storm. I spend most of the flight with my face buried against him, saying prayers I thought I'd forgotten. With every pitch and drop of the small commuter plane, I squeeze his hand. After circling for an hour, we're stranded on the mainland for the night. Everyone claps when the pilot lands in Hyannis, and we step off woozy into the dark night. John drops coins in the pay phone and wakes someone, the housekeeper at his grandmother's, to let them know we'll be spending the night. "We're set," he says. It's easy.

In the taxi on the way over, he admits he was frightened, too, but I never would have guessed it. His face showed nothing.

When we finally get to the Vineyard the next day, it's foggy. We stock up at Cronig's Market, then follow the lonely roads, ones I've never seen, past shuttered Victorians and shingled farmhouses. By Chilmark, the land turns bare and wild, and when State Road splits, we take the lower fork and turn onto an unmarked dirt road. Bert, the caretaker, has opened up the main house, and that's where we'll stay. But in the afternoon, John takes me to the Tower. It's been shut for months. He holds the door open, and I step into the new-wood smell. When I come back with him that summer, and those that follow, the Tower is where we stay.

The next morning, he takes me to the cliffs. The sun's out, and he wants to orient me. My sense of direction is usually good, but the island has me turned around. We drive up Moshup Trail. Gray heads of houses nestle in the scrub, and as we near the top, I can see the lighthouse—one I know from postcards—and its faint beam hoops over us. "Gay Head Light," he says. Outside the car, it's cold. The souvenir shops are boarded shut, but there's the smell of salt, and I can almost hear the phantom linger of wind chimes and seashell mobiles. I push my hands into the silky pockets of my coat as he strides ahead. He nods to one of the shacks and smiles. "Great chili fries."

We reach the promontory, the very western edge of the island.

The sky is as bright as water. It was called Gay Head then, all of it—the land, the township, the cliffs below. But years later, when I returned after his death, it would be known by another name, an older one—Aquinnah—for the Wampanoag people who have lived here for thousands of years and who, in summer, run the shops and sell the chili fries. In legend, a giant named Moshup created the channels and islands by dragging his toe across the land. He lived in his den in the cliffs and caught whales with his bare hands. Until the white man came, he taught his people to fish and plant, and he watched over them. Some say that he still does—that when the fog drifts in, he's there.

I lean against the railing, with the windy sea below, and he tells me these stories. And in my new coat, I'm hoping I look something like the French Lieutenant's Woman. The wrong color, I know, and there's no hood, but that's the idea anyway.

"There's Cuttyhunk." He points, his arm on my shoulder; the other holds my waist. "Nashawena, then Pasque. Naushon's the long one." Except for Cuttyhunk, these are all private islands and mostly deserted. Then he turns in the opposite direction—south toward Squibnocket Pond and his mother's beach. I follow his gaze to an island on its own some miles off. "That's Nomans Land." *Nomans*, I repeat after him, and decide I like that one best.

When it's warmer, we will sail to Cuttyhunk. When the leaves are tipped with red, we will hike on Naushon. We'll camp for a night on Nomans, a moonless sky and the Milky Way arched above our small tent.

We get a late start. On our approach to Nomans at sunset, his mother's Seacraft threatens to run aground near some old pilings, and I swim ashore with our gear piled on my head. It takes three trips. Then I watch from the beach as he dives with a knife in his teeth and after many tries succeeds in anchoring the boat. Damaged, he says, but afloat. That night, we roast bluefish, corn, and potatoes and drink wine under the stars.

In the morning, I hear engines. I nudge him awake. Outside the tent, mongrel seagulls peck at the singed tinfoil around the campfire. I look up. A plane is buzzing low. Now, in daylight, a large sign with DANGER painted in black letters glares at me. He'd told me it was illegal to land here but neglected to say that while a third of the island is a bird sanctuary, the rest is a navy bombing practice site. As I scramble, cursing, for the boat, I can hear him: "Don't stress, this is the *bird* side!" Later, his mother will berate him, and not only for the injury to the boat. "But you were with Christina," she keeps saying, to remind him that I was there, in harm's way, alongside him.

And one August morning—it may be the last summer we're together—we will kayak to the back end of Nashawena, hide the boat in the brush from the caretaker, and climb to the headlands, where the sheep are. We'll sit in the scratchy grass flecked with blue chicory and look out over Vineyard Sound, and he'll tell me the names he likes. "Flynn Kennedy—it's got a good ring. What do you think of Flynn?"

I don't like Fleur, his girl's name. I prefer Francesca, Isabel, and Kate. But Flynn I like. Or it might be the sleepy look on his face as he says it.

But all that will happen later. Right now, it's windy and his arms are around me and I can see in all directions. Which way is east? I say, and he spins me a quarter turn from where I'm guessing. Away from the sea, away from the cliffs, in the direction of Gay Head Light.

. . .

In the afternoon, the wind dies down, and we take the jeep to the beach. As soon as we cross the uplift of dune, he jumps out, scales the car, and orders me into the driver's seat.

"Just do it," he yells when I say I can't drive.

I hear him laughing on the roof, and I spin the jeep in circles, as tight and as fast as I can.

"Now you!" he says.

"I can't." But somehow he gets me up there, camel-hair coat and all. My fingers dig into the sides of the roof as he pushes down the gas. After, I catch my breath from laughing and slide down the driver's side into his arms, and we walk to the water's edge. It's a winter beach, mottled oysters, mussels the size of my thumbnail, threads of papery black and white seaweed, and the dirty foam the surf has left. Billows of it. He kicks it as we walk.

"Don't you know the story?" I ask.

"What story?"

"Mermaids have no immortal soul—they live three hundred years and then become the foam on the sea."

"What are you talking about?" He's picking up small stones and skipping them, a singsong on flat water.

I go on to tell him the Hans Christian Andersen tale, of the red flowers in the garden of the Sea King's daughter, her desire for a soul, her love of the black-eyed prince she rescues from drowning, the potion that turns her tail into legs. But each step's a sharp knife, and the cost is her tongue.

"Then what happens?" he asks. His stone skips three times, and we whistle at his prowess.

"He marries someone else and she becomes a spirit of the air."

He hands me one he likes. It's freckled, and I save it from skipping.

"You know strange things."

"It's not strange," I reply, slipping the stone into my pocket. "It's a fairy tale."

"You're a funny girl," he says. He turns to me. He's thinking of something, and his eyes get smaller.

"Funny," I say back. I was hoping for something else. Beguiling, maybe. And I imagine myself a butterfly on velvet—pinned, prodded, examined. Denuded of mystery.

"You're different. Intriguing," he continues, his voice dispassionate in a way I've never heard before.

I look away from him down the beach. The wind dries my eyes, and I fix my gaze on the tender way these shallow waves hit the shore.

After some time, he pulls me toward him, his fingers looped in the belt of my new coat. "Hey," he says, softly. "I have no doubts about you or what's happening. I have everything I want here and now. I only think I'm crazy it didn't happen sooner."

"You do?"

"I've always had a sneaker for you. Always." His forehead presses mine, and the weight calms me. The longest courtship ever, that's what he calls it. "I wanted to pounce, but every time you had a boyfriend, and they were all Marlboro men."

It's not what I remember, but I like when he says it.

We keep walking. Past a small wooden sign at the top of the highwater mark. POSTED: NO TRESPASSING. Past Zack's Beach, its bluffs blown back like a wave with a brambled top. Crusts of purple sand crack under our sneakers as we go. And near the dunes, remnants of summer—tall orange buoys speared in the sand, a chapel/fort of driftwood, a child's shoe. The wind picks up, and I pull the coat around me. He leans into me as we walk, crossing my path. Then he bounds ahead, taking giant steps. I jump between them. Everything's a game. We switch and he follows my tracks, and wonders out loud why my feet are so small. They're not. They're average. Many things about me are. But he keeps saying they're small. *You're so small.* And that winter he has dreams he will break me.

He's showing me the place he loves. I know this. Every summer his beach is different. It erodes and changes. Every summer it's new. We're near the cliffs now, the chalky face seared by color. They wrap a mile around this end of the island and stretch 150 feet up. *Iron ore, clay, gravel, sand, black lignite.* He's reeling off the reasons for the brilliant hues.

At Philbin Beach, we're close. He asks if I want to keep going, and I say yes.

"Come here." He's standing on the rubble of rocks under the cliffs. "Give me your hand," he says, pushing his own against the face. I move in over whale-colored boulders and touch. It's wet, weeping almost—Spring's pulse hidden within. I look at him, and he can tell what I'm thinking. "It's alive," he says. He runs his finger along a flaky ridge and dabs my forehead yellow. Then his own. *There*, I think.

It's cold, but the sun is strong, and he's talking about moraines and fossils, the Ice Age and clay. I smile and press my back against a dry patch of cliff and listen. What's a moraine, I ask, and he tells me. It's the end place, the farthest reach of ice, the finish of advance and retreat. He points to a round, banded rock rising from the water. It could be from Vermont—even Canada—dragged here as the ice scraped south thousands and thousands of years ago, carrying sediment and till. And in the cliffs—pieces of ancient whale and shark, a polished tooth, a rib, a jaw, a shard of wild horse, a wisp of camel. When he was younger, he used to come here with friends, and they'd strip down and paint their bodies with the clay. *Warriors.*

I look at him—his face is shining—and stretch my arm across the crumbling rock to find him. The words fall over me. I let them. The stories the bones tell. The life that was here.

I have a dream about John. It's one I've had for years. At first after he died, it came all at once, for days in a row, but now it's less frequent. It's always on a beach at dusk—the light low, the colored sky deepening. It could be Montauk, where I'm writing this book, or Zack's Beach on the Vineyard, or the great wide swath at Cumberland, or even California. But there are cliffs in the dream, red cliffs. Like in the tale he told when he first took me to Gay Head Lighthouse. Red from Moshup's whales. Black from the soot of his fires.

I look up. He's there—coming toward me, hands pushed in his pockets, grinning so wild it makes me laugh. "How are you here?" I keep saying. "How are you here?" He doesn't answer. He looks at me, proud to have come this far.

Better not waste time. I know from before that I don't have long. I think he can't touch me, but he does and he's warm. We sit together on the sand and watch the water. And next to him, in the dream, I feel I am most like myself. Then we walk fast and talk fast. All the things only that person can know. I point to a small boulder down the beach. "When we reach that rock, you will leave me," I say. As if it is too much, too selfish to have him this long, and I don't want any surprises. I tell him how my life has been, things he may not know, secrets. But he knows everything. "What my friends tell me," he says, and we leave it at that.

When we're close to the rock, I turn to ask him something. But he's gone, already in the water. I see his back, a long lean dive breaking the surface of gray-green. "Hey—come back," I shout. "Goodbye, you didn't say goodbye." Sometimes I yell, angry, "You forgot to say goodbye!" Then I laugh; it's just like him. But after a while, when the trail through the water disappears, I just stand there.

I don't know when, I tell myself in the dream, but he will come back when I least expect it, and it will be on a beach like this one.

From the shallows, Moshup watches. In legend, he watches his children and, to keep them free, turns them into sharks. I believe he watches John. And he watches the girl, he sees the girl. But if you *were looking, you would see a woman alone on an empty beach, heavier than she once was, speaking to the waves as if they hear her.*

The next day, we leave, and whatever spell's between us is still there. It's been seven months since August, since we did the play. Seven months since we met near the Ramble and the words fell between us and we began.

I put it off—the weekend away—wary that the curious alchemy of mystery and knowing might dissolve with four days in a row. But it hasn't. It's stronger. And like thick black ice, I begin to trust that it will hold me.

"I have a surprise for you," he says over breakfast. We'd flown up commercial, but he tells me he's chartered a plane back, and now we have more time. Over the years, he will say this when he does what pleases him. *A surprise for you.* And for a long time, I will find it charming. Like when he orders three breakfasts and tells the waiter two are for me.

The pilot greets us at the shingled terminal and drives us to the plane in a cart. It feels glamorous. "You're lucky," the pilot says. "Gonna be a great sunset. Clear skies all the way to New York." It's a single-engine Cessna with three passenger seats. Blue-winged, with a striped nose. The pilot checks wheels, pressure, flaps, gauges, and John follows him around the plane. He's had lessons before, and they talk shop.

When they're done, the pilot pulls me up the wing into the tilted plane, then John. Something breaks. I reach inside the pocket of my coat; there's his stone and pieces of a scallop shell I found near the cliffs the day before. We buckle in and the tower clears us. I've never been in a plane so small, and he holds my hand for take-off. His face—all of him—it's eager. Once we're up, he gives me the headphones. I listen for a moment to the monotone jumble of numbers and letters and codes I know fascinate him, then hand them back.

I'm entranced by the shapes from above—the coves and cliffs and ponds, the yellow borders of beach against the deep dark sea. I try to memorize and tuck them away like my life depends on it: I must have this snapshot of now. The pilot was right—the sky's clear, only a thin bank of violet at the horizon. The din in the cabin is a dull roar—like you're underwater. We can't hear each other and speak in an amalgam of excited gestures and facial expressions. Below, there's Gay Head and the empty islands we saw the day before from the cliffs—only now, from the sky, they're complete. *Naushon, Nashawena, Pasque.* I say the names to myself to remember. In case this is the last time. In case it's all we have. Just then the sun drops and floods the plane with ruddy light. *Look!* He lets go of my hand. He wants me to see.

The camel coat's on my shoulders. The sky's shot with red. And there's something I've never seen. Small lines—the creases at his eyes, when he's happy, when he's smiling. Like bird wings.

Acknowledgments

First: Without the love and encouragement of Jennie Moreau, Fredrika Brillembourg, and Mia Dillon, this book would not have been written. They knew that going back would not be easy, and like many of my friends, they had faith when I faltered. They persuaded me to tell my story and reminded me of the heart when I veered away. In addition, I have endless gratitude for Elizabeth Auran and Tom Diggs, who read so kindly, so carefully, and then shed light. And for Bernadette Haag Clarke and Rebecca Boyd, who knew, and always said, "Keep going!"

Profound thanks to Gary Murphy and Kirk Stambler for their counsel and keen insights; Paulette Bartlett, Rachel Resnick, and Erin Cressida Wilson for their thoughtful reads and good advice; Asaad Kelada, Arye Gross, Cordelia Richards, Daniel McDonald, and Andrew Haag for braving early drafts. And to Lynne Weinstein for her beautiful photographs and her friendship.

Heartfelt thanks to my agent, Suzanne Gluck, whose steadfast belief in my story and whose guidance at every turn have proven invaluable. And to her assistant, Caroline Donofrio, who answered my questions with cheerfulness and clarity. I am enormously grateful to the fabulous Julie Grau and the superb team at Spiegel & Grau: Sally Marvin, Avideh Bashirrad, Erika Greber, Richard Elman, Dana Leigh Blanchette, Greg Mollica. And to Evan Gaffney. Special thanks are due to Hana Landes, who kept things running smoothly, and to Dennis Ambrose, whose patience and good humor during the copyediting process meant so much.

For beginnings, I will always be grateful to Mary Jemail and Mary de Kay, my inspired eighth and tenth grade English teachers; and to Will Scheffer, Lisa Glatt, and the UCLA Extension Writers' Program. And for the beginnings of the book to playwright and actor George Furth—he badgered until I began. A big thank you to Lainey Papageorge, who provided prayers and made a cherished return possible, and to Roger Miller for Daruma.

For keeping a place at their table and, when I needed it, generously offering a quiet room to write in, I must thank Matt O'Grady and John Shaka, Matthew Sullivan and Harriet Harris, Victoria Tennant, Keir Dullea, and Jason La Padura. Your friendship and love have meant so much. Thanks also to Jonathan and Helena Stuart for providing a glittering view of the sea for several crucial weeks.

For tireless help with facts and for sharing their memories, I am indebted to Anne Korkeakivi, Tom Dunlop, Tim Monich, Laurence Maslon, Spencer Beckwith, Billy Straus, Robin Saex Garbose, Lisa Curtis, Stephanie Venditto, Katherine Swett, Sarah Miller, Susan Burke, and especially, the quicksilver Ultan Guilfoyle, who responded to each and every one of my emails, no matter how trifling. *Cumberland Island: A History* by Mary R. Bullard and *Convent of the Sacred Heart: A History in New York City* by Timothy T. Noonan were books that inspired memories of my own, and I am grateful to the authors.

Many thanks for the kindnesses of Mikel and Margaret Dunham, Karen Watson, Laney Fichera, Lynn Blumenfeld, G. Marq and Karen Roswell, Robert Haag, Elizabeth Reed, Jessica Queller, Kari Catalano, Adam Green and Elizabeth Fasolino, Stephen DiCarmine, Bob Morris, Samantha Dunn, Richard and Louise Paul, Elyn Saks, Jennifer Fraser, Christopher Clarke, Karen Balliet, Robert Levithan, Debby Stover, Diana Berry, Spencer Garrett, and my manager, Christopher Wright, who has always shown patience and support. I would also like to thank Mujah Maraini-Melehi, who made a respite happen, and Donald Antrim, whose honest words at the right time meant a great deal.

I am deeply appreciative of the Monday Night Writers Group, especially for the support of Sara Pratter, Kathleen Dennehy, and Fielding Edlow; the John Jermain Library; and the communities of Montauk and Sag Harbor, New York, which provided the welcome, seclusion, and peace I needed to complete the book.

To Father Daniel and the monks at the Hermitage: The gifts I received on the hill remain. To the nuns at Sacred Heart who encouraged us to keep journals: I listened, and years later found I had boxes full.

Finally, I would like to thank my brilliant editor and friend, Cindy Spiegel. I am humbled by your gifts. When we met again in 2006, I sensed we shared a vision. Now I know this to be abundantly true. As you once said, this was meant.

ABOUT THE TYPE

This book is set in Fournier, a typeface named for Pierre Simon Fournier, the youngest son of a French printing family. He started out engraving woodblocks and large capitals, then moved on to fonts of type. In 1736 he began his own foundry and made several important contributions in the field of type design; he is said to have cut 147 alphabets of his own creation. Fournier is probably best remembered as the designer of St. Augustine Ordinaire, a face that served as the model for Monotype's Fournier, which was released in 1925.